Essential Role of Social Science Information System in Library Science

ESSENTIAL ROLE OF SOCIAL SCIENCE INFORMATION SYSTEM IN LIBRARY SCIENCE

Anil Kumar
Ph.D. (Library & Information Science), M. Phil (Library Science), M.Lib, B.Lib Science, Master in Arts (M.V) & Master of Philosophy (M.V), PGDCA
Presently faculty at
Swift Group of Colleges, Rajpura

Ess Ess Publications
New Delhi

Essential Role of Social Science Information System in Library Science

ISBN : 978-93-87698-20-8

First Published 2019

Published by:
Ess Ess Publications
4831/24, Ansari Road,
Darya Ganj,
New Delhi-110 002.
INDIA
Phones: 23260807, 41563444
Fax: 41563334
E-mail: info@essessreference.com
www.essessreference.com

Cover Design by *Patch Creative Unit*

Printed and bound in India

Dedication

I dedicate this piece of work to the glory of God "The almighty", without whom I am nothing. To my father, mother, elder brother, sisters, wife and son for their endless support and encouragement.

Contents

Acknowledgements

Preface

UNIT-I :

STRUCTURE AND DEVELOPMENT OF SOCIAL SCIENCE

1	Social Science	3
2	Political Science	18
3	Management	29
4	Psychology	37
5	Sociology	52
6	Education	66
7	Economics	78
8	History	94
9	Public Administration	108

UNIT-II :

DOCUMENTARY SOURCES OF SOCIAL SCIENCE

10	Information System	125
11	Information Sources	136
12	Popular And Scholarly Literature	157
13	Web Based Information Sources	161

14 Study of International Encyclopedia of Social Sciences 207

15 International Encyclopedia of Social and Behavioural Sciences 209

16 International Bibliography of the Social Sciences 212

17 Social Sciences Citation Index 215

18 International Political Science Abstracts 218

19 Psychological Abstracts 222

20 Bibliography of Doctoral Dissertations 224

21 Statistical Abstracts India 226

UNIT-III :

INSTITUTIONAL SOURCES

22 Information Generation & Dissemination Institutional Resources 231

UNIT-IV :

PLANNING OF SOCIAL SCIENCE RESEARCH LIBRARY

23 Planning of Library 323

24 Information Systems and Networks in Social Sciences at National Level 337

25 Information Systems and Networks in Social Sciences at International Level 381

Acknowledgements

Success is the fruit of hard work. This success was possible due to the collective efforts of so many personalities to whom I express my gratitude.

First and foremost, I would like to humble thank almighty God for his divine intervention in my life without which I would not have been able to make this study. *It is god who arms me with strength and paves my path.*

Transcending all this, sweet love, affection and care of my grandparents Sh. Mela Ram, Smt. Maya Devi and Sh. Tek Chand, Smt. Maya Devi have been like a spring of inspiration and strength for me, which made it possible to fulfil this task efficiently.

I own heartiest thanks to my Father Sh. Som Nath and Mother Smt. Shanti Devi. Their constant inspiration and guidance kept me focused and motivated. They bore me, raised me, supported me, taught me and loved me and the support of my elder brother, Dr. Ajay Kapoor is sincerely acknowledged. Words fail to express my appreciation to my wife Pooja Kapoor & son Aryan Kapoor whose dedication and persistent confidence in me has taken the load off my shoulder.

I am thankful to my elder sisters, Mrs. Meenakshi, Sangeeta and Anju who assisted me directly or indirectly in completion of this book.

Anil Kumar

Preface

This book results from continued strong belief in the need for a text that focuses on social science information system in library science issues of present and future in a distinctive pattern. This edition is incorporated with many suggestions from both social science and library information system side, as it focuses on the critical roles of librarians and teachers. This book has been written for bachelor of library science and can be used as a reference source for post-graduate students of library and information science. This book covers all the topic of social science information system in the library science curriculum according to most of the Indian universities. This text is grounded with theoretical and practical aspects of social science and information system in library science education and library practice.

The increasing interest in the study of society and societary problems by thinkers has created a growing demand for social science courses in the colleges. In many cases, the economist, for example, is teaching that economics is the fundamental social science and that all of the other social sciences are based upon and controlled by the economic desired of man, and at the same time, the historian, it may be, is teaching thc same student that history and the historical method are primary to the understanding of human society. Thus the teachers and authorities in the field of the social sciences often present the rather strange spectacle of each claiming his own special social science as the most fundamental and ground of all other social sciences upon his own specialized field.

Social Science is a vague subject to be explored and many other books by experts in library science can be used for referral along with this book. This book can facilitate new learners to acquaint with the basic knowledge of social science and library information system which can be applied in practical experience of academics and library area. I have tried to explain the concepts in a simple and comprehensive manner to develop a foundation for the new library professionals. This book will help in library science aspects in their practical life of library profession as it will help to understand the basic concepts of social science & library information system in terms.

The chapters have been sequenced to facilitate ease in reading and understanding. This textbook is divided into four units, with each unit focusing on one the major domains of essentials role of social science information system in library science.

Unit 1: Structure & Development of Social Science

Social Science : Introduction, Meaning of Social Science, Term used of Social Science, Definition of Social Science, Nature of Social Science, Growth & development of Social Sciences, Scope of Social Science, Social Science research trends, Social Sciences in India, Social Studies, Nature of Social Science, Functional Similarities & Differences between Social Science and Social Studies, Components of Social Science information system.

Political Science : Introduction, Meaning of Political Science, Definiticn of Political Science, Scope of Political Science, Growth and landmarks of Political Science, Research trends of Political Science.

Management : Introduction, Definitions of Management, Scope of Management, Nature of Management,

Development & landmarks of Management, Research Trends of Management.

Psychology : Introduction, Meaning of Psychology, Definitions of Psychology, Scope of Psychology, Origin and history of Psychology, Landmarks of Psychology, Research trends of psychology.

Sociology : Introduction, Meaning of Sociology, Definitions of Sociology, Scope of Sociology, Landmarks of Sociology, Research trends of Sociology, Sociology in India.

Education : Introduction, Meaning of Education, Ancient period concept of Education, Definition of Education, Scope of Education, Nature of Education, Landmarks of Education, Research trends of Education.

Economics : Introduction, Origin of Economics, Meaning of Economics, Definition of Economics, Scope of Economics, History & landmarks of Economics, Research trends of Economics.

History : Introduction, Origin of History, Meaning of History, Definition of History, Scope of History, Historical background & landmarks of History, Research trends of History.

Public Administration : Introduction, Meaning of Public Administration, Definition of Public Administration, Scope of Public Administration, Historical background & landmarks of Public Administration, Research trends of Public Administration.

Unit 2: Documentary Sources of Social Science

Information System : Introduction, Information, System, Definitions of Information System, Components of Information System.

Information Sources : Introduction, Meaning of Information Sources, Definitions of Information Sources, Types of Information Sources.

Popular and Scholarly Literature : Introduction, Some examples of popular literature, Scholarly literature, some examples of academic journals.

Web Based Information Sources : Introduction, Meaning of web based information resources, Definition of web based information resources, some examples of web based information resources.

E-Journals : Introduction, Meaning of E-Journals, Definitions E-Journals, History and growth of E-Journals, Categories of E-Journals, Advantages of E-Journals, Limitations of E-Journals, Prominent online databases in Science and Technology.

E-Reference Sources : Introduction, Advantages of E-Reference sources, Effects of E-Reference Sources, Initiatives of E-Reference Sources, Factors of E-Reference Sources, Limitations of E-Reference Sources, Examples of E-Reference Sources.

Subject Gateways : Introduction, History and Current Status, Meaning of Subject Gateways, Definitions of Subject Gateways, Features of Gateway, Why Gateway, How to use Subject Gateways, When to use Subject Gateways, Characteristics of Subject Gateways, Library Related Subject Gateways.

Institutional Repositories : Introduction, Meaning of Institutional Repository, Definitions of Institutional Repository, Objectives of Institutional Repository, Institutional Repository Policy, Software for Institutional Repositories, Institutional Repository Projects.

Digital Libraries : Introduction, Meaning of Digital Library, Use of term, Definitions of Digital Library, Function of Digital Library, Purpose of Digital Library, Advantages of Digital Library, Limitation of Digital Library, Deference of Traditional & of Digital Library, Architecture of Digital Library System.

Study of International Encyclopedia of Social Science : Introduction, Features of International Encyclopedia of Social Science.

International Encyclopedia of Social and Behavioural Sciences: Introduction, Features of International Encyclopedia of Social and Behavioural Sciences, Subject Classification.

International Bibliography of the Social Sciences : Introduction, History of International Bibliography of the Social Sciences, Coverage, Availability, Online format.

Social Science Citation Index: Introduction, Database covers, Comprehensive coverage, Century of social science, Criticism.

International Political Science Abstracts : Introduction, Indexing and abstracting, Topics include, Selection guidelines, Structure, Annual subscription, Electronic database.

Psychological Abstracts : Introduction, History of psychological abstract, Publicity, CD-ROM database.

Bibliography of Doctoral Dissertation : Introduction of Bibliography of Doctoral Dissertation.

Statistical Abstracts India : Introduction, History of Statistical Abstracts India, Area of Statistical Abstracts India.

Unit 3 : Institutional Sources

Information Generation & Dissemination Institutional Resources : Introduction of Information Generation & Dissemination Institutional Resources.

ICSSR (Indian Council of Social Science Research) : History of ICSSR, Objectives of ICSSR, Programme and Services of ICSSR, Research Institute of ICSSR, Regional Centres of ICSSR, Library Service of ICSSR, Library Membership of ICSSR, Council of ICSSR.

ICWA (Indian Council of World Affairs) : History of the Council, The objects of the Council, Research Work of ICWA, ICWA Library (Sapru house library), Library Services, Publication of ICWA, ICWA Committees, CSCAP-India Committee.

IIMA (Indian Institute of Management-Ahmedabad) : Introduction, Vision and Strategic Priorities, Campus of IIMA, Awards & Honours, Academic Programmes, NICMAN, Library of IIMA, Library Services, Events of IIMA.

IIPA (Indian Institute of Public Administration) : History of IIPA, Objectives of IIPA, Activities of IIPA, Network and Collaboration, Institutional Requirements of IIPA, Academic Centres, Library of IIPA, Library Services.

NCAER (National Council for Applied Economic Research) : History of NCAER, Mission & Vision of NCAER, NCAER Activities, Research Areas Activities of NCAER, Data, Sponsors & Partners, Events of NCAER, NCAER library, Library Services, NCAER Publication.

TISS (Tata Institute of Social Science) : History of TISS, Vision of TISS, Mission of TISS, TISS library (Sir Dorabji Tata Memorial Library), SDTM library vision, SDTM library objectives, TISS library history, TISS library resources & services, Training facilities, Digital library, Campuses, Academics, Collaborations.

UNESCO (United Nations Educational, Scientific and Cultural Organization) : History of UNESCO, Vision of UNESCO, Milestones of UNESCO, Objectives and Functions of UNESCO, Activities of UNESCO, Main Activities of UNESCO, UNESCO Library, Library Services, UNESCO Publication.

ICHR (Indian Council of Historical Research) : History of ICHR, Aims and Objectives, Functions of ICHR, Mission of ICHR, Grants, ICHR library, Library services, ICHR publication, Special projects.

LSE (London School of Economics and Political Science) : History of LSE, LSE Goals, Priorities for the future, Vision of LSE, Subject Discipline, Origins of the Library, Library Services.

SSRC (Social Science Research Council) : History of SSRC, SSRC basic Commitments, Purpose of SSRC, Tools of SSRC, Programs, Fellowships and Prizes, Library Services.

Unit 4: Information Systems & Networks

Planning of Social Science Research Libraries : Introduction to Planning of Library, Tools and Techniques of Social Science Research Library Planning, Benefits of a Plan, Recipe for a Plan, Phases of a Proposed Social Science Research Library Building, Planning Responsibilities for Social Science Research Library, Other Environmental Factors, Some Conceptual Principles of Planning with Social Science Research Libraries.

Information Systems and Networks in Social Sciences at National Level:

DELNET (Developing Library Network) : Introduction, Objectives of DELNET, Database of DELNET, Services of DELNET, DELNET consortium of E-Journals, Membership fee of DELNET, Functions and Activities of DELNET, Areas of Research.

INFLIBNET (Information Library Network) : Introduction, Mission and Vision of INFLIBNET, Aims and Objectives of INFLIBNET, Physical Infrastructure of INFLIBNET, Services and Technical Activities of INFLIBNET.

NASSDOC (National Social Science Documentation Centre) : Introduction, Facilities available at NASSDOC, NASSDOC Services, Library Membership, NASSDOC Databases/Publication Programmes.

SENDOC (Small Enterprises National

Documentation Centre) : Introduction, Objectives of SENDOC, Strengths of SENDOC, Services of SENDOC, Publications of SENDOC, Library Membership of SENDOC.

Information Systems and Networks in Social Sciences at International Level:

DEVINSA (Development Information Network for South Asia) : Introduction of DEVINSA, Objectives of DEVINSA, Products and Services of DEVINSA.

DEVSIS (Development Science Information System): Introduction, Objectives of DEVSIS, Products and Services, Functions of DEVSIS, Coverage of DEVSIS.

APINESS (Asia-Pacific Information Network in Social Sciences) : Introduction of APINESS, Aims of APINESS, Evolution of APINESS, The Frame Work of APINESS, Main Constituents of APINESS, Activities of APINESS, Achievements at National level in India, Services of APINESS, Conclusion.

Hope this book will be beneficial for the library science students to maximum extent possible as a result of the dedication and hard work put up to make it more understandable for the beginner leaders and managers.

Anil Kumar

Unit-I

STRUCTURE AND DEVELOPMENT OF SOCIAL SCIENCE

1

Social Science

INTRODUCTION

The social sciences have a long history, although they became self-consciously scientific only in the nineteenth century. Early proponents of a scientific approach to the study of society and its problems, including A. Comte and J. S. Mill, proposed a positivist or naturalist program that used the same methods to study both natural and social sciences. This elicited a strong critical response from humanists, who believed that the way to understand human behavior was through interpretation, paying close attention to history. Durkheim rejected Mill's belief that laws of human behavior were ultimately based on laws of individual psychology. He used statistical methods to argue that certain facts about societies could not be explained by facts about individuals. Weber, joined with interpretivists to reject the search for laws in the human sciences, but he did propose a kind of singular causal explanation that performed its explanatory task by demonstrating the rationality of certain types of behavior. Weber also argued for an important tenet of positivism, namely, the neutrality of science with respect to values. Scientists were able, and were required, to keep their own values and prejudices separate from the issues they studied.

In the twentieth century, the positions of naturalists and interpretivists were refined, and some common ground was found. The critical theorists attacked what they saw as the naturalists' attempt to undermine human freedom with a social science that was manipulative and full of evil potential. In the 1960s, T. Kuhn's careful historical study of the growth of scientific knowledge showed the importance of interpretive work in the physical as well as the social sciences. Sociologists of science built on Kuhn's suggestions about factors other than data and logical inference that influence theory choice.

MEANING OF SOCIAL SCIENCE

Social Science is a generic term covering the scientific study of man. It is a discipline or branch of science that deals with the socio-cultural aspects of human behaviour.

TERM USED OF SOCIAL SCIENCE

The conception of a social science is due to Comte, He used the concept of social science 1837, though the term social science appears to have been first used English about 1874, However, Dr. S.R, Ranganathan rightly remarked that, it appears to have come into general use only very much later. This is evident from the following facts:

The term "social sciences" has its entry for the first time, into 1913 edition of Webster's New International Dictionary; "Social Science as the branch of science that deals with the institutions and functioning of human society and with the inter-personal relationships of individuals as member of society". As far as the adoption of the use of the term "Social Science" in the title of periodicals or serials goes, it was carried for the first time by the documentation serial "Social Science Abstracts" started in New York in 1929.

As regards the emergence of the term "Social Science" from encyclopedias in 1930 by Edwin R. A. S, named for the first time. The encyclopedia edited by him as "Encyclopaedia of the Social Sciences" According to him, social sciences is those mental or cultural sciences which deal with the activities of the individual as a member of the group.

Mitchell, in his dictionary of sociology, points out that the term social science is loosely applied to any kind of study concerning man and society.

DEFINITION OF SOCIAL SCIENCE

Social science is defined as any scholastic discipline or scientific field that investigates human society.

According to James High, "Social Sciences as those bodies of learning and study which recognizes the simultaneous and mutual action of physical and no-physical stimuli which produce social relation".

According to Charles Beard, "Social Sciences are a body of knowledge and thought pertaining to human affairs as distinguished from sticks, stones, stars and physical objects".

Bining & Bining defines Social Science as "the subject that relate to the origin, organization, and development of human society, especially to man in his association with other men".

NATURE OF SOCIAL SCIENCE

The following points may characterize the nature of social sciences:

1. Direct bearing on human activity is : Social sciences are those aspects of knowledge which have direct bearing on man's activities in different socio cultural fields.

2. Advance studies of human society : Social sciences are advance level studies of human society; and they are generally taught at higher education level.

3. Find out truths about human relationships: Social

sciences seek to find out truths about human relationships which ultimately contribute to the social utility and advancement of knowledge.

GROWTH & DEVELOPMENT OF SOCIAL SCIENCES

While 'social sciences' evolved during the eighteenth century as a formal field of study and became a part of university/higher education curriculum, 'social studies' evolved during the twentieth century in order to be included in the school or junior school curriculum. The evolution and growth of social sciences are the byproduct of modernization, industrialization, renaissance, urbanization, growth of science and many more related developments. There were many changes in human lives and living, which were hardly seen before during the eighteenth century and afterwards. The whole world took a radical turn since the eighteenth century.

Renaissance in Italy and other European countries, French revolution 1789, industrial revolutions starting from 1767, American war of independence 1776, development of new forms of capitalism, immense development in natural sciences, etc. brought both happiness and difficulties for human society in the world. For example, on the positive side, there was commercial development, development of transport and communication, multiplication of comforts, improvement of education and health condition, development of economic condition, etc.; and on the negative side, there was development of complexity in social life, political chaos, social disorganization and unrest, intellectual crisis, development of unhealthy competition among people, etc. In order to counter all these problems and challenges, social sciences originated and became the part of education/ learning system.

Social sciences originated in the eighteenth century in an effort to understand the character and future of modern society (Ross, 1991). Montesquieu Spirit of the Laws (1748), Adam Smith's Wealth of Nations (1776), Condorcet's Outline of a Historical View of the Progress of the Human Kind (1795) and J.G. Herder's Idea towards a Philosophy of History (1784-91) were exemplary texts of the social sciences. Observing the difference between modern society and its feudal and ancient forms, these social scientists envisioned social sciences that would guide modern society into the future.

Due to increasing industrialization, modernization, scientific development, etc. many new social problems are arising and affecting the whole social system and paralyzing it. While rapid growth of industrialization and modernization brings in multitude social problems including diseases, social alienation, workers exploitation etc., modern science creates germ warfare, atoms for destruction of humanity, many hazardous chemical and nuclear reaction, etc. Two wars (i.e. World War-I and World war-II) in the twentieth century brought indefinable misery for mankind. In addition to these two wars, there were numerous wars which were found in many parts of the world which were/are really bad for humanity. The misuse of science, urbanization, industrialization etc. has really become a threat to humanity in this world. The experience of severe economic depression from 1930 to 1940 created the feeling of insecurity, fear, suspicion and distrust among the people of the world.

The rapid growth of science and technology in the last hundred years has created many new social problems, though it has many positive effects. Social sciences emerged to prevent and check the evil effects of science, industrialization and modernization, etc. on the one hand and to guide the modern society for better future on the other hand. Now-a day philosophers, statesmen, scientists, politicians and many other intelligentsias have realized that social sciences are no way inferior to other sciences including physical sciences or biological sciences. The general sciences have proved that is capable of organizing the forces of the atom to cause the destruction of the entire humanity from the world by a single explosion. There is a need of studying social sciences to obstruct destruction of human society by such forces. Since social sciences have great relevance for modern day society, so, they form an important component/ part of modern day education/curriculum system.

Social sciences have become the part of university/ higher education system across the world starting from the eighteenth century. Realizing the importance of social sciences for developing healthy social and democratic citizenship qualities of individuals, they have been included in the school curriculum of most of the countries of the world especially from the twentieth century either in the name of ***'Social Studies'*** or in the name of ***'Social Sciences'***.

SCOPE OF SOCIAL SCIENCES

The word "science" is older than its modern use. The word has become a short-form for "Natural Science". It is a recent development that society has become the object of an organized body of knowledge which can be standardized and taught objectively, while following its own rules and methodology. The Social science has a wide scope.

According to Seligman, the social sciences can be divided into three classes:

1. Purely social sciences such as political science, history, economics, anthropology, jurisprudence, sociology and penology.
2. Semi social sciences such as education these are in fact not social in origin but still retain part of a social context.
3. Sciences with social implications such as biology (as applied to human beings), Medicine (as applied to social

hygiene and public health), although all these are independent in origin, yet they have acquired social context partially.

Fairchild in the Dictionary of Sociology gives the following disciplines which come under social sciences:

1. Economics
2. Government
3. Law
4. Psychology
5. Sociology
6. Anthropology

Dr. S. R. Ranganathan has stated that the following disciplines can be covered under social sciences:

1. Education
2. Geography
3. History
4. Political Science
5. Economics
6. Sociology
7. Law

H.E, Burmes thinks that the following disciplines fall under the scope of social sciences:

1. History
2. Human Geography
3. Biology
4. Social Anthropology
5. Cultural Anthropology
6. Sociology
7. Economics
8. Political Science

9. Jurisprudence
10. Ethics

E.C. Hagues enumerates the following disciplines for inclusion m the social sciences:

1. Sociology
2. Anthropology
3. Social work
4. Cultural Geography
5. Economics
6. Political Science
7. History

W. F. Ogburn and A. Goldenweiser recognizes only the following disciplines as belonging to the social sciences:

1. Anthropology
2. Economics
3. History
4. Political Science
5. Sociology

Gee Wilson admits the following disciplines under the category of social sciences:

1. Sociology
2. Economics
3. Anthropology
4. Statistics
5. Psychology
6. Jurisprudence
7. History
8. Philosophy
9. Political science

The **social sciences** comprise academic disciplines concerned with the study of the social life of human groups, animals and individuals including anthropology, archeology, communication studies, cultural studies, demography, economics, human geography, history, linguistics, media studies, political science, psychology, social work and sociology.

SOCIAL SCIENCE RESEARCH TRENDS

Though some attempts have been made in certain universities to coordinate research with other specializations in a subject, the trend is more and more to conduct research in terms of a single specialisation. Universities should establish a close contact with the society and they should not only contribute to creation of new data, but also deal with new types of analysis and presentation. Funding bodies like UGC, ICSSR, and the like should constitute high level committees in various disciplines to evaluate the quality of research work at universities and make suitable suggestions, for modification and improvement in the quality of research. Workshops organized to impart training to guide in the areas such as computer applications and new research techniques.

SOCIAL SCIENCES IN INDIA

The categories of knowledge, their meaning control and the methodology have the influences of the social and historical forces of the time. In the Indian context, the colonial experience was unique. During the colonial period, the analyses of Indian society were Eurocentric in their concepts. Concepts are such as "caste" "tribe" "community" "family" and "kinship" were defined in the socio-historical equivalents of the European society. Such a historical and segmental treatment *of* concepts can be seen in the colonial administrator tuned sociologist Sir Henry Meine, who formulated the concept of "community" as equivalent to the Indian notion of "Sangha" (Community). The missionary view saw roots of degeneration in Indian society in its religion. The administrative point viewed traditional institution in India as barrier to the development of national modern society.

By early twentieth century an alternative paradigm of national awakening has been built in Indian social science which has proposed to be the "Paradigm of pupil's progression". It treated the processes in Indian society in a dynamic historical perspective. The sociologists of this generation turned to issues of sociology as a science in general on the one hand and of cultural and national liberation on the other. The national awakening orientation was followed by changes in the world-level ideology of social science. The philosophical and historical orientations of European sociologists came to an end. The importance of empirical field studies, operational tools and experiments increased in India. During this period, studies of Indian rural communities by American social anthropologists were carried out. At the same time a number of studies on rural change, problems of institution were initiated by Indian sociologists who aimed at contributing to policy formation and development.

Such studies were followed by a new trend of indigenization in India. The uniqueness of Indian civilization and its past glory were forefront. The UGC sponsored workshops in social sciences and several social scientists emphasized the need for indigenization of some of the basic concepts in order to understand India's structure, since western models were inadequate. This trend is continuing to the present day thought. It has not led too much change in the general orientation of social scientists. The subject of study may be indigenous yet methods employed to study were borrowed from American sociologists. No thought was given to the construction of an alternative methodology suited to the study of Indian situation. By and large, the structural functionalists approach was employed by Indian sociologists, perhaps with little variation. New developments like critical sociology and phenomenology in the world level sociology was incorporated in Indian studies. However, with the coming up of new areas of interests, it may be expected that alternative approaches in social sciences will develop.

SOCIAL STUDIES

The concept of 'Social Studies' is of recent origin. Social studies originated and developed in order to be considered as the part of school curriculum. The wide spread use of social studies started in America since 1916. Its use in India can be traced back to the formulation of Gandhiji's Basic Education in 1937.

According to John V. Michaela's, "The social studies are concerned with man and his interaction with his social and physical environment; they deal with human relationships. The central function of the social studies is identical with the central purpose of education–development of democratic citizenship".

NATURE OF SOCIAL STUDIES

The following points may characterize the nature of social studies:

1. Social studies are concerned with human study in relation to socio-cultural environment.
2. Social studies have been evolved from social sciences as an instructional area in order to be taught at school level for promoting healthy social/democratic living among learners.
3. Social studies establish the relationship among present, past and future.
4. Social studies stress more on contemporary human life and its problems than the past history of man.

5. Social studies aims at enabling students to adjust to their socio-cultural environment which includes family, community, state, nation and at large the entire humanity.
6. Social studies are a realistic course or deals with practical aspects of society.
7. Social studies are now at growing and developing stage. It is trying to make its scope broader and wider.
8. Social studies are considered now as a core subject at school level for developing necessary competencies relating to healthy social living.

FUNCTIONAL SIMILARITIES & DIFFERENCES BETWEEN SOCIAL SCIENCES & SOCIAL STUDIES

Social Sciences and social studies are two sides of the same coin. They are related with each other as well as different from each other in many ways. Let us find out their similarities and differences.

SIMILARITIES

1. Both social sciences and social studies are the outcomes of same genus/parenthesis.
2. Both of them share a common body of course contents.
3. In case of both, the central focus is woman's/man's relationship with woman/ man and her/his environment.
4. Human relationship is the common denominator in case of both social sciences and social studies.
5. Both focus on woman/man engaging in variety of activities for the purpose of meeting her/his basic needs, communicating her/his ideas and feeling, producing and consuming the necessities of life and saving human and natural resources.

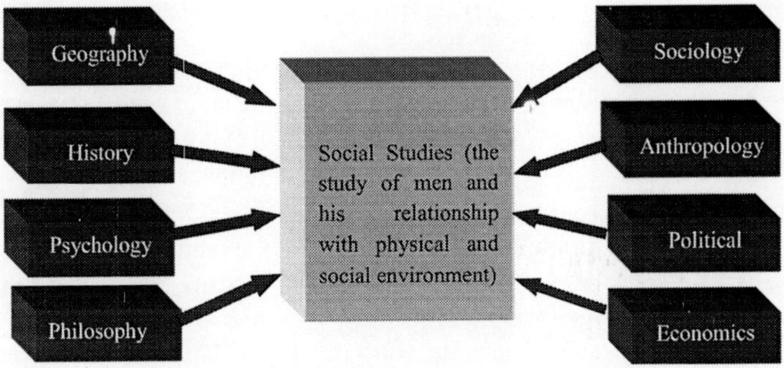

Fig. 1.1. Functional relationship of Social studies with Social Sciences

Source : **John Jarolimek- "Social studies in elementary education", The MacMillan Company (1959), New York.**

DIFFERENCE BETWEEN SOCIAL SCIENCE AND SOCIAL STUDIES

Sr. No	*Points of Difference*	*Social Science*	*Social Studies*
01	Derivation	Social Sciences are the genesis or the parent discipline of social studies.	Social studies is the outcome or product of social sciences
02	Approach	Social sciences represent an adult approach.	Social studies represent a child approach.
03	Area of affairs	Concerned with theoretical aspects of human affairs.	Concerned with practical aspects of human affairs.
04	Area of affaire	Social sciences seek social utility.	Social studies seek instructional utility.
05	Approach	Social sciences are studied through idealistic approach.	Social studies are studied through pragmatic approach.
06	Aim	Social science aim at contributing knowledge and increasing the intellectual horizon.	Social studies aim at acquiring knowledge for solving various practical problems of the society.
07	Composition	Social sciences include large number of subjects	Social studies draws its contents from large

	like history, political science, sociology, anthropology, economics etc.	number of social sciences and label them under three of four broad heads (i.e. history, economic etc.) to be taught at school or junior school level.
08 Nature of Composition	Social sciences are the mixture of different subjects where each and every subject has special identity and one subject can easily be differentiated from others.	Social studies are a compound rather than mixture where something new emerges out of combinations. It is very difficult to separate the parts of social studies in clear cut ways.
09 Reader	The readers of social sciences are very few. Only those who are competent and interested then can study social sciences.	Since citizenship preparation is the main aim of social studies, so, it is studied by everybody.
10 Stage of study	Social sciences are advanced study of human society. They are basically taught at high university level.	Social studies are the simplified aspect of social sciences which is basically taught at school or junior school stage.
11 Scope	The scope of each social science subject is limited within its own field. For example, economics is related with such kind of activities which touch economic field.	Social studies touch all the aspects of human social life in a compound manner.
12 Scope	Social sciences have vast scope since they include numerous subjects.	Social studies are the part of social sciences. So, it is narrower than social sciences.
13 Complexity	Social sciences are the complex study of social phenomena.	Social studies are the simplified aspect of social sciences taught to the school or junior students.

REFERENCES

- Comte, Auguste (1896). Positive philosophy of Auguste Comte. Translated & condensed by Harriet Martinece. Vol. 3. London; Bell.
- Jarolimek, John (1959). Social studies in elementary education, The MacMillan Company, New York.
- Kochhar, S. K. (1984). The Teaching of Social Studies.
- Mitchell (1950). Dictionary of sociology. England.
- Rajan, Mohan. P. A (1990). Paradigm for Social Science India: In Social Science information Proven and Prospects. New Delhi; Vikas Publishing.
- Seligman, E.R.A (1948). Encvclopaodia of Social Sciences. Vol.15. New York; Macmillan, p. 3

2

Political Science

INTRODUCTION

Political science is that branch of the social sciences that studies the state, politics, and government. Political Science deals extensively with the analysis of political systems, the theoretical and practical applications to politics, and the examination of political behavior. Many political scientists view themselves as being engaged in fleshing out the connections between political events and conditions, and by this understanding they hope to construct a system of general principles that posit the way the world of politics works. Political science is not a standalone field and it intersects many other branches like sociology, economics, history, anthropology, public policy among others. Political scientists are much sought after these days because of the changing landscape of politics across the world and since the society wants to understand how the political world works, they need someone to explain the nuances of the political economy. Any casual perusal of the newspapers and the television channels reveals that political scientists are at the forefront of debates and discussions for their knowledge and expertise.

MEANING OF POLITICAL SCIENCE

In the third century BCE, the Greek philosopher Aristotle was perhaps the first scholar to think systematically about how different forms of government led to different political outcomes: such as stability or rebellion in the city states in Ancient Greece. In fact, if science is the systematic building and organisation of knowledge with the aim of understanding and explaining how the world works, then Aristotle was probably the first 'political scientist'.

The term 'Political Science' consists of two words, i.e. Political and Science. The word 'Politics' is derived from the Greek word 'Polis' which means the city-state. In ancient Greece, the basic unit of political organization was the city-state. It was the Greeks who first embarked upon the study of state as distinct from the church. The foundations of political thinking were laid by the great Greek philosophers, Socrates, Plato and Aristotle. Plato was the author of the book "The Republic". Aristotle the father of political science firstly used the term 'politics' and converted the subject into an academic discipline.

Science : is the systematic study of the structure and behavior of the physical and natural world through observation, evidence and experiment. So political science is the branch of knowledge that deals with systematic study of the structure and behavior of the state and political institutions through scientific analysis. Politics refers to the subject matter of our study; science denotes the methodology or the way of studying the process of politics. The first term seeks to answer the question "what is studied" and the second term refers to "how is it studied". Therefore, the political phenomenon which should be studied in accordance with a definite plan or system is called political science.

DEFINITION OF POLITICAL SCIENCE

It is difficult to give a precise definition to political science, because of its varying scope in different situations. Let us examine some of those definitions.

According to Paul Janet : "Political science is that part of science which treats of the foundations of state and the principles of government".

According to H.J Laski : "The study of politics concerns itself with the life of man in relation to organized states".

According to Lasswell : "political science is the study of shaping and sharing of power".

According to David Easton : "Political science is the study of the authoritative allocation of values for a society".

According to COBUILD Advanced English Dictionary: "Political science is the study of the ways in which political power is acquired and used in a country".

According to Garner, "Political Science begins and ends with the state"

According to Aristotle, "Science of polis".

According to Gettle, "Science of state"

SCOPE OF POLITICAL SCIENCE

The scope of political science is vast and experts have divided the field of political science into five sub-disciplines that are political theory, public administration, comparative politics, international relations, and public law. It needs to be noted that these sub-disciplines cover the entire gamut of the modern political economy and provide the basis for the study and understanding of how the global political economy works. The study of the matters concerning the allocation and distribution as well as the transfer of power is one of the main preoccupations of political scientists. The success or otherwise of the governance structures is gauged by political scientists who examine the multifaceted and multilayered factors at work that contribute to good or bad governance. The scope of the political scientists has now been broadened to include the realm of the study of the democratic elections across the world. In other words, with the explosion in the political systems all over the world, political scientists, and their scope of study has been considerably enhanced.

GROWTH AND LANDMARKS OF POLITICAL SCIENCE

The study of politics has had a long tradition. As a matter of fact, Political Science has its roots in ancient Greece. The Greeks used the term "Politika" to describe the numerous activities of the "Polis" or city-states in which they lived. Thus, it was the Greek thinkers who laid the foundation for the development of a systematic science of politics. They were mainly concerned with questions of morality and ethics and tried to define an ideal state. The first efforts to systematically study politics can be traced in the works of the two famous political thinkers from ancient Greece, namely, Plato and Aristotle. Later, Christian religious thinkers like St. Augustine and St. Thomas Aquinas, also dwelt upon the idea of an ideal state and sought to derive moral and ethical principles regarding the same. Accordingly, in the classical (Greek) and Christian formulations, Political Science was more in the realm of political philosophy focusing on the study of state.

In the fifteenth century, Niccolo Machiavelli, the Italian political thinker, started the tradition of studying existing and historical political institutions. It marked a departure from the classical and Christian traditions of political philosophy. Efforts were made to identify institutional arrangements that would maintain social order and political stability. Accordingly, political thinkers subsequently tried to deal with the historical origins of different political institutions and the r structural frameworks.

However, it must be mentioned here that the origin of Political Science as an academic discipline is not very old. Many thinkers have contributed towards the growth of Political Science as a discipline. In this context, the name of **Francis Lieber**, who was a professor of History and Political Science at Columbia University, needs special mention. His work 'Civil Liberty and Self Government' has made significant contribution towards the growth of Political Science as an academic discipline.

Another landmark in the growth of Political Science was the establishment of a school of Political Science at Columbia University at the initiative of **John. W. Burgess** in 1880. It was called the Faculty of Political Science. In 1886 this school inaugurated the Political Science Quarterly which was the first scholarly journal of Political Science as a discipline. It heralded a new era in the growth of the discipline as it gave scholars a new platform to express their views in writing.

The establishment of Johns Hopkins University in 1876 was another milestone in the growth of Political Science. In this context, the establishment of Johns Hopkins Historical and Political Science Association in 1877 and The Johns Hopkins Studies in Historical and political science are worth mentioning. Accordingly, the above two universities-Columbia and Johns Hopkins, contributed significantly towards the growth of Political Science as an academic discipline. The studies and research carried out in these universities also widened the scope of Political Science which was earlier confined to the study of political institutions and historical origin. The subject subsequently began to embrace various concepts like rights, justice, law, sovereignty while analyzing the functioning of governments. The political thinkers also started discussing the merits and demerits of various forms of governments, political institutions etc.

The establishment of the American Political Science Association in 1903 provided a boost towards the strengthening of Political Science as a discipline. It soon became a leading organization for the study of political science and provided a platform for different scholars, departments and institutions from the discipline of Political Science. It also widened the scope of Political Science beyond the study of political philosophy and institutions.

During the 1920s, Political Science made a paradigm shift in the form of the positivist movement. It sought to make the study of Political Science scientific by applying empirical and statistical methods. The Social Science Research Council was chartered in 1923 to encourage scientific research in Economics, Sociology and Political Science. The positivist movement culminated in the behavioural revolution of the 1950s. The growth of behaviouralism can be regarded as the major landmark in the growth of Political Science as a discipline. The behaviouralists put emphasis on making the study of Political Science scientific. They were influenced by the developments and research in different disciplines and they tried to make the study of Political Science inter-disciplinary. In order to draw scientific conclusions the behaviouralism advocated the use of statistical methods and tools in the study of Political Science. Thus, with the emergence of behaviouralism the character of Political Science had changed to a large extent. Behaviouralism shifted the focus of Political Science from the study of political institutions to the study of day today behaviour of the individuals in a political society. Political thinkers like David Easton, Charles E. Merriam, and Arthur Bentley contributed significantly through their writings and research towards the growth of behavioural revolution in Political Science.

After the Second World War and in the early fifties of the twentieth century, Political Science was highly influenced by sociologists like Tocqueville, G. Mosca, Max Weber, Talcott Parsons etc. Such an interaction between political scientists and sociologists helped to bring the study of Political Science closer to society. For instance, the concept of the state, which had been central to Political Science, gave way to the new concept of the "political system," developed by **David Easton**. The new concept highlighted the interaction between the society and the political process.

During this period the behavioural revolution in Political Science became popular and various methods of research and techniques of data collection were identified by the political thinkers. The Social Science Research Council of United States set up in the early twenties of twentieth century continued to play an important role in popularizing behavioural ideas in the post second world war era.

Political Science entered a new phase towards the late 1960s in the form of the Post-behavioural revolution. The rise of behaviouralism clearly introduced a scientific vigor in the study of political phenomena. However, it soon came to be realized that too much emphasis was being laid on adoption of scientific techniques in the field of Political Science. In the process, Political Science was losing touch with the real social and political issues. Therefore, post-behaviouralists made an effort to make Political Science relevant to the society. However, it must be remembered that post-behaviouralism cannot be separated from behaviouralism as it has emerged out of behaviouralism. Through using different techniques and methods, the post-behaviouralists have tried to overcome the drawbacks of behaviouralism and make the study of Political Science more relevant to the society. Thus, we can see that the Political Science which emerged as a study of the state and government has undergone tremendous changes in the later period. Because of the contribution of different scholars its scope is widening and its nature is changing. In the present time, the focus of Political Science shifts from the study of the state and government to the political system as a whole.

RESEARCH TRENDS OF POLITICAL SCIENCE

During the late 20th century the American practice of the discipline has become dominant worldwide. The analytical methods favored by the behaviorists continue to influence political scientists, who have developed rational choice theory to predict and explain the behavior of people when they interact in a political context. Political scientists have also reconsidered some of the most basic building blocks of society, such as the state and the institutions it comprises.

1. Rational Choice Theory

The latest initiative to make political science more self-consciously scientific involves the use of rational choice theory, which attempts to deduce what will happen when individuals are faced with a political situation. The theory borrows from economics the assumption that all individuals are *rational egoists*. People are assumed to be rational in their capacity to devise, choose, and put into practice effective means to clear ends; they are egoists because the ends in question generally refer to the self-interest of that individual. Rational choice theory can be applied to everything from decisions made by small committees to complex negotiations between governments.

Rational choice theory has proven limited in its ability to predict real-world behavior. For example, rational choice theory cannot explain why intelligent people vote in elections when the chances of their vote being decisive in determining the winner of the election are near zero. Some observers believe that the results of rational choice theory are best thought of as a set of warnings about what would happen if people behaved as rational egoists, rather than an explanation of how the world actually works.

2. New Institutionalism

New Institutionalists have reinvigorated the study of institutions. In political science, institutions can be defined as systems of formal rules or informal understandings that coordinate the actions of individuals. Examples of institutions include the U.S. Congress and global agreements that seek to limit damage to the earth's ozone layer. New Institutionalists claim that the behavioral revolution of the 1950s led political scientists to overemphasize the behavior of individuals, to the neglect of the institutional contexts in which these individuals operate. New Institutionalists claim to have more-sophisticated theories about how institutions work than did the "old" Institutionalists of the early 20th century.

3. Return of the State

From the 19th century to the 1940s many political scientists regarded the state as a unified, organic entity that integrated government, society, and political organizations. During the behavioral revolution, this concept of a unified, goal-directed state was discredited, in favor of a looser and more open concept of the political system. Behaviorists contended that the idea of the state was unscientific and mocked it as mystical. They claimed that political systems, in contrast, are real and observable, composed of various inputs and outputs. According to the behaviorists, the inputs in a political system include influences such as lobbying by interest groups and bargaining between the executive and legislative branches, and the outputs are public policies.

The concept of the state, now more precisely defined as the set of officials legally authorized to make binding decisions for a society, made a comeback in the 1980s. States are viewed as having certain functions or imperatives that they must perform—for example, maintaining the confidence of financial markets—regardless of the desires of their political leaders, the wishes of voters, pressure from interest groups, or bargaining within government.

4. Democracy and Democratization

During the 1980s and 1990s increasing numbers of political scientists studied democracy and its development in societies that had formerly been ruled by authoritarian governments. The wave of democratization that followed the end of the Cold War inspired political theorists to develop new models of democracy, and political scientists to study the role of citizenship and citizen education in democratic governments.

5. Challenges to the Discipline

Marxists challenged conventional political science through most of the 20th century, charging that the discipline overlooked oppressive political relationships in the capitalist economy. According to Marxists, formal democracy is a sham because the dominant economic class in society always controls the government.

REFERENCES

- https://www.managementstudyguide.com/political-science.htm
- https://www.quora.com/With-examples-what-is-the-definition-of-political-science

3

Management

INTRODUCTION

Management is the scientific art of achieving the results of goals by effective utilization of the resources. Management is a science which has made tremendous contributions to the improvement of all the industry including library science. As the library is a core industry in today's world and we are having united resources, so it has become a great need to use these resources efficiently with meticulous managerial skills. Management generally lays emphasis on control i.e. control of personnel, control of cost, time, salaries, overtime, inventory etc. Management is required to plan, organize, co-ordinate and control the affairs of the organization. It brings the human and material resources together and motivates people for achievement of the objectives of the organization. Management is a universal process in all social and economic activities. Management is involved to some extent in all activities of human life.

DEFINITIONS

Management in general can be defined as all the activities and tasks undertaken by one or more persons for the purpose of planning and controlling the activities of others in order to achieve an objective or complete an activity that could not be acting independently.

According to F.W. Taylor, "Management is the art of knowing what you want to do and then seeing that they do it in the best and the cheapest may."

According to Peter Drucker, "Management is a multipurpose organ that manages a business and manages Managers and manages Workers and work."

According to George R. Terry, "Management Is a distinct process consisting of planning, organizing, actuating and controlling, utilizing in each both science and art, and followed in order to accomplish pre-determined objectives."

According to Harold Koontz, "Management is the art of getting things done through others and with formally organized groups."

According to Mary Parker Follett, "Management is the art of getting things done through people."

SCOPE OF MANAGEMENT

Although it is difficult to precisely define the scope of management, yet the following areas are included in it:

1. Subject-matter of management : Planning, Organizing, Directing, Coordinating, Controlling are the activities included in the subject matter of management.

2. Functional areas of management : These include:

- ***Financial management*** : Financial management includes accounting, budgetary control, quality control, financial planning and managing the overall finances of an organization.
- ***Personnel management*** : Personnel management includes recruitment, training, transfer promotion, demotion, retirement, termination, labor-welfare and social security industrial relations.
- ***Purchasing management*** : Purchasing management

includes inviting tenders for raw materials, placing orders, entering into contracts and materials control.

- ***Production management*** **:** Production management includes production planning, production control techniques, quality control and inspection and time and motion studies.
- ***Maintenance management*** **:** Maintenance management involves proper care and maintenance of the buildings, plant and machinery.
- ***Transport management*** **:** Transport management includes packing, warehousing and transportation by rail, road and air.
- ***Distribution management*** **:** Distribution management includes marketing, market research, price-determination, taking market- risk and advertising, publicity and sales promotion.
- ***Office Management*** **:** Office Management includes activities to properly manage the layout, staffing and equipment of the office.
- ***Development management*** **:** Development management involves experimentation and research of production techniques, markets, etc.

3. Management is an inter-disciplinary approach : For the correct implementation of the management, it is important to have knowledge of commerce, economics, sociology, psychology and mathematics.

4. Universal application : The principles of management can be applied to all types of organizations irrespective of the nature of tasks that they perform.

5. Modern management is an agent of change : The management techniques can be modified by proper research and development to improve the performance of an organization.

6. Essentials of management : Three essentials of management are:

- Scientific method
- Human relations
- Quantitative technique

NATURE OF MANAGEMENT

1. Management is a scientific process by which objectives of an organization are observed in a planned way.
2. Management is a process to allocate and utilize the resources efficiently.
3. Management is the managerial process of forming a strategic vision, setting objectives, crafting a strategy and then implementing and executing the strategy.
4. Management means deciding what is to be done and getting the work done by other people who are brought into a group to work harmoniously and efficiently to accomplish common laid down organizational objectives.
5. Management focuses on the entire organizational process from both a short and a long term perspective.
6. Management is a functional concept and persons performing management are designated as managers or executives.

DEVELOPMENT & LANDMARKS OF MANAGEMENT

Management thought has a long history. It is as old as human civilization itself. Management in one form or the other has been a significant feature of economic life of mankind throughout ages. Management thought is an evolutionary concept it has develop along with and in line with the growth of social, political, economic and scientific institutions. Management thought has its origin in the ancient times. It developed gradually along with other socioeconomic developments. The contributor's to management though are many. They include Management philosophers, management practitioners and scholars. Modem management is based on the solid foundations laid down by management thinkers from the early historical period.

The Sumerian : The recorded use of organised management dates back to 5000 B.C. when the agricultural revolution had taken place. These agricultural civilizations existed in India, China and Egypt According to Peter Drucker these irrigation civilizations "were not only one of the great ages of technology, but it represented also mankind's most productive age of social and political innovation". As the villages grew and civilizations evolved, the managers too grew and evolved. They became the priests, the kings, the ministers holding power and wealth in the society. Written documents found in the Sumerian civilization which flourished some 5000 years ago, contains evidence of management control practices.

The Egyptians : As early as 4000 B.C., the Egyptians were aware of the importance of planning, organising and controlling. The huge pyramids of Egypt stand a mute testimony to the managerial and organizational abilities of the ancient Egyptian civilization. One pyramid required 1,00,000 men working for 20 years, covering 13 acres, using 2.3 million blocks, each weighing an average of 2.5 tons. To produce such a monument required proper planning, work allocation, organising, directing, controlling and decision making.

The Grecian : In the Grecian civilization we find the origin of the Scientific Method in the famous Socratic discourses. The Romans who built a vast empire extending from Britain in the west to Syria in the east ruled it for many years only because of their superior and advanced managerial abilities.

The Ancient Aryans : In ancient India Kautilya wrote his Arthashastra in about 321 B.C. the major theme of which was political, social and economic management of the State. The study of administration of the cities of Mohenjodaro and Harappa of the ancient Aryans in 2000 B. C., Buddha's order and the Sangha in 530 B. C., provide evidence about the use of the principles of management.

The 13th and 14th centuries : During the 13th and 14th centuries AD the large trading houses of Italy needed a means of keeping records of their business transactions. To satisfy their needs Luca Pacioli published a treatise in 1494 describing the Double Entry System of Book-keeping for the first time.

Management thought is an evolutionary concept. New theories and principles were suggested along with new developments in the business field. The new thoughts supplemented the existing thoughts and theories. This is how developments are taking place continuously in regard to management thoughts. Management thinkers and thinkers from other fields such as economics, psychology, sociology and mathematics have also made their contribution in the evolution of management thought.

RESAERCH TRENDS OF MANAGEMENT

This includes analyzing current research trends from the following perspectives:

1. Emerging corporate management best practices.
2. The broadening applications of actuarial science.
3. Management recruiting and education.
4. Management consultant offerings.
5. Advisory services from insurance consultants and brokers.
6. Sources for risk information and risk data.
7. Industry standards.

8. Government regulations.
9. Ratings agency assessments.
10. Technology advances supporting.
    - Enterprise Risk Management (ERM).
    - Data acquisition.
    - Data mining.
    - Data management.
    - Data analytics.
    - Decision support.
    - Decision rule management.
    - Data visualization.
    - Reporting and communication.

The combination of advances in business school risk education, risk data sources, information technology, actuarial science, risk consultant advice, and insurance advisory services is vastly changing business management discipline today. Collectively they will break down the barriers of organizational silos and politics that have been preventing more effective assessments and management of corporate challenges.

As the digitization of corporate information grows exponentially, the IT products and applications in development today will enable companies to better meet the rising risk management efficiency expectations of shareholders, industry standards, the SEC, and other regulatory agencies.

Intelligent Management Trends analyzes and reports on the latest management concepts, education, actuarial science, services vendors, technology vendors, and risk information sources that are carrying us forward to the next crest of business management proficiency.

REFERENCES

- https://www.managementstudyhq.com/nature-and-scope-of-management.html
- http://kalyan-city.blogspot.com/2010/06/management-functions-process management. html

4

Psychology

INTRODUCTION

Psychology is the academic and applied study of the human mind and behavior. Perhaps there are no more salient topics in the information age and the global economy than a comprehensive understanding of how learning takes place and what predicts and determines human behavior. Students interested in the subject of psychology are interested in why people do, say and think what they do. They have questions about how learning takes place, how genetics dictate certain traits but not others, how memories are formed, where to draw the line between normality and disorder, whether a damaged brain can regain function and the predictors of addiction.

MEANING OF PSYCHOLOGY

The word psychology was used by 'Rudolf Goeckle' in 1590.

It is derived from two Greek Words 'Psyche' and 'logos'. Psyche means 'Spirit' or 'Soul' or 'Human mind'. The word 'Soul' means the spiritual or immortal elements in a person. The words 'Logos' means Knowledge or study like all "Logies". The first Greek letter psi in psyche is used as the international symbol for psychology.

DEFINITIONS OF PSYCHOLOGY

Oxford American Dictionary, "Psychology is the scientific study of mental processes and behavior. It is the study of mind and how it works".

According to Woodworth, "Psychology is the science of the activities of the individual in relation to the environment".

According to Watson, "Psychology is the positive science of behaviour".

According to McDougall, "Psychology is the positive science of conduct and behaviour".

Concise Oxford Dictionary, "Psychology is the scientific study of the human mind and its functions, especially those affecting behavior in a given context".

According to Sir W. Hamilton, "Psychology is the science of human and animal behavior which includes the application of this science to solve human behavior. Psychology is defined as a science about the phenomena of the mind, conscious subject or self".

SCOPE OF PSYCHOLOGY

Psychology is a broad and diverse field. A number of different subfields and specialty areas have emerged. The subject matter of psychology can be grouped into different branches for the sake of convenience and specialized study. We divide it into wo broad categories, namely, pure psychology and applied psychology.

Pure science provides the framework and theory. Its contents deal with the formulation of psychological principles and theories. It suggests various methods and techniques for the analysis assessment, modification and improvement of behavior.

In applied psychology, the theory generated and discussed through pure psychology finds its practical shape.

Here, we discuss the ways and means of the applications of psychological rules, principles, theories and techniques with reference to real practical situations. The branches of pure and applied psychology are as follows:

Branches of Pure Psychology

1. General Psychology : General psychology is relatively a large area or field of psychology which deals with the fundamental rules, principles and theories of psychology in relation to study of behaviour of normal adult human beings.

2. Abnormal Psychology : Abnormal psychology is the study of abnormal behaviour and psychopathology. This specialty area is focused on research and treatment of a variety of mental disorders and is linked to psychotherapy and clinical psychology. Mental health professional typically utilize the diagnostic and statistical manual of mental disorders to diagnose mental disorders.

3. Social Psychology : Social psychology is a discipline that uses scientific methods to study social influence, social perception, and social interaction. Social psychology studies diverse subjects including group behaviour, social perception, leadership, nonverbal behaviour, conformity, aggression and prejudice.

4. Experience Psychology : Experimental psychology described and explains the ways and means of carrying out psychological experiments following scientific methods in controlled or laboratory situations for the study of mental processes and behaviour. It picks up animals, birds and human beings as subjects for these experiments.

5. Physiological/Biological Psychology : Physiological Psychology also known as biopsychology, studies how biological processes influence the mind and the behaviour. This area is closely linked to neuroscience and utilizes tools such as MRI and PET scans to look at brain injury or brain abnormalities.

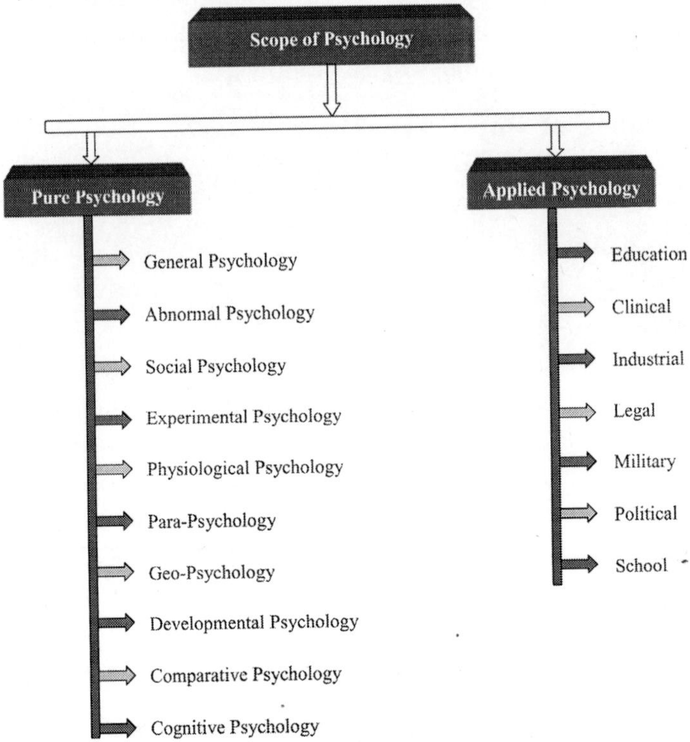

6. Para-Psychology : Para-Psychology deals with extra sensory perceptions, cases of rebirth, telepathy and applied problems.

7. Geo-Psychology : Geo-Psychology describes and explains the relation of physical environment particularly weather, climate, soil and landscape with behaviour.

8. Developmental Psychology : Developmental Psychology is the branch of psychology that looks at human growth and development over the lifespan. Theories often focus on the development of cognitive abilities, morality, social functioning, identity, and other life areas. For convenience, it is further divided into branches like child psychology, adolescent psychology and adult psychology.

9. Comparative Psychology : Comparative Psychology is the branch of psychology concerned with the study of animal behaviour. The study of animal behaviour can lead to a deeper and broader understanding of human psychology.

10. Cognitive Psychology : Cognitive Psychology is the study of human thought processes and cognitions. Cognitive psychologists study topics such as attention, memory, perception, decision-making, problem solving, and language acquisition.

Branches of Applied Psychology

1. Education Psychology : Education Psychology is that branch of applied psychology which tries to apply the psychological principles, theories and techniques to human behaviour in educational situation. The subject matter of this branch covers psychological ways and means of improving all aspects of the teaching learning process including learner, learning process, learning material, learning environment and the teacher.

2. Clinical Psychology : Clinical Psychology is focused on the assessment, diagnosis, and treatment of mental disorders. It explains the causes of mental illness or abnormal behaviour of a patient attending to a clinic or hospital and suggests individual or group therapy for the treatment and effective adjustment of the affected person in the society.

3. Industrial Psychology : Industrial Psychology is the area of psychology that uses psychological research to enhance work perfor4mance, select employee, improve product design and enhance usability. This branch tries to seek application of the psychological principles, theories and techniques for the study of human behaviour in relation to industrial environment. It includes topics like ways and means of knowing and improving the taste and interest of the consumers, advertising and sale of products, selection training and placement of personnel, solving labour problems, establishing harmonious relationships between the employee and employer, strengthening morale of workers and increasing production etc.

4. Legal Psychology : Legal Psychology tries to study the behaviour the persons like clients, criminals, witnesses etc. with the help of psychological principles and techniques. It studies improving the ways and means of crime detection, false witnesses and other complex phenomena. The root causes of the crime, offense, dispute or any legal case can be properly understood through the use of this branch of psychology.

5. Military Psychology : Military psychology is concerned with the use of psychological principles and techniques in the world of military science. i.e. how to keep the morale of the soldiers and citizens high during war time, how to fight war of propaganda and intelligence services, how to secure better recruitment of personnel for the armed forces, how to improve fighting capacities and organizational climate and leadership.

6. Political Psychology : Political psychology related itself with the use of psychological principles and techniques in studying the politics and deriving political gains. i.e. knowledge of dynamics of group behaviour, judgment of public opinion, qualities of leadership, psychology of propaganda and suggestions, the art of diplomacy etc.

7. School Psychology : School psychology is the branch of psychology that works within the educational systems to help children with emotional, social and academic issues.

ORIGIN AND HISTORY OF PSYCHOLOGY

Origin of Psychology (387 BC to Present)	
335 BC	Aristotle suggested that the heart is the mechanism of mental processes.

387 BC	Plato suggested that the brain is the mechanism of mental processes.
1793	Philippe Pinel released the first mental patients from confinement in the first massive movement for more humane treatment of the mentally ill.
1861	French physician Paul Broca discovered an area in the left frontal lobe that plays a key role in language development.
1869	Sir Francis Galton, influenced by Charles Darwin's 'Origin of the Species' publishes 'Hereditary Genius,' and argues that intellectual abilities are biological in nature.
1874	Carl Wernicke published his work on the Frontal lobe, detailing that damage to a specific area damages the ability to understand or produce language.
1878	G. Stanley Hall received the first American Ph.d in psychology. He later founded the American Psychological Association.
1879	Wilhelm Wundt founded the first formal laboratory of psychology at the University of Leipzig, making the formal beginning of the study of human emotions, behaviours and cognitions.
1883	The first laboratory of psychology in America is established at Johns Hopkins University.
1885	Herman Ebbinghaus introduced the non-sense syllable as a means to study memory processes.
1886	Sigmund Freud began performing therapy in Vienna, marking the beginning of personality theory.
1890	The team, "Mental Tests" was coined by James Cattell, beginning the specialization in psychology now known as psychological assessment.
1890	Sir Francis Galton developed the technique known as the correlation to better understand the interrelationships in his intelligence studies.
1890	New York state passed the State Care Act. Ordering indigent mentally ill patients out of poor-houses and into state hospitals for treatment and developing the first institution in the U.S for psychiatric research.
1892	Foundation of American Psychological Association headed by G. Stanley Hall, with an initial membership of 42.
1895	Alfred Binet founded the first laboratory of psychodiagnosis.

1896 The first psychological clinic was developed at the University of Pennsylvania marking the birth of clinical psychology.

1900 Sigmund Freud published 'Interpretation of Dream' marking the beginning of psychoanalytic thought.

1905 Alfred Binet's intelligence test was published in France.

1906 Ivan Pavlov published the first studies on classical conditioning.

1911 Edward Thorndike published first article on animal intelligence leading to the theory of operant conditioning.

1912 William Stern developed the original formula for the intelligence Quotient (IQ) after studying the scored on Binet's intelligence test. The formula is IQ

$$= \frac{\text{Mental Age (MA)}}{\text{Chronological Age (CA)}} \times 100$$

1912 Max Wertheimer published research on the perception of movement, marking the beginnings of Gestalt Psychology.

1913 Carl G. Jung departed from Freudian views and developed his own theories citing Freud's inability to acknowledge religion and spirituality. His new school of thought became known as Analytical Psychology.

1927 Anna Freud, daughter of Sigmund Freud, published her first book expanding her father's ideas in the treatment of children.

1932 Jean Piaget published 'The Moral Judgement of Children' beginning his popularity as the leading theorist in cognitive development.

1935 Thematic Apperception Test (TAT) was published by Henry Murray.

1942 Carl Rogers published 'Counseling and Psychotherapy' suggesting that respect and a non-judgement approach to therapy is the foundation for effective treatment of mental health issues.

1942 Minnesota Multiphasic Personality Inventory (MMPI) was developed and fast became the most widely researched and widely accepted psychological assessment device.

1950 Erik Erikson published 'Childhood and society, 'where he expands Freud's Theory to include social aspects of personality development across the lifespan.

1952 A study on psychotherapy efficacy was published by Hans

	Eysenck suggesting that therapy is no more effective that no treatment at all. This prompted an onslaught of outcome studies which have since shown psychotherapy to be an effective treatment for mental illness.
1952	The Diagnostic and Statistical Manual of Mental Disorders (DSM) was published by the American Psychiatric Association marking the beginning of modern mental illness classification.
1953	Code of Ethics for psychologists was developed by the American Psychological Association.
1954	Abraham Maslow helped to found Humanistic Psychology and later developed his famous 'Hierarchy of Needs'.
1968	First doctor of psychology professional degree program in clinical psychology was established in the department of psychology at the University of Illinois Urbana/Champaign.
1971	First Ph.d awarded University of Illinois Urbana/ Champaign.
1973	APA endorsed the Psy.D. Degree for professional practice in psychology.
1988	American Psychological Society established.
1990	The emergence of managed care prompts the APA to become more political, leading to the idea of prescribing psychologist and equity in mental health coverage.
1995	First psychologist prescribes medication through the U.S military's psychopharmacology programme.
1997	Deep Blue, the supercomputer at the time, beats the world's best chess player, Kasparov, marking a milestone in the development of artificial intelligence.
1998	Psychology advances to the technological age with the emergence of e-therapy.
2002	New Mexico becomes the first state to pass legislation allowing licensed psychologists to prescribe psychotropic medication.

LANDMARKS AND RESEARCH TRENDS OF PSYCHOLOGY

Historically, the evolution of the subject psychology can be conveniently studied by breaking the period, into three heads:

1. Pre-scientific Age
2. Scientific Age
3. Present Contemporary Age

1. Pre-Scientific Age

The age of the Pre-Scientific Psychology (stretched up to the middle of the 19th century) witnesses the following trends:

- In the earliest age of superstitions, causes and forms of human behavior were being located in something outside the human beings i.e. planets or demons, spirits, and other supernatural power.
- Subsequently, philosophers like Socrates, Plato and Aristotle etc. with their philosophical viewpoints tried to do away with the evils of superstition. Especially after the renaissance in the 17th century, there emerged quite a dominating philosophical basis of behavior in the philosophies like dualism propagated by Descartes and empiricism advocated by Locke and Kant. According to dualism theory, mind and body are separate entities. The body is merely a machine that works automatically but human beings, however, possess a mind in addition to their bodies. Mind, rather than being automatic is capable of free thought, imagination and memory. Therefore, human behavior can be explained through the mode of inter actions between the mind and the body. Another point, from the angle of historical importance in Descartes' teaching was his belief in innate ideas i.e. certain necessary truths or axioms which he supposed were inherent in man's nature.
- In the 19th century the viewpoint of Locke, Kant and their successors gave birth to associationism, the first

school of psychology-in Great Britain, emphasizing a direct connection between sensation and idea. According to this doctrine, there is a direct connection between sensation and idea. If sensation has often been experience, together, the corresponding ideas will tend to occur together; if A has been associated with B, C, and D in sensory experience, the sensory experience A, occurring alone will tend to arouse the ideas of B, C, and D which accompanied it (Heidbreder, 1971).

- As a reaction towards too much intellectualization brought about by associationism and empiricism, there arose a wave of naturalism propagated by Rousseau, Pestalozzi and Froebel and the idea of faculty psychology propagated by German thinkers like Christian wolf. The naturalists tried to revolt against too much intellectualization brought about by rationalists and empiricists. They insisted on the role of feelings and emotions and rejected the notion that man is essentially a creature of ideas and reason.
- The faculty psychology was opposed and replaced by Herbartion psychology propagated by a nineteenth century German professor Johann Friedrich Herbart. If particularly emphasized the doctrine of apperception.

2. The Modern age of Scientific Psychology

From the late 1800's until the 1930's psychologists were divided about what they should study and how they should study it. Four major schools were developed.

Structuralism : Structuralism grew out of the works of James, Wundt and their associates. These psychologists believed the chief purpose of psychology was to describe, analyse and explain conscious experience, particularly feelings and sensations. The sturcturalists attempted to give a scientific analysis of conscious experience by breaking by breaking it down into its specific components or structures.

For example, they identified four basic skin sensations: warmth, cold, pain, and pressure. They analyses the sensation of wetness as the combined experience of cold and smoothness.

The structuralism primarily used a method of research called introspection. In this technique, subjects were trained to observe and report as accurately as they could their mental processes, feelings and experiences.

Behaviorism : Behaviorism was introduced in 1913 by Jond B. Watson, an American psychologist. Watson and his followers believed that observable behavior, not inner experience, was the only reliable source of information. This concentration on observable events was a reaction against the sturcturalists' emphasis on introspection. The behaviourists also stressed the importance of the environment in shaping an individual's behavior. They chiefly looked for connections between observable behavior and stimuli from the environment.

The behaviourist movement was greatly influenced by the work of the Russian physiologist Ivan P. Pavlov. In a famous study, Pavlov rang a bell each time he gave a dog some food. The dog's mouth would water when the animal smelled the food. After Pavlov repeated the procedure many times, the dog's saliva began to flow whenever the animal heard the bell, even if no food appeared. This experiment demonstrated that a reflex such as the flow of saliva can become associated with a stimulus other than the one that first produced it in this case, the sound of a bell instead of the smell of food. The learning process by which a response becomes associated with a new stimulus is called conditioning.

Watson and the other behaviourist realized that human behavior could also be change by conditioning. In fact, Watson believed he could produce almost any response by controlling an individual's environment. During the mid

1900's, the American psychologist, B.F Skinner gained much attention for behaviourist ideas. In his book 'Walden Two (1948)', Skinner describes how the principles of conditioning might be applied to create an ideal planned society.

Gestalt psychology : Gestalt psychology, like behaviouism, developed as a reaction against structuralism. Gestalt psychologists believed that human beings and other animals perceive the external world as an organized pattern, not as individual sensations. For example, a film consists of thousands of individual still picture, but we see what looks like smooth continuous movement. The German word 'Gestalt' means pattern, form, or shape. Unlike the behaviourists, the Gestaltists believed that behavior should be studied as an organized pattern rather than as separate incidents of stimulus and response. The familiar saying "The whole is greater than the sum of its parts" expresses an important principle of the Gestalt movement. Gestalt psychology was founded about 1912 by Max Wertheimer, a German psychologist. During the 1930's, Wertheimer and two colleague took the Gestalt movement to the United States.

Psychoanalysis : Psychoanalysis was founded during the late 1800's and early 1900's by the Austrian doctor, Sigmund Freud. Psychoanalysis was based on the theory that behavior is determined by powerful inner forces, most of which are buried in the unconscicus mind. According to Freud and other psychoanalysts, from early childhood people repress (force out of conscious awareness) any desires or needs that are unacceptable to themselves or to society. The repressed feelings can cause personality disturbance, self destructive behavior, or even physical symptoms.

Freud developed several techniques to bring repressed feelings to the level of conscious awareness. In a method called free association, the patient relaxes and talks about anything that comes to mind while the therapist listens for clues to the person's inner feelings. Psychoanalysts also try to interpret dreams, which they regard as a reflection of unconscious drives and conflicts. The goal is to help the patient understand and accept repressed feelings and find ways to deal with them.

Modern Psychology : Modern Psychology has incorporated many teachings of the earlier schools. For example, though many psychologists disagree with certain of Freud's ideas, most accept his concept that the unconscious plays a major role in shaping behaviour. Similarly, most psychologists agree with the behaviorists that environment influences behaviour and that they should study chiefly observable actions. However, many psychologists object to pure behaviourism. They believe that it pays too little attention to such processes as reasoning and personality development.

Psychology today has continued to develop in several directions. A group of extreme behaviourists called the stimulus-response school believe all behaviour is a series of responses to different stimuli. According to these psychologists, the stimulus connected with any response can eventually be identified. As a result, stimulus-response psychologists regard behaviour as predictable and potentially controllable.

3. Recent trend in Contemporary Psychology

The present world of psychology is dominated by a mixed trend involving so many schools of thought. Some schools worth mentioning are: behaviourism, psycho-analysis, humanist psychology, transpersonal psychology and cognitive psychology.

Cognitive Psychology : Cognitive Psychology has its roots in the cognitive outlook of the Gestaltists. The names of psychologists like Edward Tolman and Jean Piaget are associated with the further propagation of the ideas of this psychology. They believe there is more to human nature than a series of stimulus response connections. These psychologists concentrate on such mental processes as thinking, reasoning, self awareness. They investigate how a person gathers information about the world, processes the information, and plans responses.

Humanist Psychology : Humanist Psychology advocated by the contemporary psychologists like Maslow, Rogers, Arthur Combs, and Gordon Allport reflects the recent human trends in psychology. A school called humanistic psychology developed as an alternative to behaviourism and psychoanalysis. Humanistic psychologists believe individuals are controlled by their own values and choices and not as psychoanalysts believe. The goal of humanistic psychology is to help people function effectively and fulfill their own unique potential. The supporters of this approach include the American psychologist Abraham H. Maslow and Carl R. Rogers. Many psychologists do not associate themselves with a particular school or theory. Instead, they select and use what seems best from a wide variety of sources. They approach is called eclecticism.

REFERENCES

- https://allpsych.com/timeline/
- https://www.quora.com/Whats-the-scope-of-psychology
- http://www.psychologydiscussion.net/notes/psychology-notes/notes-on-psychology-definition-scope-and-methods/1945

5

Sociology

INTRODUCTION

Sociology is the scientific study of the individual and group behavior within society. Sociology has many sub-sections of study, ranging from the analysis of conversations to the development of theories to try to understand how the entire world works. A standard textbook approach emphasizes several theoretical approaches to understanding human behavior; however, there are four main approaches: Structural-Functionalism, Social-Conflict, Symbolic-Interactionalism and Feminism. Post- Modernism is also a theoretical perspective characteristic of Sociology, though not often deemed a major perspective is nonetheless a field of study of concentration, with extensive roots in the sociological tradition of research and understanding human behavior.

MEANING OF SOCIOLOGY

The term sociology was coined by 'Auguste Comte', a French philosopher in 1839. The word sociology is derived from the Latin word 'Societus' meaning 'Society' and the Greek word 'Logos' meaning 'Study or Science'. The etymological meaning of 'Sociology' is thus the 'Science of Society'. It is considered as a social science. All human beings have to interact with other human beings in order to survive.

DEFINITIONS OF SOCIOLOGY

There are numerous definitions from the various points of view of the respective groups of sociologist.

According to L. T. Hobhouse, "The subject matter of sociology is the inter-action of human minds".

According to L.W. Ward, "Sociology is the science of society or of social phenomena".

According to M. Ginsberg, "Sociology is the study of human inter-action and interrelation their conditions and consequences".

According to H. M. Johnson, "Sociology is the science that deals with social groups their internal forms or modes of organisation, the processes that tend to maintain or change these forms of organisation and relations between groups".

According to Von Wiese, "Sociology is a special social science concertrating on inter human behaviour, on processes of sociation, on association and dissociation as such".

According to H. P. Fairchild, "Sociology is the study of the relationships between man and his human relationships".

According to R.E. Park & F. W. Burgess, "Sociology is the science of collective behaviour".

According to Max Weber, "Sociology is the science which attempts the interpretive understanding of social action".

However, the common idea underlying them all is that Sociology is concerned with human relationships. Its emphasis is on the 'Social' aspect of these relationships.

SCOPE OF SOCIOLOGY

Sociology as a science and particularly as a separate field of study is of recent origin.

Scope means the subject matter or the areas of study. Every science has its own field of inquiry. It becomes difficult to study a science systematically unless its boundary or scope is determined precisely. Sociology as a social science has its own scope or boundaries. But there is no one opinion about the scope of Sociology. However, there are two main schools of thought regarding the scope of Sociology: (1) The Specialist or Formalistic school and (2) the Synthetic school. There is a good deal of controversy about the scope of Sociology between the two schools. The supporter of first school believes that Sociology is a specific science and the scope should be limited whereas others believe that it is a general science and its scope is very vast.

1. Specialistic school

The supporters of this school of thought are George Simmel, Vierkandt, Max Weber, Vonwise, and F. Tonnies. The main views of the school regarding the scope of Sociology are:

- Sociology is a specific, pure and independent social science.
- Sociology studies the various forms of social relationships.
- Scope of Sociology is very narrow and limited.
- Sociology deals with specific form of human relationship.
- Sociology need not study all the events connected with social science.
- Simmel believes that it is a specific social science and it should deal with social relationships from different angles.

Criticism

- Sociologist alone does not study the forms of social relationships. Other social scientists also do that.
- The distinction between the forms of social relations and their contents is not practicable.
- Thirdly, the formalistic school has narrowed down the scope of Sociology.
- Finally, the conception of pure Sociology is imaginary.

2. Synthetic school

The supporters of synthetic school are the sociologists like Ginsberg, Durkheim, Comte, Sorokin, Spencer, F. Ward, and L.T. Hobhouse.

According to this school:

- Sociology is a general and systematic social science.
- Scope of Sociology is very vast.
- Sociology needs help from other social sciences.
- It is a synthesis of social science.
- Sociology is closely related with other social sciences.

LANDMARKS AND RESEARCH TRENDS OF SOCIOLOGY

Historically, the evolution of the subject sociology can be conveniently studied by breaking the period.

The Greeks : it is true that science of sociology as we understand it today definitely emerged very late but it does not mean that no attempts were made to explain human relations and behaviour earlier than 1839. As has already been mentioned, attempts to understand social phenomena have been made since earliest times, though they were more of a speculative rather than of scientific nature. The earliest attempts at systematic thought regarding social life in the west may be said to have begun with the ancient Greek philosophers Plato (427-347 B.C) and his disciple Aristotle (384-322 B.C). Plato's republic is an analysis of the city community in all its aspects, and in Aristotle's Ethics and Politics we find the first major attempts to deal systematically with the law, the society and the state. But one defect of Greek approach was that it lacked the concepts of community as distinct from the state, that is, the study of social relationships was dominated by political aspects. Furthermore, though Aristotle showed more realistic approach to social phenomena than did Plato, who was his teacher, yet their Investigations resulted in depicting the character of an ideal social order. They used their wisdom in bolstering up a cause, never to find "the cause" of social life itself. Since they were either attacking or defending their own social systems, their interpretation of the facts of social life was prejudiced. Plato vastly underestimated the complexity of social organisation. In his plan, everything was to go on according to plan, but in social life nothing ever goes quite according to plan. Aristotle's philosophy, since it supported the status quo was highly conservative in character. The only evidence that Aristotle advanced to prove the natural basis for society, was existence of society, he explained society in terms of itself.

The Romans : Among the Romans, the most outstanding author is Cicero who in his book De Officus (On Justice) transmitted to the western world the treasures of Greek learning in philosophy, politics, law and sociology. But the Romans were mainly occupied with giving Europe 'The Law and hence they did not think in terms of non legalistic aspect of society. They have produced few original social philosophies.

The Scholastics : The period thereafter was overshadowed and overwhelmed by scholastic thinking. The scholastics propounded the Biblical thesis that man is a special creation of God. He is subject to no laws but those of

God. The church men are God's earthly representatives empowered by him to interpret his decrees and enforce his will. The social system existing at the time was the divinely sanctioned one. Anyone who thought of changing it was a heretic. The scholastic philosophy was a conservative philosophy. It gave theological interpretation to social attitudes. The scholastics have been proved false in their thesis that nothing social can be changed since men have been constantly changing their societies.

The Moderns : It was not until the sixteenth century that clear cut distinction was made between state and society and there appeared writers who treated life's problems on a more realistic level. The most notable among these were Hobbes and Machiavelli. 'The Prince' of Machiavelli is an objective discussion of the state and statecraft and is devoted chiefly to an exposition of the principles governing the successful state, which he had been able to formulate on the basis of historical data. Sir Thomas More was another notable author of this period who had in his book 'Utopia', published in 1515, tried to deal with every day social problems albeit by means of depicting an ideal social order, which presumably was meant for emulation. More's technique of presenting a picture of the ideal life as a way of pointing out what real life ought to be was utilized by several other writers un their works for example by Thomas Campanella in his city of the sun, Sir Francis Bacon in his new Atlantis and James Harrington in The Commonwealth of Nations.

Italian writer Vico & the French writer Montesquieu deserve special mention for their notable contribution towards the scientific investigation of special phenomenon. Vico in his book The New Science contended that society was subject to definite laws which can be observed through objective observation and study. Montesquieu in his celebrated work The Spirit of Laws had analyzed the role that external factors, especially climate, play in life of human societies. According to Montesquieu "Laws were an expression of national character and the spirit which they geographical condition under which men lived". Climate is the principal determinant of social life. Montesquieu's conclusions were little better than those of the speculative philosophers. His fault was that he tried to know the whole truth about social life on the basis of one element alone. Like Aristotle he arrived at the very conservative conclusion that what is, it must be.

Auguste Comte (1798–1857) the Father of Sociology

Auguste Comte is considered by many to be the father of sociology. The term sociology was first coined in 1780 by the French essayist Emmanuel-Joseph Sieyès (1748–1836) in an unpublished manuscript (Fauré et al. 1999). In 1838, the term was reinvented by Auguste Comte (1798-1857). Comte originally studied to be an engineer, but later became a pupil of social philosopher Claude Henri de Rouvroy Comte de Saint-Simon (1760-1825). They both thought that social scientists could study society using the same scientific methods utilized in natural sciences. Comte also believed in the potential of social scientists to work toward the betterment of society.

He held that once scholars identified the laws that governed society, sociologists could address problems such as poor education and poverty (Abercrombie et al. 2000).

Comte named the scientific study of social patterns Positivism. He described his philosophy in a series of books called 'The Course in Positive Philosophy' (1830-1842) and A General View of Positivism (1848). He believed that using scientific methods to reveal the laws by which societies and individuals interact would usher in a new "positivist" age of history. While the field and its terminology have grown, sociologists still believe in the positive impact of their work.

Harriet Martineau (1802–1876)-the First Woman Sociologist

Harriet Martineau was a writer who addressed a wide range of social science issues. She was an early observer of social practices, including economics, social class, religion, suicide, government, and women's rights. Her writing career began in 1931 with a series of stories titled *Illustrations of Political Economy*, in which she tried to educate ordinary people about the principles of economics (Johnson, 2003).

Martineau was the first to translate Comte's writing from French to English and thereby introduced sociology to English-speaking scholars (Hill, 1991).

She is also credited with the first systematic methodological international comparisons of social institutions in two of her most famous sociological works: Society in America (1837) and Retrospect of Western Travel (1838). Martineau found the workings of capitalism at odds with the professed moral principles of people in the United States; she pointed out the faults with the free enterprise system in which workers were exploited and impoverished while business owners became wealthy. She further noted that the belief in all being created equal was inconsistent with the lack of women's rights. Much like Mary Wollstonecraft, Martineau was often discounted in her own time by the male domination of academic sociology.

Karl Marx (1818–1883)

Karl Marx was one of the founders of sociology. His ideas about social conflict are still relevant today. Karl Marx (1818–1883) was a German philosopher and economist. In 1848 he and Friedrich Engels (1820–1895) coauthored the Communist Manifesto. This book is one of the most influential political manuscripts in history. It also presents Marx's theory of society, which differed from what Comte proposed.

Marx rejected Comte's positivism. He believed that societies grew and changed as a result of the struggles of different social classes over the means of production. At the time he was developing his theories, the Industrial Revolution and the rise of capitalism led to great disparities in wealth between the owners of the factories and workers. Capitalism, an economic system characterized by private or corporate ownership of goods and the means to produce them, grew in many nations.

Marx predicted that inequalities of capitalism would become so extreme that workers would eventually revolt. This would lead to the collapse of capitalism, which would be replaced by communism. Communism is an economic system under which there is no private or corporate ownership: everything is owned communally and distributed as needed. Marx believed that communism was a more equitable system than capitalism. While his economic predictions may not have come true in the time frame he predicted, Marx's idea that social conflict leads to change in society is still one of the major theories used in modern sociology.

Herbert Spencer (1820–1903)

In 1873, the English philosopher Herbert Spencer published The Study of Sociology, the first book with the term "sociology" in the title. Spencer rejected much of Comte's philosophy as well as Marx's theory of class struggle and his support of communism. Instead, he favored a form of government that allowed market forces to control capitalism. His work influenced many early sociologists including Émile Durkheim (1858–1917).

Georg Simmel (1858–1918)

Georg Simmel was a German art critic who wrote widely on social and political issues as well. Simmel took an anti-positivism stance and addressed topics such as social conflict, the function of money, individual identity in city life, and the European fear of outsiders (Stapley, 2010). Much of his work focused on the micro-level theories, and it analyzed the dynamics of two-person and three-person groups. His work also emphasized individual culture as the creative capacities of individuals. Simmel's contributions to sociology are not often included in academic histories of the discipline, perhaps overshadowed by his contemporaries Durkheim, Mead, and Weber (Ritzer & Goodman, 2004).

Emile Durkheim (1858–1917)

Durkheim helped establish sociology as a formal academic discipline by establishing the first European department of sociology at the University of Bordeaux in 1895 and by publishing his Rules of the Sociological Method in 1895. In another important work, Division of Labour in Society (1893), Durkheim laid out his theory on how societies transformed from a primitive state into a capitalist, industrial society. According to Durkheim, people rise to their proper levels in society based on merit.

Durkheim believed that sociologists could study objective "social facts" (Poggi 2000). He also believed that through such studies it would be possible to determine if a society was "healthy" or "pathological." He saw healthy societies as stable, while pathological societies experienced a breakdown in social norms between individuals and society. In 1897, Durkheim attempted to demonstrate the effectiveness of his rules of social research when he published a work titled Suicide. Durkheim examined suicide statistics in different police districts to research differences between Catholic and Protestant communities. He attributed the differences to socioreligious forces rather than to individual or psychological causes.

George Herbert Mead (1863–1931)

George Herbert Mead was a philosopher and sociologist whose work focused on the ways in which the mind and the self were developed as a result of social processes. He argued that how an individual comes to view himself or herself is based to a very large extent on interactions with others. Mead called specific individuals that impacted a person's life significant others and he also conceptualized "generalized others" as the organized and generalized attitude of a social group. Mead's work is closely associated with the symbolic interactionist approach and emphasizes the micro-level of analysis.

Max Weber (1864–1920)

Prominent sociologist Max Weber established a sociology department in Germany at the Ludwig Maximilians University of Munich in 1919. Weber wrote on many topics related to sociology including political change in Russia and social forces that affect factory workers. He is known best for his 1904 book, The Protestant Ethic and the Spirit of Capitalism. The theory that Weber sets forth in this book is still controversial. Some believe that Weber argued that the beliefs of many Protestants, especially Calvinists, led to the creation of capitalism.

Others interpret it as simply claiming that the ideologies of capitalism and Protestantism are complementary.

Weber believed that it was difficult, if not impossible, to use standard scientific methods to accurately predict the behavior of groups as people hoped to do. They argued that the influence of culture on human behavior had to be taken into account. This even applied to the researchers themselves, who, they believed, should be aware of how their own cultural biases could influence their research. To deal with this problem, Weber and Dilthey introduced the concept of verstehen, a German word that means to understand in a deep way. In seeking verstehen, outside observers of a social world an entire culture or a small setting attempt to understand it from an insider's point of view.

In his book The Nature of Social Action (1922), Weber described sociology as striving to "interpret the meaning of social action and thereby give a causal explanation of the way in which action proceeds and the effects it produces." He and other like-minded sociologists proposed a philosophy of antipositivism whereby social researchers would strive for subjectivity as they worked to represent social processes, cultural norms, and societal values. This approach led to some research methods whose aim was not to generalize or predict (traditional in science), but to systematically gain an in-depth understanding of social worlds.

The different approaches to research based on positivism or antipositivism are often considered the foundation for the differences found today between quantitative sociology and qualitative sociology. Quantitative sociology uses statistical methods such as surveys with large numbers of participants. Researchers analyze data using statistical techniques to see if they can uncover patterns of human behavior. Qualitative sociology seeks to understand human behavior by learning about it through in-depth interviews, focus groups, and analysis of content sources (like books, magazines, journals, and popular media).

RESEARCH TRENDS OF SOCIOLOGY

Research trends in the pattern of sociology are:

- Team research work.
- Flexibility in research, i.e. collaboration of workers in all fields of sociology.
- Advancement on the front of scientific knowledge.
- Inter-disciplinary research.

- Consolidating advances by large-scale cooperative research.
- Application of existing theory.
- Permanent revision of theory.
- Symbiosis between fundamental and applied research.
- Development of research methodology.

SOCIOLOGY IN INDIA

The study of sociology in India started in 1919 at the University of Bombay, but it was in 1930 that its study as a separate discipline was started. Now it being taught at a number of universities and it is getting popular among the students. Some Indian writers like G.S. Ghurye, R. K. Mukerjee & H. T. Mazumdar have also made original contribution to sociological studies. These studies pertain to Indian villages, caste system, marriage, kinship, family and social disorganization.

REFERENCES

- https://courses.lumenlearning.com/alamo-sociology/chapter/reading-the-history-of-sociology/
- https://www.scribd.com/doc/93541909/A-Historical-Sketch-of-Sociological-Theory
- http://www.preservearticles.com/201101173438/what-is-the-scope-of-sociology.html

6

Education

INTRODUCTION

Man today is at the peak civilization. It transformed itself from the Stone Age and cave man to the position of governing & observing the phenomena in space, hyperspace & stars & in the depth of oceans and the earth. Computer revolutionized the human life and world is now just like a village which is called globalization. It is universal fact that the present century is well known for scientific discoveries, research and information technology. So, in this development & progressive period everything is changing and increasing day by day. So education is lifelong and dynamic process. It begins at birth and continues throughout life. Education is life and all of the life is education.

Education is as old as the human race and has strong relation with the social patterns, economical systems, cultural values and emotions of human beings. Quest for knowledge is an innate quality of human beings which makes them distinct from all other species on this planet. So, the various attempts to recognize knowledge leads to the development of present educational system. The term "Education" is used commonly in our day to day life. Different people have different view point and interpretation regarding the term education. Education is a process in which and by which the knowledge, characters and behavior of the human being are shaped and molded. Education is lead to the enlightenment of mankind.

Education is the process of facilitating learning or the acquisition of knowledge, skill, values, beliefs and habits. This process includes various educational methods such as storytelling, discussion, teaching, training and directed research. Education frequently takes place under the guidance of educators, but learners may also educate themselves. Education can take places in formal or informal settings and any experience that has a formative effect on the way one thinks, feels or acts may be considered educational.

MEANING OF EDUCATION

Etymologically, the word education is derived from the Latin 'Educare' 'bring up', which is related to educere 'bring out', "bring forth what is within", "bring out potential" & ducere, "to lead". The word meaning denotes that education brings out the best from within the students.

ANCIENT PERIOD CONCEPT OF EDUCATION

Considering the Sanskrit word for Education, the commonly known word is 'Shiksha' which is derived from the word "Shas" which means to discipline. The word "Vidya" which denotes the subject matter of the body of knowledge is derived from the verb root "Vid" to know.

Hence in its simplest analysis the term "Education" means the process of raising up and drawing out the best in a person, through the art of teaching or training.

Education is the process by which people learn:

1. Instruction : Instruction refers to the facilitating of learning, usually by a teacher.

2. Teaching : Teaching refers to the actions of a real live instructor to impart learning to the student.

3. Learning : Learning refers to learning with a view toward preparing learners with specific knowledge, skills, or abilities that can be applied immediately upon completion.

DEFINITION OF EDUCATION

Education as something that is important is not independent of the number of opinion and assumptions about the meaning and definition of true education. Education being an important social activity, its meaning has been changing through the ages due to change in social and physical conditions. Following definitions are the opinion of experts on education which of course will vary:

According to Chanakya, "Education means training for the country and love for the nation".

According to Shankaracharya, "Education is realization of self".

According to Guru Nanak Dev Ji, "Education is self realization and service of the people".

According to Swami Vivekanand, "Education is manifestation of divine perfection already existing in man".

According to Mahatma Gandhi, "Education is all round drawing out of best in child and man body, mind and spirit".

According to Aristotle, "Education is the creation of a sound mind in a sound body".

According to John Dewey, "Education is the development of all those capacities in the individual which will enable him to control his environment and fulfill his possibilities".

According to Tagore, "Education makes man's life in harmony with all existence".

Hence in its simplest analysis the definition "Education is the natural, harmonious and progressive development of man's innate power".

SCOPE OF EDUCATION

Scope means range of view outlook field or opportunity of activity operation and application. Education has a wider meaning and application.

1. Educational philosophy : Philosophy of education covers aims of education, nature of education, importance of education, and function of education its very old and essential part of education.

2. Educational psychology : Main aim of education is the development of child. Psychology helps to understand the child better and development of child with respect of physical, mental, emotional, social adjustment, individual difference, personality, thinking, reasoning, problem solving.

3. Educational sociology : A child lives in the society so it's important for him to know about the society the nature of society, type of society, interdependence between culture and society.

4. History of education : It is also important to know background, origin, development, growth and aspect of the subjects. And also education system method of teaching during ancient period, medieval period, British period and modern period.

5. Economics of education : For the growth of business and market the world class economical education is important for each and important.

6. Method of teaching : In ancient time the pupil was passive listeners but now they actively participate with the teacher in the process of education. So the skill and proficiency of difference teaching methods needs to be developed.

7. Educational administration and supervision : The educational institution and the system have to be supervised and administrated smoothly so that the process of education goes well.

8. Problems of education : This scope includes problems of teaching management of education and also suggestion and remedies for it.

9. Population education : Viewing at the undesirable growth of population, awareness is created through population education.

10. Environmental education : Ecological in balances have drown the attentions of intelligence today. So looking at the environmental problems study of environment education has great importance.

NATURE OF EDUCATION

The natures of education are:

1. Education is life-long process : Education is life long process because every stage of life of an individual is important from educational point.

2. Education is a systematic process : It refers to transact its activities through a systematic institution and regulation.

3. Education is development of individual and the society : It is called a force for social development, which brings improvement in every aspect in the society.

4. Education is modification of behavior : Human behavior is modified and improved through educational process.

5. Education is training : Human senses, mind, behavior, activities; skills are trained in a constructive and socially desirable way.

6. Education is instruction and direction : It directs and instructs an individual to fulfill his desires and needs for exaltation of his whole personality.

7. Education is life : Life without education is meaningless and like the life of a beast. Every aspect and incident needs education for its sound development.

8. Education is continuous reconstruction of our experiences : As per the definition of John Dewey education reconstructs and remodels our experiences towards socially desirable way.

9. Education is a power : Education is a power and treasure in human being through which he is entitled as the supreme master on the earth.

Therefore, the role of education is countless for a perfect society and man. It is necessary for every society and nation to bring holistic happiness and prosperity to its individuals.

LANDMARKS AND RESEARCH TRENDS OF EDUCATION

Education began in prehistory, as adults trained the young in the knowledge and skills deemed necessary in their society. In pre-literate societies, this was achieved orally and through imitation. Story-telling passed knowledge, values, and skills from one generation to the next. As cultures began to extend their knowledge beyond skills that could be readily learned through imitation, formal education developed. Schools existed in Egypt at the time of the Middle Kingdom.

The Plato : Plato founded the Academy in Athens, the first institution of higher learning in Europe. The city of Alexandria in Egypt, established in 330 BCE, became the successor to Athens as the intellectual cradle of Ancient Greece. There, the great Library of Alexandria was built in the 3rd century BCE. European civilizations suffered a collapse of literacy and organization following the fall of Rome in CE 476.

The Confucius : In China, Confucius (551-479 BCE), of the State of Lu, was the country's most influential ancient philosopher, whose educational outlook continues to influence the societies of China and neighbours like Korea, Japan, and Vietnam. Confucius gathered disciples and searched in vain for a ruler who would adopt his ideals for good governance, but his Analects were written down by followers and have continued to influence education in East Asia into the modern era.

The Aztecs : The Aztecs also had a well-developed theory about education, which has an equivalent word in Nahuatl called "The Act of Strengthening or Bringing up Men". It means "the art of raising or educating a person" or "the art of strengthening or bringing up men." This was a broad conceptualization of education, which prescribed that it begins at home, supported by formal schooling, and reinforced by community living. Historians cite that formal education was mandatory for everyone regardless of social class and gender. There was also the word Neixtlamachiliztli, which is "The act of giving wisdom to the face". These concepts underscore a complex set of educational practices, which was oriented towards communicating to the next generation the experience and intellectual heritage of the past for the purpose of individual development and his integration into the community.

Fall of Rome : After the Fall of Rome, the Catholic Church became the sole preserver of literate scholarship in Western Europe. The church established cathedral schools in the Early Middle Ages as centres of advanced education. Some of these establishments ultimately evolved into medieval universities and forebears of many of Europe's modern universities. During the High Middle Ages, Chartres Cathedral operated the famous and influential Chartres Cathedral School. The medieval universities of Western Christendom were well-integrated across all of Western Europe, encouraged freedom of inquiry, and produced a great variety of fine scholars and natural philosophers, including Thomas Aquinas of the University of Naples, Robert Grosseteste of the University of Oxford, an early expositor of a systematic method of scientific experimentation, and Saint Albert the Great, a pioneer of biological field research. Founded in 1088, the University of Bologne is considered the first, and the oldest continually operating university.

Middle Ages : Elsewhere during the Middle Ages, Islamic science and mathematics flourished under the Islamic caliphate which was established across the Middle East, extending from the Iberian Peninsula in the west to the Indus in the east and to the Almoravid Dynasty and Mali Empire in the south.

Johannes Gutenberg : The Renaissance in Europe ushered in a new age of scientific and intellectual inquiry and appreciation of ancient Greek and Roman civilizations. Around 1450, Johannes Gutenberg developed a printing press, which allowed works of literature to spread more quickly. The European Age of Empires saw European ideas of education in philosophy, religion, arts and sciences spread out across the globe. Missionaries and scholars also brought back new ideas from other civilizations-as with the Jesuit China missions who played a significant role in the transmission of knowledge, science, and culture between China and Europe, translating works from Europe like Euclid's Elements for Chinese scholars and the thoughts of Confucius for European audiences. The Enlightenment saw the emergence of a more secular educational outlook in Europe.

UNESCO : In most countries today, full-time education, whether at school or otherwise, is compulsory for all children up to a certain age. Due to this the proliferation of compulsory education, combined with population growth, UNESCO has calculated that in the next 30 years more people will receive formal education than in all of human history thus far.

RESEARCH TRENDS OF EDUCATION

Research trends in the pattern of education are:

1. Team Teaching : Putting two instructors in one classroom is known as team teaching, collaborative team teaching or co-teaching. This model provides benefits and presents challenges to both teachers and students. Kids in co-teaching classrooms observe teamwork in action and learn to see concepts from more than one perspective. They have the chance to learn from teachers with diverse backgrounds and can delve deeper into subjects thanks to the opportunity for more one-on-one instruction time. However, conflicting personalities and the tendency of students to favor one teach over the other can threaten the stability of this model.

2. Individualized Instruction : A great deal of research is being done on how diversification of instruction to cater to the unique needs of students may help them to better grasp core subjects. This type of instruction moves away from the traditional lecture model of teaching and offers students a way to learn at their own pace. Slower learners can take the time they need to develop a solid understanding of material while more advanced students don't have to wait to move on to the next concept. This better addresses individual learning styles and allows teachers to utilize diverse platforms to provide instruction.

3. Mixed-Age Teaching : The potential benefits of putting kids of different ages together in the same classroom are still being researched, but many schools have been using this teaching method for years with good results. In a mixed-age classroom, young students learn how to interact with older ones and benefit from observing their academic abilities. Collaboration between age groups facilitates further development. Achieving advanced competencies at a young age increases confidence. Teachers also benefit from mixed-age classrooms in that they're able to track their students through more than one grade to get a clearer picture of academic growth.

4. Brain-Based Teaching : Based on neuroscience research that shows consistent practice of a concept creates strong pathways between neurons, brain-based teaching takes advantage of the power of the developing mind to create the greatest amount of positive changes during the short period that kids are in school. Kids work in groups, participate in games that address specific concepts and engage in lessons built around central themes, all with the goal of improving their understanding of important academic skills and ideas. Physical education is included to facilitate the growth and development of new neuronal pathways.

5. Critical Thinking Skills : Although memorization of fundamental facts is critical to building a foundation of knowledge in the early grades, kids also need to be taught how to apply those facts in a multitude of situations. Research into critical thinking skills is driving new ways of teaching that include encouraging students to ask questions, develop problem-solving skills by working in groups and discuss the outcomes of their experiments. These methods of discovery give kids a more active role in their education and teach them how to make decisions by applying the facts they've learned to the problem at hand.

6. Paedocentric : in this present world the focus is on the student and not on the subject. It is based on the learners need and their interest. It involves more of students input and thus focusing on the whole child and not a part of the student. The modern teacher focuses on the child's need and helps him to grow like a plant with his fullest capabilities and abilities.

7. Teacher's role : No more the teacher is considered as the dominating or the pivotal figure in the school. The modern teacher prepares the children to enable themselves to participate in the teaching learning process. Teachers are rather known as the facilitators, mentors etc.

8. Activity centered : The focus of modern teaching is on activity based learning. They emphasis on task oriented programs which help the students to better understand the subject i.e. simulations, projects, experiment etc. these tasks helps the students to gain knowledge as well as skills.

9. Creative education : Another latest trend in today's school is encouragement on innovation or creativity. Creativity is a thought in our mind and by enhancing creativity they enable the child's thoughts to give a concrete shape through the intervention of his thoughts.

10. Community participation : Enhancing the parent teacher association in every school is the best example of community participation and this participation reciprocates in solving many miscommunication and problems.

11. Latest technology : Technology plays a vital role in the teaching and learning process. Technology not only simplifies our life but it provides a vivid range of knowledge and experience to the students. There are wide use of computer assisted learning, computer assisted instructions, which has enabled the students for wider knowledge within their own accessibility and affordability.

12. Methods of appraisal : The latest methods of

evaluation are based on a vision of learning and well defined performance indicators. In addition the cognitive aspect and other abilities of the student is been taken into account.

13. Innovations in teaching learning : Many innovations are on the process for the better teaching learning process which will help them to develop their intellectual, social and career development.

REFERENCES

- http://letseduodisha.blogspot.com/2014/11/meaning-nature-and-scope-ofeducation. html
- https://en.wikipedia.org/wiki/Education
- https://www.masters-in-special-education.com/lists/5-trending-disciplines-in-educational-research

7

Economics

INTRODUCTION

Economics is the social science of studying the production, distribution and consumption of goods and services. It is a complex social science that spans from mathematics to psychology. At its most basic, however, economics considers how a society provides for its needs. Its most basic need is survival; which requires food, clothing and shelter. Once those are covered, it can then look at more sophisticated commodities such as services, personal transport, entertainment, the list goes on.

Today, this social science known as "Economics" tends to refer only to the type of economic thought. Today, the economics is that branch of knowledge in which those activities of human beings are studied in which they undertake to acquire scarce means (that is wealth) which are capable of satisfying their unlimited wants.

ORIGIN OF ECONOMICS

The origin of economics goes back to the period of Chandre Gupta Mourya, a famous ruler of Mouryan Dynasty. Kautilya, a famous financial adviser to Chandre Gupta Mourya wrote "Arthashastra" (In Kannada language) means Economics. During early days, Economics was called political economics as it was applied by famous kings to govern the state or city. Prof. Alfred Marshall, a famous economist, first used the term economics instead of political economy. The use of the Economics results in two advantages according to Sir Dennis Robertson (1) The termination-ICS indicates that our study is or aspires to be a science, like Physics, Dynamics and so forth and (2) The dropping of the word 'Political' emphasizes that our ultimate concern is with individual human beings, not with states. The father of economics called is name Adam Smith (1723-1790).

MEANING OF ECONOMICS

The term "Economics" is taken from Greek Words "Oikos" and "Nomos". "Oikos" means household & "Nomos" means management. So, Economics means household management, i.e. managing a household, using the limited funds available in the most economical manner possible.

In other words, it means managing the desires and aspirations of family through wise allocation of resources (money) in order to achieve maximum satisfaction in life.

DEFINITION OF ECONOMICS

According to Adam Smith, "Economics enquires into the nature & causes of the wealth of nations".

According to Ricardo, "Economics studies, how the produce of the earth is distributed, that is, economics deals with the distribution of income and wealth".

According to Marshall, "Economics is a study of mankind in the ordinary business of life and examines that part of individual and social action which is connected with material requisites of well being.

According to J.B. Say (1803), "distinguishing the subject from its public-policy uses, defines it as the science of production, distribution, and consumption of wealth".

According to Paul A Samuelson, "Economics is the study of how men and society choose, with or without the use of money, to employ scarce productive resources which could have alternative uses, to produce various commodities over time and distribute them for consumption now and in the future among various people and groups of society".

To sum up the concluded that the definition of economics can be had in the following words: "Economics is the science which studies the activities to the most efficient consumption, production, exchange and distribution of the scarce means, having alternative uses, for the maximum satisfaction of the human wants, for increasing welfare and for economic development'.

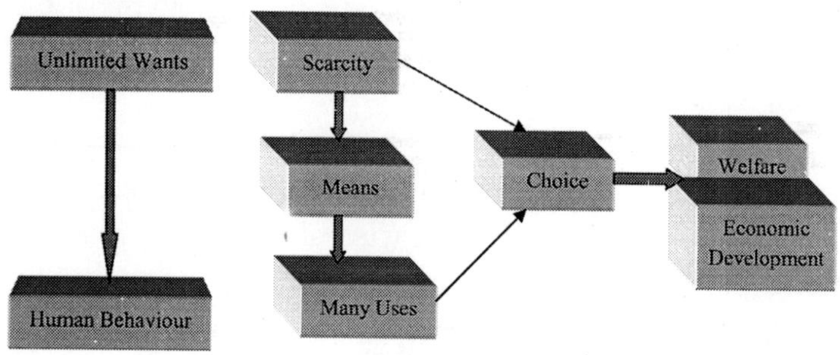

Fig. 1. Good Definition

SCOPE OF ECONOMICS

Scope means province or field of study. In discussing the scope of economics, we have to indicate whether it is a science or an art and a positive science or a normative science. It also covers the subject matter of economics.

1. Economics - A Science and an Art

(a) Economics is a science : Science is a systematized body of knowledge that traces the relationship between cause and effect. Another attribute of science is that its phenomena should be amenable to measurement. Applying these characteristics, we find that economics is a branch of knowledge where the various facts relevant to it have been systematically collected, classified and analyzed. Economics investigates the possibility of deducing generalizations as regards the economic motives of human beings. The motives of individuals and business firms can be very easily measured in terms of money. Thus, economics is a science.

(b) Economics -A Social Science : In order to understand the social aspect of economics, we should bear in mind that labourers are working on materials drawn from all over the world and producing commodities to be sold all over the world in order to exchange goods from all parts of the world to satisfy their wants. There is, thus, a close inter-dependence of millions of people living in distant lands unknown to one another. In this way, the process of satisfying wants is not only an individual process, but also a social process. In economics, one has, thus, to study social behaviour i.e., behaviour of men in-groups.

(c) Economics is also an art : An art is a system of rules for the attainment of a given end. A science teaches us to know; an art teaches us to do. Applying this definition, we find that economics offers us practical guidance in the solution of economic problems. Science and art are complementary to each other and economics is both a science and an art.

2. Positive and Normative Economics

Economics is both positive and normative science.

(a) Positive science : It only describes what it is and normative science prescribes what it ought to be. Positive science does not indicate what is good or what is bad to the society. It will simply provide results of economic analysis of a problem.

(b) Normative science : It makes distinction between good and bad. It prescribes what should be done to promote human welfare. A positive statement is based on facts. A normative statement involves ethical values. For example, "12 percent of the labour force in India was unemployed last year" is a positive statement, which could is verified by scientific measurement. "Twelve percent unemployment is too high" is normative statement comparing the fact of 12 percent unemployment with a standard of what is unreasonable. It also suggests how it can be rectified. Therefore, economics is a positive as well as normative science.

3. Methodology of Economics

Economics as a science adopts two methods for the discovery of its laws and principles i.e. Deductive Method & Inductive Method.

(a) Deductive method : Here, we descend from the general to particular, i.e., we start from certain principles that are self-evident or based on strict observations. Then, we carry them down as a process of pure reasoning to the consequences that they implicitly contain. For instance, traders earn profit in their businesses is a general statement which is accepted even without verifying it with the traders. The deductive method is useful in analyzing complex economic phenomenon where cause and effect are inextricably mixed up. However, the deductive method is useful only if certain assumptions are valid. (Traders earn profit, if the demand for the commodity is more).

(b) Inductive method : This method mounts up from particular to general, i.e., we begin with the observation of particular facts and then proceed with the help of reasoning founded on experience so as to formulate laws and theorems on the basis of observed facts. E.g. Data on consumption of poor, middle and rich income groups of people are collected, classified, analyzed and important conclusions are drawn out from the results. In deductive method, we start from certain principles that are either indisputable or based on strict observations and draw inferences about individual cases. In inductive method, a particular case is examined to establish a general or universal fact. Both deductive and inductive methods are useful in economic analysis.

4. Subject Matter of Economics

Economics can be studied through (a) traditional approach and (b) modern approach.

(a) Traditional Approach : Economics is studied under five major divisions namely consumption, production, exchange, distribution and public finance.

1. ***Consumption*** : The satisfaction of human wants through the use of goods and services is called consumption.
2. ***Production*** : Goods that satisfy human wants are viewed as "bundles of utility". Hence production would mean creation of utility or producing (or creating) things for satisfying human wants. For production, the resources like land, labour, capital and organization are needed.
3. ***Exchange*** : Goods are produced not only for self-consumption, but also for sales. They are sold to buyers in markets. The process of buying and selling constitutes exchange.
4. ***Distribution*** : The production of any agricultural commodity requires four factors, viz., land, labour, capital and organization. These four factors of production are to be rewarded for their services rendered in the process of production. The land owner gets rent, the labourer earns wage, the capitalist is given with interest and the entrepreneur is rewarded with profit. The process of determining rent, wage, interest and profit is called distribution.
5. ***Public finance*** : It studies how the government gets

money and how it spends it. Thus, in public finance, we study about public revenue and public expenditure.

(b) Modern Approach : The study of economics is divided into: 1) Microeconomics and 2) Macroeconomics.

1. ***Microeconomics*** analyses the economic behaviour of any particular decision making unit such as a household or a firm. Microeconomics studies the flow of economic resources or factors of production from the households or resource owners to business firms and flow of goods and services from business firms to households. It studies the behaviour of individual decision making unit with regard to fixation of price and output and its reactions to the changes in demand and supply conditions. Hence, microeconomics is also called price theory.
2. ***Macroeconomics*** studies the behaviour of the economic system as a whole or all the decision-making units put together. Macroeconomics deals with the behaviour of aggregates like total employment, gross national product (GNP), national income, general price level, etc. So, macroeconomics is also known as income theory. Microeconomics cannot give an idea of the functioning of the economy as a whole. Similarly, macroeconomics ignores the individual's preference and welfare. What is true of a part or individual may not be true of the whole and what is true of the whole may not apply to the parts or individual decision making units. By studying about a single small-farmer, generalization cannot be made about all small farmers, say in Tamil Nadu state. Similarly, the general nature of all small farmers in the state need not be true in case of a particular small farmer. Hence, the study of both micro and macroeconomics is essential to understand the whole system of economic activities.

Conclusion the Scope of Economics

To sum up the concluded that the scope of economics can be had in the: Economics is concerned with human well-being as well as ethical values. It is science and an art, since the scientific principles are applied practically. It is both positive and normative science since the actual happening and the future happenings are dealt. Hence the scope and nature of economics deals in with all the above as explained by the economists.

HISTORY & LANDMARKS OF ECONOMICS

Economic writings date from earlier Mesopotamian, Greek, Roman, Indian subcontinent, Chinese, Persian, and Arab civilizations. Economic precepts occur throughout the writings of the Boeotian poet Hesiod and several economic historians have described Hesiod himself as the "first economist". Other notable writers from Antiquity through to the Renaissance include Aristotle, Xenophon, Chanakya (also known as Kautilya), Qin Shi Huang, Thomas Aquinas, and Ibn Khaldun. Joseph Schumpeter described Aquinas as "coming nearer than any other group to being the "founders' of scientific economics" as to monetary, interest, and value theory within a natural-law perspective.

Two groups, later called "mercantilists" and "physiocrats", more directly influenced the subsequent development of the subject. Both groups were associated with the rise of economic nationalism and modern capitalism in Europe. Physiocrats, a group of 18th-century French thinkers and writers, developed the idea of the economy as a circular flow of income and output. Physiocrats believed that only agricultural production generated a clear surplus over cost, so that agriculture was the basis of all wealth. Thus, they opposed the mercantilist policy of promoting manufacturing and trade at the expense of agriculture, including import tariffs. Physiocrats advocated replacing administratively costly tax collections with a single tax on income of land owners. In reaction against copious mercantilist trade regulations, the physiocrats advocated a policy of laissez-faire, which called for minimal government intervention in the economy.

Adam Smith (1723–1790) was an early economic theorist. Smith was harshly critical of the mercantilists but described the physiocratic system "with all its imperfections" as "perhaps the purest approximation to the truth that has yet been published" on the subject.

Classical Economy

1. Adam Smith (1723-1790) : The publication of Adam Smith's The Wealth of Nations in 1776 has been described as "the effective birth of economics as a separate discipline." The book identified land, labour, and capital as the three factors of production and the major contributors to a nation's wealth, as distinct from the physiocratic idea that only agriculture was productive.

Smith discusses potential benefits of specialization by division of labour, including increased labour productivity and gains from trade, whether between town and country or across countries. His "theorem" that the division of labor is limited by the extent of the market" has been described as the "core of a theory of the functions of firm and industry" and a "fundamental principle of economic organization." To Smith has also been ascribed "the most important substantive proposition in all of economics" and foundation of resource-allocation theory – that, under competition, resource owners (of labour, land, and capital) seek their most profitable uses, resulting in an equal rate of return for all uses in equilibrium.

2. Rev. Thomas Robert Malthus (1798) used the concept of diminishing returns to explain low living standards. Human population, he argued, tended to increase geometrically, outstripping the production of food, which increased arithmetically. The force of a rapidly growing population against a limited amount of land meant diminishing returns to labour. The result, he claimed, was chronically low wages, which prevented the standard of living for most of the population from rising above the subsistence level. Economist Julian Lincoln Simon has criticized Malthus's conclusions.

3. David Ricardo (1817) : While Adam Smith emphasized the production of income, David Ricardo (1817) focused on the distribution of income among landowners, workers, and capitalists. Ricardo saw an inherent conflict between landowners on the one hand and labour and capital on the other. He posited that the growth of population and capital, pressing against a fixed supply of land, pushes up rents and holds down wages and profits. Ricardo was the first to state and prove the principle of comparative advantage, according to which each country should specialize in producing and exporting goods in that it has a lower relative cost of production, rather relying only on its own production. It has been termed a "fundamental analytical explanation" for gains from trade.

4. John Stuart Mill (1848) : Coming at the end of the classical tradition, John Stuart Mill (1848) parted company with the earlier classical economists on the inevitability of the distribution of income produced by the market system. Mill pointed to a distinct difference between the market's two roles: allocation of resources and distribution of income. The market might be efficient in allocating resources but not in distributing income, he wrote, making it necessary for society to intervene.

5. Marxism : Marxist (later, Marxian) economics descends from classical economics. It derives from the work of Karl Marx. The first volume of Marx's major work, Das Kapital, was published in German in 1867. In it, Marx focused on the labour theory of value and the theory of surplus value which, he believed, explained the exploitation of labour by capital. The labour theory of value held that the value of an exchanged commodity was determined by the labour that went into its production and the theory of surplus value demonstrated how the workers only got paid a proportion of the value their work had created.

Neo-Classical Economics

At the dawn as a social science, **economics** was defined and discussed at length as the study of production, distribution, and consumption of wealth by Jean-Baptiste Say in his *Treatise on Political Economy or, The Production,*

Distribution, and Consumption of Wealth (1803). These three items are considered by the science only in relation to the increase or diminution of wealth, and not in reference to their processes of execution. Say's definition has prevailed up to our time, saved by substituting the word "wealth" for "goods and services" meaning that wealth may include non-material objects as well. 130 years later, Lionel Robbins noticed that this definition no longer sufficed, because many economists were making theoretical and philosophical inroads in other areas of human activity. In his *Essay on the Nature and Significance of Economic Science*, he proposed a definition of economics as a study of a particular aspect of human behaviour, the one that falls under the influence of scarcity, which forces people to choose, allocate scarce resources to competing ends, and economize (seeking the greatest welfare while avoiding the wasting of scarce resources). For Robbins, the insufficiency was solved, and his definition allows us to proclaim, with an easy conscience, education economics, safety and security economics, health economics, war economics, and of course, production, distribution and consumption economics as valid subjects of the economic science."

1. Citing Robbins : "Economics is the science which studies human behavior as a relationship between ends and scarce means which have alternative uses". After discussing it for decades, Robbins' definition became widely accepted by mainstream economists, and it has opened way into current textbooks. Although far from unanimous, most mainstream economists would accept some version of Robbins' definition, even though many have raised serious objections to the scope and method of economics, emanating from that definition. Due to the lack of strong consensus, and that production, distribution and consumption of goods and services is the prime area of study of economics, the old definition still stands in many quarters.

A body of theory later termed "neoclassical economics" or "marginalism" formed from about 1870 to 1910. The term "economics" was popularized by such neoclassical economists as Alfred Marshall as a concise synonym for "economic science" and a substitute for the earlier "political economy". This corresponded to the influence on the subject of mathematical methods used in the natural sciences.

Neoclassical economics systematized supply and demand as joint determinants of price and quantity in market equilibrium, affecting both the allocation of output and the distribution of income. It dispensed with the labour theory of value inherited from classical economics in favour of a marginal utility theory of value on the demand side and a more general theory of costs on the supply side.[131] In the 20th century, neoclassical theorists moved away from an earlier notion suggesting that total utility for a society could be measured in favour of ordinal utility, which hypothesizes merely behaviour-based relations across persons.

In microeconomics, neoclassical economics represents incentives and costs as playing a pervasive role in shaping decision making. An immediate example of this is the consumer theory of individual demand, which isolates how prices (as costs) and income affect quantity demanded. In macroeconomics it is reflected in an early and lasting neoclassical synthesis with Keynesian macroeconomics.

Neoclassical economics is occasionally referred as *orthodox economics* whether by its critics or sympathizers. Modern mainstream economics builds on neoclassical economics but with many refinements that either supplement or generalize earlier analysis, such as econometrics, game theory, analysis of market failure and imperfect competition, and the neoclassical model of economic growth for analyzing long-run variables affecting national income.

Neoclassical economics studies the behaviour of

individuals, households, and organizations (called economic actors, players, or agents), when they manage or use scarce resources, which have alternative uses, to achieve desired ends. Agents are assumed to act rationally, have multiple desirable ends in sight, limited resources to obtain these ends, a set of stable preferences, a definite overall guiding objective, and the capability of making a choice. There exists an economic problem, subject to study by economic science, when a decision (choice) is made by one or more resource-controlling players to attain the best possible outcome under bounded rational conditions. In other words, resource-controlling agents maximize value subject to the constraints imposed by the information the agents have, their cognitive limitations, and the finite amount of time they have to make and execute a decision. Economic science centres on the activities of the economic agents that comprise society. They are the focus of economic analysis.

An approach to understanding these processes, through the study of agent behaviour under scarcity, may go as follows:

The continuous interplay has done by economic actors in all markets sets the prices for all goods and services which, in turn, make the rational managing of scarce resources possible. At the same time, the decisions (choices) made by the same actors, while they are pursuing their own interest, determine the level of output (production), consumption, savings, and investment, in an economy, as well as the remuneration (distribution) paid to the owners of labour (in the form of wages), capital (in the form of profits) and land (in the form of rent). Each period, as if they were in a giant feedback system, economic players influence the pricing processes and the economy, and are in turn influenced by them until a steady state (equilibrium) of all variables involved is reached or until an external shock throws the system toward a new equilibrium point. Because of the autonomous actions of rational interacting agents, the economy is a complex adaptive system.

2. Keynesian Economics : Keynesian economics derives from John Maynard Keynes, in particular his book *The General Theory of Employment, Interest and Money* (1936), which ushered in contemporary macroeconomics as a distinct field. The book focused on determinants of national income in the short run when prices are relatively inflexible. Keynes attempted to explain in broad theoretical detail why high labour-market unemployment might not be self-correcting due to low "effective demand" and why even price flexibility and monetary policy might be unavailing.

The term "revolutionary" has been applied to the book in its impact on economic analysis.

Keynesian economics has two successors. Post-Keynesian economics also concentrates on macroeconomic rigidities and adjustment processes. Research on micro foundations for their models is represented as based on real-life practices rather than simple optimizing models. It is generally associated with the University of Cambridge and the work of Joan Robinson.

New-Keynesian economics is also associated with developments in the Keynesian fashion. Within this group researchers tend to share with other economists the emphasis on models employing micro foundations and optimizing behaviour but with a narrower focus on standard Keynesian themes such as price and wage rigidity. These are usually made to be endogenous features of the models, rather than simply assumed as in older Keynesian-style ones.

RESEARCH TRENDS OF ECONOMICS

- Improving financial access and financial inclusion through sectoral reforms.
- Maintaining fiscal discipline and subsidy management.
- Improving efficiency of public expenditure management.
- Balancing growth and inclusion objectives.
- As part of inclusiveness, more social development schemes unveiled, largely piggy backing on the rewards from growth policies
- However, growth policies are neglected with no new policy reform towards that direction.
- Team research work.
- Flexibility in research, i.e. collaboration of workers in all fields of economic.
- Advancement on the front of scientific knowledge.
- Inter-disciplinary research.
- Consolidating advances by large-scale cooperative research.
- Application of existing theory.
- Permanent revision of theory.
- Symbiosis between fundamental and applied research.
- Development of research methodology.

REFERENCES

- http://elearn.luanar.ac.mw/repoz/AECO141/lec01.pdf
- https://www.pluraleoekonomik.de/fileadmin/redakteure/bund/pdf/Materialien/History.pdf
- https://en.wikipedia.org/wiki/Economics#History

8

History

INTRODUCTION

History is the analysis and interpretation of the human past enabling us to study continuity and changes that are taking place over time. It is an act of both investigation and imagination that seeks to explain how people have changed over time. Historians use all forms of evidence to examine, interpret, revisit, and reinterpret the past. These include not just written documents, but also oral communication and objects such as buildings, artifacts, photographs, coins and paintings. Historians are trained in the methods of discovering and evaluating these sources and the challenging task of making historical sense out of them. History is a means to understand the past and present. History is, or should be an attempt to re-think the past.

Without the knowledge of history we cannot have the background of our religion, customs institutions, administration and so on. History thus helps us to understand the present day problems both at the national and international level accurately and objectively. While cause & effect relationship between the past and the present are lively presented in the history.

ORIGIN OF HISTORY

The origin of the word History is associated with the Greek word 'Historia' which means 'information' or 'an inquiry designed to elicit truth'.

MEANING OF HISTORY

For others history has become a "General" term meaning the study of "Everything" that is known about the human past (But even this barrier is being challenged by new fields such as Big History).

DEFINITION OF HISTORY

According to Burckhardt, "History is the record of what one age finds worthy of note in another."

According to Henry Johnson, "History, in its broadest sense, is everything that ever happened."

According to Smith, V. S, "The value and interest of history depend largely on the degree in which the present is illuminated by the past."

According to Rapson, "History is a connected account of the course of events or progress of ideas."

According to Jawaharlal Nehru, "History is the story of Man's struggle through the ages against Nature and the elements; against wild beasts and the jungle and some of his own kind who have tried to keep him down and to exploit him for their own benefit."

According to NCERT, "History is the scientific study of past happenings in all their aspects, in the life of a social group, in the light of present happenings."

According to John Jacob Anderson (1821–1906), "History is a narration of the events which have happened among mankind, including an account of the rise and fall of nations, as well as of other great changes which have affected the political and social condition of the human race".

According to Arnold J. Toynbee (1889–1975), "History not used is nothing, for all intellectual life is action, like practical life, and if you don't use the stuff well, it might as well be dead."

To sum up the concluded that the definition of history can be had in the following words: The History as a significant records of events of the past, a meaningful story of mankind depicting the details of what happened to man and why it happened. Mainly it deals with the human world.

SCOPE OF HISTORY

The scope of History is vast; it is the story of man in relation to totality of his behavior. The scope of history means the breadth, comprehensiveness, variety and extent of learning experiences, provided by the study. History which was only limited to a local saga, has during the course of century become universal history of mankind, depicting man's achievements in every field of life-political, economic, social, cultural, scientific, technological, religious and artistic etc., and at various levels-local, regional, national, and international. It starts with the past; makes present & points to the future. Events like wars, revolutions, rise and fall of empires, fortunes and misfortunes of great empire builders as well as the masses in general are all the subject matter of history.

History is a comprehensive subject and includes-History of Geography, History of Art, History of Culture, History of Literature, History of Civilization, History of Religion, History of Mathematics, History of Physics, History of Chemistry, History of Education, History of Biology, History of Atom, History of Philosophy-in fact history of any and every social, physical and natural science we are interested in. History today has become an all-embracing, comprehensive subject with almost limitless extent. The basis points of scope are given below:

1. A study of the present in the light of the past : The present has evolved out of the past. Modern history enables us to understand how society has come to its present form so that one may intelligently interpret the sequence of events. The causal relationships between the selected happenings are unearthed that help in revealing the nature of happenings and framing of general laws.

2. History is the study of man : History deals with man's struggle through the ages. History is not static. By selecting "innumerable biographies" and presenting their lives in the appropriate social context and the ideas in the human context, we understand the sweep of events. It traces the fascinating story of how man has developed through the ages, how man has studied to use and control his environment and how the present institutions have grown out of the past.

3. History is concerned with man in time : It deals with a series of events and each event occurs at a given point in time. Human history, in fact, is the process of human development in time. It is time which affords a perspective to events and lends a charm that brightens up the past.

4. History is concerned with man in space : The interaction of man on environment and vice versa is a dynamic one. History describes about nations and human activities in the context of their physical and geographical environment. Out of this arise the varied trends in the political, social, economic and cultural spheres of man's activities and achievements.

5. Objective record of happenings : Every precaution is taken to base the data on original sources and make them free from subjective interpretation. It helps in clear understanding of the past and enables us to take well informed decisions.

6. Multisided : All aspects of the life of a social group are closely interrelated and historical happenings cover all these aspects of life, not limited only to the political aspect that had so long dominated history.

7. History is a dialogue between the events of the past and progressively emerging future ends : The historian's interpretation of the past, his selection of the significant and the relevant events, evolves with the progressive emergence of new goals. The general laws regulating historical happenings may not be considered enough; attempts have to be made to predict future happenings on the basis of the laws.

8. Not only narration but also analysis : The selected happenings are not merely narrated; the causal relationships between them are properly unearthed. The tracing of these relationships lead to the development of general laws that are also compared and contrasted with similar happenings in other social groups to improve the reliability and validity of these laws.

9. Continuity and coherence are the necessary requisites of history : History carries the burden of human progress as it is passed down from generation to generation, from society to society, justifying the essence of continuity.

10. Relevant : In the study of history only those events are included which are relevant to the understanding of the present life.

11. Comprehensiveness : According to modern concept, history is not confined to one period or country or nation. It also deals with all aspects of human life-political, social, economic, religious, literary, aesthetic and physical, giving a clear sense of world unity and world citizenship.

HISTORICAL BACKGROUND & LANDMARKS OF HISTORY

Traditionally, historians have recorded events of the

past, either in writing or by passing on an oral tradition, and have attempted to answer historical questions through the study of written documents and oral accounts. For the beginning, historians have also used such sources as monuments, inscriptions, and pictures. In general, the sources of historical knowledge can be separated into three categories: what is written, what is said, and what is physically preserved, and historians often consult all three. But writing is the marker that separates history from what comes before.

Traditionally Historians

Herodotus of Halicarnassus (484 BC-CA. 425 BC) : Herodotus of Halicarnassus has generally been acclaimed as the "father of history". However, his contemporary Thucydides (ca. 460 BC – ca. 400 BC) is credited with having first approached history with a well-developed historical method in his work the History of the Peloponnesian War. Thucydides, unlike Herodotus and other religious historians, regarded history as being the product of the choices and actions of human beings, and looked at cause and effect, rather than as the result of divine intervention. In his historical method, Thucydides emphasized chronology, a neutral point of view, and that the human world was the result of the actions of human beings. Greek historians also viewed history as cyclical, with events regularly recurring.

Thucydides (460-396 BC) : Thucydides was another great Greek historian who was the contemporary of Herodotus. When the Peloponnesian war broke out, he kept the record of it from the day to day. But before completing

the whole work, the History of Peloponnesian War, he died. His style was different. He concentrated on the cause and effect relationship of every incident and that is why he is known as the father of scientific history. He is also known as the first economic historian in the world as he tried to analyze the influence of economic conditions in the history of Athens.

Sima Qian (145–90 BC) : There were historical traditions and sophisticated use of historical method in ancient and medieval China. The groundwork for professional historiography in East Asia was established by the Han Dynasty court historian known as Sima-Qian (145–90 BC), author of the Shiji (Records of the Grand Historian). For the quality of his timeless written work, Sima Qian is posthumously known as the Father of Chinese Historiography. Chinese historians of subsequent dynastic periods in China used his Shiji as the official format for historical texts, as well as for biographical literature.

Medieval Historians

The Medieval Historiography is moulded by the dogmas of Christianity (Dogmas means: that the one God is three Persons-Father, Son, and Holy Spirit). It was nothing to do with the Greeco-Roman traditions. We cannot see any rapport with this classical tradition. The medieval historiography was not based on rational thinking. It is also called the Church historiography.

Saint Augustine (354-430AD) : Saint Augustine was influential in Christian and Western thought at the beginning of the medieval period. Through the Medieval and Renaissance periods, history was often studied through a sacred or religious perspective. Around 1800, German philosopher and historian Georg Wilhelm Friedrich Hegel brought philosophy and a more secular approach in historical study.

Arab Historian

Ibn Khaldun (1332-1406AD) : Ibin Khaldun is the greatest Arab historian. He is considered as the exponent of the scientific approach in history. His most important work book is 'The Universal History' (7 Volumes). But he is famous with the preface of the work which is known as 'Muqquadama'. Ibn Khaldun warned of seven mistakes that he thought that historians regularly committed. In this criticism, he approached the past as strange and in need of interpretation.

The originality of Ibn Khaldun was to claim that the cultural difference of another age must govern the evaluation of relevant historical material, to distinguish the principles according to which it might be possible to attempt the evaluation, and lastly, to feel the need for experience, in addition to rational principles, in order to assess a culture of the past.

Ibn Khaldun often criticized "idle superstition and

uncritical acceptance of historical data."

As a result, he introduced a scientific method to the study of history, and he often referred to it as his "new science". His historical method included role of state, communication, propaganda and systematic bias in history, However Ibn Khaldun had no followers and established no school; his work was unknown in the west until the 19thcentury and had no influence there.

Modern Historians

Vico (1668-1744AD) : Giambattista Vico is one of the greatest modern historians, hails from Italy. His book is known as 'The New Science'. He interprets history as a new science. When natural science indulges the external affairs of man, social science depicts the internal affairs. A historian uses a tool much different from that of a natural scientist. He also supports the cyclical theory of history.

He divides this process in to certain phase's namely bestial stage, Age of Gods and Age of Heroes. The fourth phase is the Age of Man which denotes the struggle between the patricians and plebeians. The beginning of democratic age is with the victory of the plebeians over the patricians. Then the cyclical process ends with a decay of the existing society.

Auguste Comte (1795-1857AD) : Comte was a French philosopher stood against the Church domination in every affair. Basically he was a humanist. He propagated historical objectivity through two important works namely 'The Course of Positive Philosophy', and 'The System of Positive Policy'. He called history a social physics. He believed that it is only through history that one can understand the society. He freed history from the domination of theology and metaphysics.

Ranke (1795-1885AD) : Leopold Von Ranke is considered as the first modern historian. He introduced a method of criticism (both internal and external) in historiography and that paved the way for a new era in historiography based on the criticism of sources. Ranke brought a professional touch in history. Objectivity is an inevitable part of history. His first historical work is known as 'Histories of Roman and Tentonic People'. Ranke conducted serious researches in history of Europe. He says that the duty of every historian is to approach the events and sources with an objective mind.

The following are the famous works of Ranke: 'History of Popes', 'History of Reformation in Germany', 'History of France', 'and History of England', and 'History of Prussia'. Ranke tells that God has His own part in history. The contribution of Ranke and his followers are known as the Berlin Revolution in history

Academic Historians

In the 20th century, academic historians focused less on epic nationalistic narratives, which often tended to glorify the nation or individuals, to more objective and complex analyses of social and intellectual forces. A major trend of historical methodology in the 20th century was a tendency to treat history more as a social science rather than as an art, which traditionally had been the case. Some of the leading advocates of history as a social science were a diverse collection of scholars which included Fernand Braudel, E.H. Carr, Fritz Fischer, Emmanuel Le Roy Ladurie, Hans-Ulrich Wehler, Bruce Trigger, Marc Bloch, Karl Dietrich Bracher, Peter Gay, Robert Fogel, Lucien Febvre and Lawrence Stone. Many of the advocates of history as a social science were or are noted for their multi-disciplinary approach. Braudel combined history with geography, Bracher history with political science, Fogel history with economics, Gay history with psychology, Trigger history with archeology while Wehler, Bloch, Fischer, Stone, Febvreand Le Roy Ladurie have in varying and differing ways amalgamated history with sociology, geography, anthropology, and economics.

In opposition to the claims of history as a social science, historians such as Hugh Trevor-Roper, John Lukacs, Donald Creighton, Gertrude Himmelfarb and Gerhard Ritter argued that the key to the historians' work was the power of the imagination, and hence contended that history should be understood as an art. French historians associated with the Annales School introduced quantitative history, using raw data to track the lives of typical individuals, and were prominent in the establishment of cultural history. Intellectual historians such as Herbert Butterfield, Ernst Nolte and George Mosse for the significance of ideas in history. American historians, motivated by the civil rights era, focused on formerly overlooked ethnic, racial, and socio-economic groups. Another genre of social history to emerge in the post-WW-II era was all tags geschichte (History of Everyday Life). Scholars such as Martin Broszat, Ian Kershaw and Detlev Peukert sought to examine what everyday life was like for ordinary people in 20thcentury Germany, especially in the Nazi period.

Marxist Historians

Marxist historians such as Eric Hobsbawm, E. P. Thompson, Rodney Hilton, Georges Lefebvre, Eugene D.

Genovese, Isaac Deutscher, C. L. R. James, Timothy Mason, Herbert Aptheker, Arno J. Mayer and Christopher Hill have sought to validate Karl Marx's theories by analyzing history from a Marxist perspective. In response to the Marxist interpretation of history, historians such as François Furet, Richard Pipes, J. C.D. Clark, Roland Mousnier, Henry Ashby Turner and Robert Conquest have offered anti-Marxist interpretations of history. Feminist historians such as Joan Wallach Scott, Claudia Koonz, Natalie Zemon Davis, Sheila Rowbotham, Gisela Bock, Gerda Lerner, Elizabeth Fox-Genovese, and Lynn Hunt have argued for the importance of studying the experience of women in the past. In recent years, postmodernists have challenged the validity and need for the study of history on the basis that all history is based on the personal interpretation of sources. In his 1997 book In Defence of History, Richard J. Evans, a professor of modern history at Cambridge University, defended the worth of history. Another defence of history from post-modernist criticism was the Australian historian Keith Windschuttle's 1994 book, *The Killing of History.*

RESEARCH TRENDS OF HISTORY

1. The History Encompasses Many Subfields : As a field of study, history encompasses many subfields and ancillary fields. These include chronology, historiography, genealogy, paleography, and clinometric, among many others.

2. The Sources of Historical Research : The sources of historical knowledge can be separated into three categories: what is written, what is said, and what is physically preserved, and historians often consult all three.

3. The Research Study of the Human Past : The research study of the human past has naturally led scholars to divide that time into manageable pieces for study. There are a variety of ways in which the past can be divided, including chronologically, culturally, and topically.

4. The Research of Academic Professionalism : The research of academic professionalism and the creation of new scientific fields in the 19thand 20th centuries brought a flood of new information that challenged this notion. Archaeology, anthropology and other social sciences were providing new information and even theories about human history. Some traditional historians questioned whether these new studies were really history, since they were not limited to the written word. Anew term, prehistory, was coined, to encompass the results of these new fields where they yielded information about times before the existence of written records

5. The Historical Method : The historical method comprises the techniques and guidelines by which historians use primary sources and other evidence to research and then to write history.

6. The Post-Modernists Challenge of Validity : In recent research, postmodernists have challenged the validity and need for the study of history on the basis that all history is based on the personal interpretation of sources.

REFERENCES

- https://www.scribd.com/doc/22797322/History-scope-and-Definition
- http://ddceutkal.ac.in/Syllabus/MA_Education/Education_Paper_5_history.pdf
- http://www.universityofcalicut.info
- https://en.wikipedia.org/wiki/Economics#History

9

Public Administration

INTRODUCTION

Public Administration as independent Subject of a social science has recent origin. Public administration is the implementation of government policy and also an academic discipline that studies this implementation and prepares civil servants for working in the public service. As a "field of inquiry with a diverse scope" whose fundamental goal is to "advance management and policies so that government can function".

Traditionally Public Administration was considered as a part of political science. But in Modern age the nature of state-underwent change and it became from police stale to social service state. As a consequence, the Public Administration, irrespective of the nature of the political system, has become the dominant factor of life. The modern political system is essentially 'bureaucratic' and characterized by the rule of officials. Hence modern democracy has been described as 'executive democracy'. The administrative branch, described as civil service or bureaucracy is the most significant component of governmental machinery of the state.

MEANING OF PUBLIC ADMINISTRATION

Administer is a English word, which is originated from the Latin word 'ad' and 'Ministrare'. It means to serve or to manage. Administration means management of affairs, public or private.

DEFINITION OF PUBLIC ADMINISTRATION

According to Paul H. Appleby, "Public leadership of public affairs has directly responsible for executive action. In a democracy, it has to do with such leadership and executive action in terms that respect and contribute to the dignity, the worth, and the potentials of the citizen."

According to L. D. White, "Public Administration consists of all those operations having for their purpose the fulfillment of public policy as declared by authority." Both above definitions are done from traditional viewpoint and related only to the functions and actions of Administration."

According to Simon, "By Public Administration is meant the activities of the executive branches of the national, state, & local governments."

According to Willough, "Public Administration in broadest sense denotes the work involved in the actual conduct of governmental affairs, and in narrowest senses denotes the operations of the administrative branch only."

According to Gullick, "Public Administration is that part of the science of administration which has to do with government and thus, concerns itself primarily with the executive branch where the work of the government is done."

According to Waldo, "Public Administration is the art and science of management as applied to the affairs of the state."

To sum up the concluded that the definition of Public Administration can be had in the following words: Public Administration is a detailed and systematic application of law.

SCOPE OF PUBLIC ADMINISTRATION

We should understand various perspectives about the scope of Public Administration. Following are the three important perspectives about the scope of Public Administration.

1. Narrow perspective or POSDCORD perspective.
2. Broad perspective or subject matter view.
3. Prevailing view.

1. Narrow perspective or POSDCORD perspective

Luther Gullick is the main exponent of this perspective. According to him the scope of public administration is narrow or limited. It is also regarded as POSDCORD view. It insists that the Public Administration is concerned only with those aspects of administration which are related with the executive branch and its seven types of administrative functions.

These seven types of functions which show the scope of Public Administration are as follows:

- **'P'** Stands for Planning
- **'O'** Stands for Organization
- **'S'** Stands for Staffing.
- **'D'** Stands for Directing.
- **'Co'** Stands for Co-ordination.
- **'R'** Stands for Reporting
- **'B'** Stands for Budgeting

1. 'P' stands for Planning : Planning is the first step of Public Administration i.e. working out the broad outline of the things that need to be done.

2. 'O' stands for organization : It means establishment of the formal structure of authority through which the work is sub-divided, arranged and co-ordinate for the defined objective.

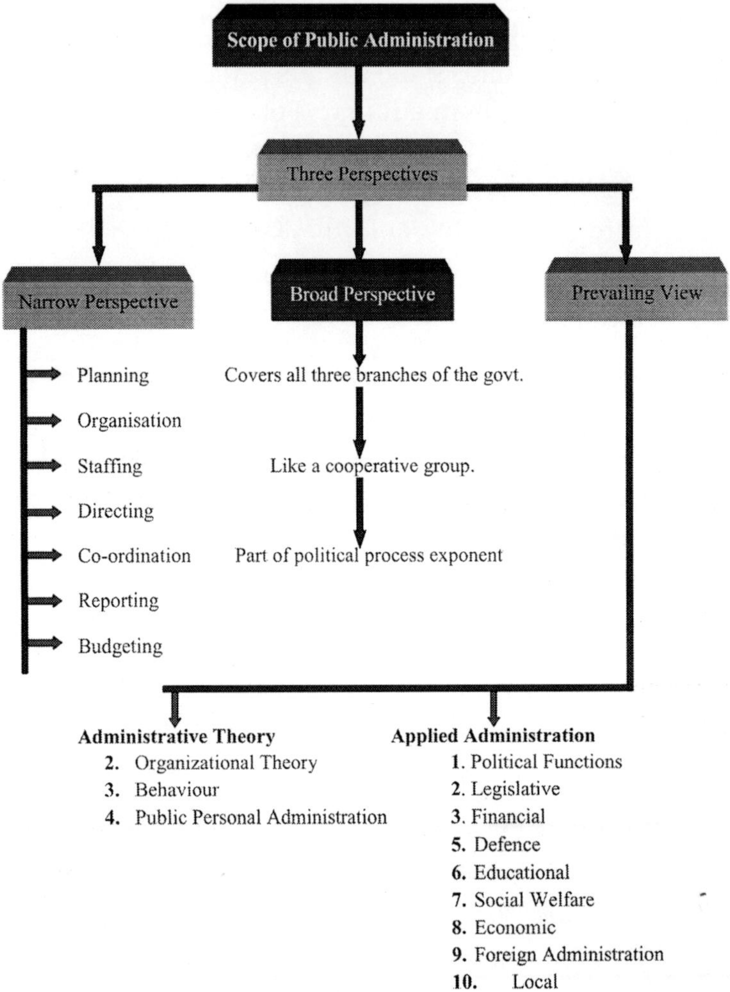

3. 'S' stands for staffing : It means the recruitment and training of the staff and maintenance of favorable conditions of work for the staff.

4. 'D' stands for Directing : It means the continuous task of making decisions and embodying them in specific and general orders and instructions, and thus guiding the enterprise.

5. 'Co' stands for Co-ordination : It means inter-relating the various parts of organization such as branches, divisions, and sections of the work and elimination of overlapping.

6. 'R' stands for Reporting : It means informing the authority to whom the executive is responsible as to what is going on.

7. 'B' stands for Budgeting : It means accounting, fiscal planning and control.

Evaluation

POSDCORB Perspective about the Scope of Public Administration is limited and narrow. It stressed on the tools of Public Administration. It does not show the substance of administration. It is a technique oriented perspective, not a subject oriented.

2. Broad perspective or subject-oriented perspective

Prof. Woodrow Wilson, L D While is main exponent of this perspective. They have taken a very broad approach about the scope of Public Administration. According to them:

(a) Public Administration covers all three branches of the government. The Legislative, Executive, Judicial and their inter-relationship. Legislative organ makes the laws, Executive organ of the government implements the laws. And judicial organ of the government interprets the laws. There is interrelationship between these three organs.

(b) Scope of Public Administration is like a cooperative group. It consists of all from class one officer to class four employees.

(c) Public Administration is a part of the political process. It has an important role in the formulation of public policy at all levels, from national to grass root. It is closely associated with numerous private groups and individuals in providing services to the community. It has been influenced in recent years by the human relations approach.

3. Prevailing view

Prevailing view divides the scope of Public Administration into two parts:

1. Administrative theory
2. Applied administration

1. Administrative theory : It includes the following aspects.

(a) ***Organizational Theory*:** The Structure, organization, functions and methods of all types of public authority engaged in administration, whether national, regional or local and executive.

(b) ***Behaviour*:** The functions of administrative authorities and the various methods appropriate to different types of functions. The various forms of control of administration.

(c) ***Public Personal Administration*** **:** The problems concerning personnel e.g. recruitment, training, promotion, retirement etc. and the problems relating to planning, research, information and public relation services.

2. Applied administration : It includes the following aspects:

(a) ***Political functions*** **:** It includes the executive - legislative relationship, administrative activities of the cabinet, the minister and permanent official relationship.

(b) ***Legislative function*** **:** It includes delegated legislation and the preparatory work done by the officials in connection with the drawing up of bills.

(c) ***Financial functions*** **:** It includes total financial administration from the preparation of the budget to its execution, accounting and audit etc.

(d) ***Defence*** **:** Functions relating to military administration.

(e) ***Educational function*** **:** It includes functions relating to educational administration.

(f) ***Social welfare administration*** **:** It includes the activities of the departments concerned with food; housing, social security and development activities.

(g) ***Economic Administration*** **:** It is concerned with the production and encouragement of industries and agriculture.

(h) ***Foreign administration*** **:** It includes the conduct of foreign affairs, diplomacy, international cooperation etc.

(i) ***Local administration*** **:** It concern with the activities of the local self-governing institutions.

HISTORICAL BACKGROUD & LANDMARKS OF PUBLIC ADMINISTRATION

Aristotle, the Greek's scholar, who is regarded as the father of political science, also discussed some aspects of administration in his famous book The Politics. During the middle age which is dubbed as dark period in the human history, nothing substantial happened in this regard. However, in the renaissance era there appeared Machiavelli's The Prince which is considered as a treatise on the art of government and administration. In modern times also many scholarly works on Political Science and memoirs of statesmen deal extensively with administrative matters. But despite all this, there has not been clear recognition of Public

Administration as a separate and distinct subject of study. Even the term Public Administration was used for the first time in the closing years of 18th century when Hamilton contributed a paper defining the meaning and scope of the discipline. Likewise, the first book on public administration was "Principles d Administration Publique" written by Charles Jean Bounin, a French scholar in 1812.

In 1887, Woodrow Wilson has written the book on "The Study of Public Administration", and laid the foundation of the science of Public Administration. After that it had underwent rapid transformation in its scope, nature and role. The evolution of public administration was into the following five phases.

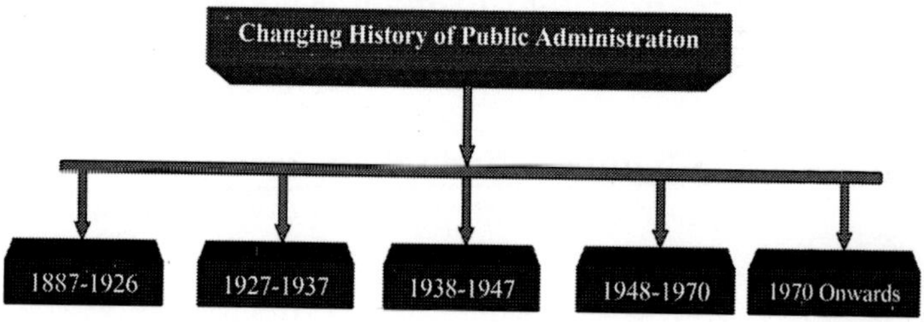

Time Periods

1. 1887 To 1926
   - Period of Dichotomy
2. 1927 To 1937
   - Developed as independent discipline,
   - POSDCORD,
   - Developed Principles of administration,
   - Science
3. 1938 To 1947
   - Behavioural Challenge
4. 1948 To 1970
   - Crisis of Identity

5. 1971 To Onwards
    - New Public administration
    - Public Policy Perspective

Phase I: 1887-1926

About the changing nature of Public Administration, in this phase following changes came out:

- Separation of Public Administration from political science
- Public Administration is the visible side of Government.
- Prof. Woodrow Wilson has given definition, nature, role and importance of Public Administration.
- L. D. White has written the first textbook on the subject i.e. 'Introduction to the study of Public Administration.'

Professor **Woodrow Wilson** is called the 'Father of Public Administration' because the genesis of the subject can be traced back to Wilson's book "The study of Public Administration" published in 1887. In this book he made a distraction between political - Science and Public Administration. Before this, it was treated as a branch of political science. Secondly, while commenting on the role of Public Administration, he said Administration is the most obvious part of government. It is government in action and the most visible side of the government. Hence, he defined "Public Administration as detailed and systematic application of law. It consists of all those operations having for their purpose the enforcement of public policy as declared by authority."

He argued for a science of administration "Which shall seek to straighten the paths of government." Thus, Wilson had projected the dichotomy view, which was picked up by other writers.

In 1900, **Frank J. Goodnow** published his book "Politics and Administration". In his book he developed the Wilson theme. He argued that "Politics and administration were two distinct functions of a government." According to him politics formulate the policies and administration executes these policies. Thus, Goodnow made a technical distinction between politics and administration.

In 1926, L.D.While published the first text-book on the subject. This book reflects the theme of dichotomy between politics and administration. He emphasized that politics and administration are to be kept separate. He also visualized involvement of administration in policy matters and through policy with politics.

Conclusion

It may be seen that the dominant feature of the first period was a passionate belief in politics administration dichotomy.

Phase II: 1927-1937

In the changing nature of public Administration this period can be called as principles of Administration and established the discipline of Public Administration as an independent science. In 1927, W.F. Willough has written a book "Principles of Public Administration." The title of the book indicates the new thrust in thinking and established the subject as an independent science.

This period witnessed publication of a number of important works on this subject. The more important among them are:

1. Mary Parker Folleft's "Creative Experience"
2. Henri Fayol's "Industrial and General Mangement."
3. Mooney's "Principles of Organisation".
4. Luther Gulick "Science of Administration."

Gulick explained the principles of administration. These are seven principles known as POSDCORB.

Conclusion

Thus in this period subject acquired:

1. The Status of separate subject of social science
2. Secondly. It was considered, as the science of administration.
3. Developed the principles of administration and theories. These theories and principles were in great demand both in government and business.

Phase III: 1938-1947

This period brought new changes in the nature of public administration.

1. Some thinkers refuted politics administration dichotomy.
2. They challenged the claim of Public Administration as a science.
3. Emphasized the environmental effects on administrative behaviour.

While public administration was taking shape as an independent discipline, C. I. Barnard, Simon, Robat Dahl challenged the claim of Public Administration as a science of administration. These thinkers disagree with the stand taken by Gullick. Simon, in 1947 published his book "Administrative Behaviour". In that he said there is no such thing as principles of administration; what are paraded as 'Principles' are in truth no better than proverbs. There is lack of scientific validity and universal relevancy in Public Administration.

Robert Dahl emphasizes the need to take into account normative considerations, human behaviour and sociological factors while defining the parameters of public administration. He brought behaviouralism in Public Administration. He emphasized the environmental effects on administrative behaviour.

Conclusion

Hence this period is called as era of challenge to Public Administration.

Phase IV: 1948 to 1970

Owing to the challenge posed by the behaviouralists, the discipline of Public Administration passed through the crisis of identity in the fourth phase. Because pre 1947 viewpoint upheld the politics administration dichotomy and the post 1947 view point adocated their fusion. Pfiffner stated that politics and administration are so intermingled and confused that a clear distinction is difficult.

Kingsley saw administration as a branch of Politics. Paul Appleby upheld the fusion view, He said at higher levels administration is more generalized, takes on a greater political character and has a total governmental significance. At lower levels, it is less political and more particularistic. Waldo in his Administrative State (1948) widened the orientation of Public Administration to include policy issues and decision making processes. On the other hand, many political scientists began to argue that the true objective of Public Administration was "intellectualized understanding" of the executive. There was also a talk of continued 'dominion of political science over Public Administration.'

In Short, this period witnessed the spectacle of Political Science not only letting Public Administration separate itself from it, but also not fostering and encouraging its growth and development within its own field. Therefore, in the post world war II period, the credentials of Public Administration to being a science and a distinct discipline and apart from political, - Science were questioned. This led to the twin development of Public Administration being viewed as political science an also as an Administration science.

Phase V: 1971 onwards

In this period Public Administration registered great progress and enriched vision.

1. Focus on the dynamics of administration.
2. It is considered as inter-disciplinary.
3. Talk of New Public Administration
4. New trends emerged in the subject of Public Administration i.e.
    - Comparative Administration
    - Development Administration
    - Market orientation - State and Market

1. Focus on the dynamics of administration : It is focusing its attention on the dynamics of administration. It is also drawing heavily on the management sciences.

2. It is considered as inter-disciplinary : Public Administration has attracted within its fold scholars from various disciplines and thus is becoming inter-disciplinary in its nature.

RESEARCH TRENDS OF PUBLIC ADMINISTRATION

- A narrow focus on technocratic, managerial approaches in an attempt to provide solutions for more effective and efficient government.
- A multidisciplinary approach to addressing complex social problems or "wicked policy" problems across

narrow specialized interests for "greater principles" of society.

- Respond proactively to the "New Governance".
- Strategic manpower development issues in public sector.
- Issues in research and doctoral programs.
- Methodological pluralism in the study of government, which may add to the depth or fragmentation of the discipline.
- A conceptual understanding of public administration, public management, NPM and governance.
- A historical and contemporary perspective of the discipline.
- A critical perspective of research and scholarship that will provide a debate on the state of discipline.
- Improving efficiency with business-like practices and attitudes toward daily operations.
- Improving the effectiveness of public service through management and by training civil servants, merit-based assessment.

REFERENCES

- http://archive.mu.ac.in/myweb_test/SYBA%20Study%20Material/pol_sc-III.pdf
- https://en.wikipedia.org/wiki/Public_administration

Unit-II

DOCUMENTARY SOURCES OF SOCIAL SCIENCE

10

Information System

INTRODUCTION

Information Systems is an academic study of systems with a specific reference to information and the complementary networks of hardware and software that people and organizations use to collect, filter, process, create and also distribute data. An emphasis is placed on an information system having a definitive boundary, users, processors, storage, inputs, outputs and the aforementioned communication networks.

INFORMATION

Common definition of information is data. However, data is no true information. Data gets its meaning and significance if only it is information. Information is represented with data, symbols and letters.

SYSTEM

In a system, network of components work towards a single objective, if there is lack of co-ordination among components, it leads to counterproductive results.

DEFINITIONS OF INFORMATION SYSTEM

According to *David Kroenke*, "An information system

(IS) is a group of components that interact to produce information."

According to Jessup & Joseph, "Information Systems is an academic study of systems with a specific reference to information and the complementary networks of hardware and software that people and organizations use to collect, filter, process, create and also distribute data. An emphasis is placed on an information system having a definitive boundary, users, processors, storage, inputs, outputs and the aforementioned communication networks".

An information system (IS) is an organized system for the collection, organization, storage and communication of information. More specifically, it is the study of complementary networks that people and organizations use to collect, filter, process, create and distribute data.

COMPONENTS OF INFORMATION SYSTEM

Information System consists of a number of organs or components. These organs or components work in harmony to achieve the define purposes. The main components of Information Systems are:

1. Libraries
2. Documentation Centres
3. Information Centres
4. Data Banks
5. Data Centres
6. Information Analysis Centres
7. Referral Centres
8. Clearing Houses
9. Translation Centres, etc.

1. Libraries : Libraries are by far the oldest institutions charged with the responsibility of collecting, storing and disseminating of information. Library is a collection of books or other written or printed materials, as well as the facility in which they are housed and served the reader within an institution that is responsible for their maintenance. According to Ranganathan, the father of library science in India "A library is a public institution or establishment charged with the care of collection of books, the duty of making them accessible to those who require the use of them and the task of converting every person in its neighborhood into a habitual library goers and reader of books."

Libraries are established by the government, academic institutions or by some other special organizations. Libraries can be grouped into three major divisions i.e. Public (State Central Library, District Library, Sub divisional Library, Rural Library), Academic (University Library, College Library), School and Special (Libraries attached to industries, Doordarshan Kendra, All India Radio, etc).

(a) *Collections*: In ancient day libraries gathered huge collection of manuscripts and preserved them most efficiently for the posterity. Modern libraries may contain a wide range of materials, including manuscripts and pamphlets, posters, photographs, motion pictures, and videotapes, sound recordings, and computer databases in various forms.

(b) *Services*: Libraries are the carriers of information from one generation to the next generation. Most of the new technology based information businesses are still largely dependent on the library for their survival which includes information broker, consultants, referral centre. In the days of IT also libraries continue to serve millions of grateful users in new and improved ways and it is hoped that in neat future also it will be the only affordable source of information.

The change in structure of libraries comes as an information system that consists of a number of organs or components. These organs or components work in harmony to achieve the define purposes. It is advantageous to discuss the changing role of library and information centers on the basis of such information unit or change in structure of the libraries.

2. Documentation Centres : ASLIB adopted the definition of the term documentation for the Journal of Documentation in 1945 as "recording, organization and dissemination of specialized knowledge". Late Dr. S. C. Bradford defines it as "the art of documentation is the art of collecting, classifying and making readily accessible the records of all kinds of intellectual activities".

(a) *Origin of Documentation Centres* : Books were not able to communicate latest scientific thought as a result importance of scientific periodicals had increased. With the acceleration of research scientific periodicals gained further importance. Along with the scientific periodicals new kind of literature like conference proceedings, annual reviews, patents, standards and specification, theses, secondary periodicals like indexing and abstracting journals, directories, research reports, etc. started appearing in big way. Further these paper based information sources are supplemented by CD, DVD, etc. As a result libraries started acquiring all these materials along with books. To have a comprehensive term for all these media of communication "Documentation" was brought into vogue. The reader for this kind of new literature steadily increases but the nature of complexity of information sources led to the demand of services that are outside the domain of traditional libraries and the traditional library techniques were found to be unsuitable hence, a new breed of organization known as documentation centres paved the way.

(b) *Services* : Documentation centres find out new vistas in serving the need of the user. It gives emphasis towards provision of information contained in document rather than serving the document themselves. It analyses the content of the documentation in finer details, provide indexing, abstracting, union catalogue, translation, etc.

services to meet the need of the specialist users. Another basic function of any documentation centres is that it brings to the notice of specialist user, current and recent literature of value to them. Services of documentation centres are designed to satisfy the existing and anticipated needs of its users. The main purposes served by these units are:

- To answer the queries
- To help in finding the primary document
- To identify as accurately as possible all information of potential interest to users
- To see that the user receive the information.

3. Information Centres : An information centre can be defined as "An organization that

(a) Select, acquire stores and retrieve specific information in response to requests.

(b) Announces, abstract, extract and indexes information.

(c) Disseminate information in response to requests from documents or in anticipation".

Meltzer defines the information centre as "The Special library with added functions of analyzing and synthesizing information needed by management, staff and the technical personnel of the organization". Thus information centres gives emphasis towards the provision of information contained in the document rather than document themselves which is the main consideration of traditional libraries.

A library handles and provides address of a document containing information but an information centre gives information that is inside the document and also processes and disseminates it. The information centre differs from the library in following main areas:

- Degree of delegation by the user i.e. the task of searching and evaluating information is dome by the staff.

- Exercise of judgment and evaluation as to the importance of the retrieved material in relation to the client's request.
- The giving of information itself rather than document.
- The processing of search input into a variety of search products.
- Provides information to not only user of parent organization but also outside the organization too.
- Not only acquire, process, store and retrieve information (the library function) but also reduce analyse and present information/data.

4. Data Banks : Data Banks are usually concerned with a broader field. They are very precise grids to extract the raw data from data collection and the relevant literature which they arrange in structured files so as to be ready for subsequent processing to answer user queries. The essential characteristic of data bank is storing information in a form (so data should be in a machine readable files i.e. for storing and retrieving of data computer should be used) which will allow continuous updating, augmentation and approach from different points of view and which has the capacity of supporting simultaneously a number of user at remote locations. To use the analogy of a bank, a user can deposit or withdraw from several branches.

Satmana defines a data bank as an open information system with sets of data known as files. It is composed of the following elements:

- The basic files known as data base.
- A filing system that makes to integrate data from different files, relative to the same entities
- A data processing system that allows users to extract relevant information from the files adopted to their needs and in a form suited to their decision pattern.

Data centre and data banks are dissimilar only regarding the subjects they deals and type of data they handle. Simply stated data centres handle only numerical data and mostly for science and technology. Data banks are multidisciplinary and deal with all types of data particularly administrative, statistical, techno-economics, census and survey, and similar other that are produced by several institutions. Data banks handle data only while data centres handle data themselves or literature about data.

5. Data Centres : According to UNESCO a data centre "constitutes an organization handling quantitative numerical data" Such centers take the primary function of collecting, organizing, and disseminating data (mainly numerical) and also provide a measurement service and are in a position to advance relevant measurement techniques. They store data on a narrow field of specification. Data centres try to collect arrange and store numerical data pertaining to a specific subject field or to answer specific queries. Data centre activities are anticipatory operations planned keeping in view the requirements of its user. It also checks systematically all available data and organizes them into a number of categories for the purpose of showing the current state of knowledge together with comments on the precision or reliability of the data in regard to the various aspects of a product or phenomena. It may be stated here that the activities of a data centre may comprise of the following:

- Data Collection.
- Data Control.
- Data Codification.
- Data Organization and structuring into a database.
- Data Retrieval.

Example of data centre includes National Data Centre for Crystallography, University of Madras, India.

6. Information Analysis Centres : The COSATI

standing panel wrote the following comprehensive definition of Information Analysis Centre (IAC) "An information analysis centre is a formally structured organizational unit, specifically (but not necessarily exclusively) established for the purpose of acquiring, selecting, storing, retrieving, evaluating, analyzing an synthesizing a body of information and / or data in a clearly defined specialized field or pertaining to a specified mission with intent of compiling, digesting, repackaging or otherwise organizing and presenting pertinent information and / or data in a form most authoritative, timely and useful to a society of peers and management".

The key activities of IAC s are analysis, interpretation, synthesis, evaluation and repackaging of information carried out by subject specialists, resulting in the production of new, evaluated information in the form of critical reviews, state of art, monographs or data compilation as well as substantive, evaluated responses to queries for the purpose of assisting a community of users more broadly representative than the staff of the parent institutes of laboratories.

These centres have to closely monitor the literature produced in the field, evaluate the utility of each piece of information so gathered and the information are communicate to the users in a directly usable form. The results of analysis are communicated either through a regular publication or by way of sporadic reports. It is very much essential that these centres should verify the information so gathered with regard to the validity, reliability and accuracy before dissemination.

7. Referral Centres : These do not provide the user with the documents. Instead it refers or directs them to the source from where they can get the data or the documents. Mostly to secondary publication, information centres, professional organizations, research institutions, clearing houses and individual scientist, etc. They maintain files of sources, directories, etc. The referral centre may even bring out such documents. So, in simple referral centre provide switching mechanism among different types of information institutions. The referral service may be one of the activities of a documentation centre and it is difficult to find units performing this function exclusively. To achieve its objectives a referral centre has to perform certain basic operations. These includes:

- A referral centre possesses an inventory of all significant information resources in different disciplines.
- It compiles and publishes directories of scientific and technical information resources.
- It analyzes the operating relationships that exist in the scientific information.

8. Clearing Houses : A clearing house is a central agency for collection, classification and distribution of information. It may include specialized information centres as well as conventional libraries. It represents a depository for document with the additional objectives of servicing as a central agency engaged in the distribution of information. It also includes such functions as collecting and maintaining records of research and development.

Clearing houses provide a single point of access to documents originating from a number of sources from different places, in different languages. The producers of the documents inform the clearing house about the bibliographical details of the document and usually send them a copy. The clearing houses circulate the description of the documents to the organization that are interested in the field and to the participating organizations. They may provide a copy of these documents as well on request if available. These units are organized either on a cooperative basis or by an international or national agency.

Most of the clearing houses have specialized as well as they developed collections. They have information gathering network to acquire documents in their subject areas. They also provide specialized information services in some selected areas. They answer specific and general type of questions and may act as central searching places for enquiry especially for research and development areas.

The difference between a documentation center and a clearing house is that the documentation centre deals with conventional documents, whereas the clearing house deals with the non-conventional documents like conference proceedings, scientific reports, document of limited circulation, etc.

9. Translation Centres : In modern times in any discipline literature are published in many languages as a result, scientist in need of particular information find it difficult to be able to understand the contents of the documents. To solve the problem, some national and international level organization comes forward to help the scientist in this regard. They translate the content of the documents from one language to another to meet the needs of the user. In the field of science and technology following centre provides translation services:

- National Translation Centre, Chicago, America
- International Translation Centre, Delft, Netherlands
- British Library Lending Division, Boston

10. Data Consolidation and Evaluation Centre : It is an advance form of information units which check systematically all available data and organize them into a number of categories for the purpose of showing the current state of knowledge together with comments on the precision or reliability of the data in regard to the various aspects of a product or phenomenon.

REFERENCES

- Jessup, L. M., & Joseph, S. V (2008). Information Systems Today. 3rd Ed. Pearson Publishing, 416.
- Kroenke, David (2015). MIS Essentials. 4th Ed. Boston: Pearson, 10.

11

Information Sources

INTRODUCTION

Literature of a subject is its foundation. It represents a record of achievements of human race. Literature is diverse, complex and multilingual in nature. It is becoming more and more inter-disciplinary. It is growing at a fast pace. In sciences, it is almost doubling itself in every very few years according to some studies. In social Sciences, it is doubling at the rate of every eight to twelve years. Literature serves the informational needs of various kinds of Users. It forms source of Information. Traditionally Specking, information sources would include primarily books, periodicals and newspapers. However, the number and forms of source are continuously increasing. In addition, unpublished sources are becoming increasingly important to scholars. Occasions will arise, especially in a special library of University library, when information would be required by a user without precondition about the form of document. In such a situation, what matters is the finding of information not the sources of information.

MEANING OF INFORMATION SOURCES

An information source is a person, thing, or place from which information comes, arises, or is obtained.

DEFINITIONS

According to Wong, "Information source might then inform a person about something or provide knowledge about it. Information sources are divided into separate distinct categories, primary, secondary, tertiary".

An Information Source is a source of information for somebody, i.e. anything that might inform a person about something on provides knowledge to somebody. Information sources may be observations, people speeches, documents, pictures, organizations etc.

An information source is where you got your information from; this can be a book or a website. Information sources are the various means by which information is recorded for use by an individual or an organization. It is the means by which a person is informed about something or knowledge is availed to someone, a group of people or an organization. Information sources can be observations, people, speeches, documents, pictures, organizations. Information sources can be in print, non-print and electronic media or format.

TYPES OF INFORMATION SOURCES

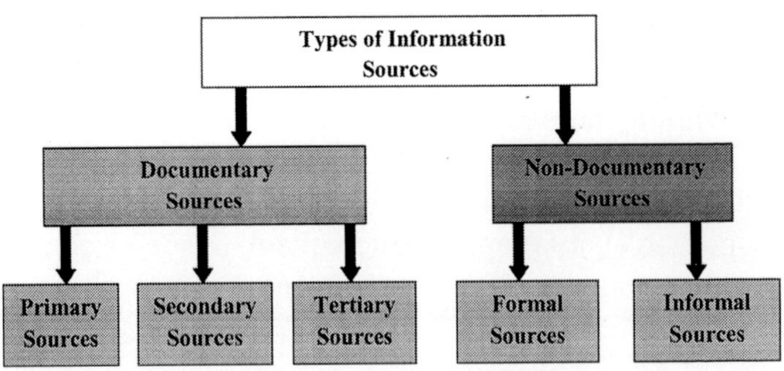

Different epistemologies have different views regarding the importance of different kind of information sources. Empiricism regards sense data as the ultimate information sources, while other epistemologies have different views

(Kragh, 1989). The various types of information sources can be divided into two broad categories.

Documentary Sources : These are generally published or recorded documents of knowledge. Documentary sources may be as under:

1. ***Primary Sources*** **:** Primary sources of information are the first published records of original research and development or description of new application or new interpretation of an old theme or idea. There are original documents representing unfiltered original ideas.

Primary sources are unorganized sources, which are rather difficult to use by them, the secondary sources helps us to use these. These are important sources of information. A subject becomes a discipline in its own right when independent primary sources begin to be produced in that area. The rate of growth of a discipline to a large extent depends upon the amount of literature being produced in the form of primary sources reporting development in the concerned field.

Primary sources are distinguished from secondary sources, which cite, comment on, or build upon primary sources. Though the distinction is not a sharp one "Primary and secondary are relative terms, with sources judged primary or secondary according to specific historical contexts and what is being studied." (Kragh, 1989).

For Example:

- Periodicals
- Conference Papers
- Research Monographs
- Newspapers
- Research Reports
- Patents
- Standards

- Thesis
- Industrial and Trade literature
- Manuscripts
- Web sites
- Video Recordings Speeches
- Unpublished Sources:
  - Memoranda Laboratory notebooks
  - Diaries,
  - Company Files
  - Portraits
  - State Papers
  - Autobiographies and memoirs

A. ***Periodicals*** **:** Periodicals are publications such as journals, newspapers, or magazines published on a regular basis - daily, weekly, bi-weekly, monthly, bimonthly, quarterly, yearly, etc. The information in periodicals covers a wide variety of topics and is very up-to date. Other hand all periodicals do not report original work. There are a number of periodicals which specialize in interpreting and providing opinions on developments reported in primary sources of information.

B. ***Research Monographs*** **:** Research Monographs are "separately published reports on original research that are too long, too specialized, or otherwise unsuitable for publication in one of the standard journals. Each Monograph is self-contained, frequently summarizes existing theory or practice before presenting the author's original and previously unpublished work, and is likely to be one of a series of such research monographs in the same field." However, it may be added that ordinarily a monograph is a short treatise. It differs from a treatise in the same that it is a work done on a more limited scale. Otherwise both have the same features and serve same purposes. A research monograph presents results of original research.

C. ***Newspapers*** **:** Newspaper articles are short and written in non-technical language. They provide first-hand account of an event and so are primary sources. Newspapers come in different forms and are designed for the general public and are business in nature. Newspaper articles are usually short and written in an easy to understand language by staff reporters and reviewed by staff within the organization. Newspapers are also good sources for secondary information. However, not all information in newspapers is reliable. Newspapers are published daily, weekly or monthly.

D. ***Patents*** **:** In 1852, patents were interpreted as scientific and technical literature. At this time the patents legislation was passed. Accordingly, all approved patents should be printed. The word 'Patent' means an official right given to a person to make, use or sell a product, process, design, etc. invented by him/her for a fixed number of years. In fact, this is a settlement between state and researchers, under which state researcher guarantees to use it till a certain time and instead receives royalty from the government. Patents are a facility provided by the government, under which new exploration is given monopoly for a certain period. This is a personal certificate of agreement between the Government and the Investigator. It is monopolized by the investigator for a certain period to create, sell and use any new or useful machine composition created by the manufacturer.

This type of certificate provides a certificate for scholar and workers, to innovate work or produce and promote. Patents have all the details regarding the creation of the object and accordingly according to it, the person who has the title has to construct a comprehensive Vaastu. Thus, patents are an important part of primary sources, as the exploration is new and the ideas of this exploration are unpublished, etc. Patents are of great use especially for chemistry, chemistry, medicine manufacturing. There is an agency for this type of publication in each country. In India, Indian patent office is the agency responsible for giving a monopoly letter. Currently, I receive 3000 monopoly papers every year. Patents are regularly included in the indexing and abstracting service.

E. ***Conference*** **:** An important avenue for reporting new research or developments. Papers presented may or may not be subject to editorial scrutiny. Conference papers can be: not published at all, published only in abstract form, published in advance of the conference as a preprint, published in book form, or as a special issue of a journal.

F. ***Standards*** **:** A standard is something set up and established by authority as a rule for the measure of quantity, weight, extent, value or quality. The standard is such an official criteria, which is prepared by an industrialist, businessmen or a specialist to test the size, importance, etc. of any object. It develops very much after the research program. Normally there are some standard pages that include definitions, methods, attributes, measurements etc. The table and the pictures are also painted. They can be classified as follows:

1. *Dimensional Standard* : These standards are formulated to secure uniformity, interchangeability, and simplification of the types and sizes of one product. i.e. ISO/R169–1960. Sizes of photocopies (on paper) readable without optical devices.

2. *Quality Standard*: These standards are meant for generating quality products. A product manufactured according to the standard will do or perform whatever it is expected to do or perform. For example, a pressure cooker manufactured in accordance with a standard will not burst under excessive pressure. The excess pressure will automatically come out through the pressure valve. Example: IS: 3253-1965.
3. *Standard Test Methods* : These standards prescribe standard methods for testing, chemical analysis, determination of constituents in a chemical compound, and so on. Example: IS: 2188-1962.
4. *Code of Practice* : These standards are meant for correct application of materials and appliances; installation, operation, maintenance of machinery, plants, and so on. Example: IS: 3916-1966. Code of practice for pig housing.
5. *Standard Terminology*
6. *Physical and Scientific Standard* : This record is very important for research. National level organizations in different countries have been set up only for humanization, like British Standards Institution, Indian Standards Institution, this institution provides 300 standards per year, International Standard Organization.

G. ***Research Reports*** **:** Presently research reports are being used more than the magazines. According to a study, more than 10% of all documents taken in this type of report in the first decade were. Thus research reports have become a powerful medium of scientific communication. After the Second World War, the research report was triggered. Due to the emergence of such documents, there is lack of paper, limited distribution and more time for publication in the magazine publication. Therefore, it was considered to develop such a medium which can be distributed in limited copies of paper and at fast speed and this document would be very useful.

H. ***Thesis*** **:** detailed accounts of research conducted for the awarding of higher academic degrees. The research is assessed by external examiners before the degree is awarded. In many cases, it will also be later reported in a condensed form as a journal article.

I. ***Manuscripts*** **:** In relation to ancient subjects, the museum material, coin, ancient relics, inscriptions, statues, genealogy etc. are important place for research. Apart from these, the handwritten texts, manuscripts, unprinted texts, mementos, memos etc. were included in the historical material. The National Library in India, Calcutta, Archive Library Delhi, Oriental Research Library Pune, Khuda Bakhsh Oriental Public Library Patna, Govt. Oriental Manuscripts Library Madras etc. are working.

J. ***Industrial & Trade Literature*** **:** Business literature is important sources for getting information about a specific production. When no such material is found, then specific trading literature becomes useful as a primary source. The main objective of business literature is to provide detailed information of its production. The main reason for this is that in order to increase the sales of its production, credibility occurs in the market before production. These notifications are given by producers and dealers. These literatures are available in the form of Technical Bulletin, Prices List, Datasheet, Book Lists, Handbooks and Institution Magazines etc.

K. ***Diaries*** : Writers, scientists, scholars and many others maintain diaries. These diaries provide most authentic biographical material and plenty of other information. Normally these diaries are handwritten and sometimes depending on their importance they are published also. The diaries of Fanny Burney, English novelist, titled Early Diary 1768-78, and Diary and Letters 1778 - 1840 beautifully depict the background of the period.

L. ***Letters*** : The practice of writing letters for communicating messages is very old. Even today this practice is continuing though with the spread of telephones and mobile phones it is showing signs of decline especially in the case of personal letters. With the advent of Internet, the channel of communication has also undergone change. Now, a huge number of letters has taken the form of e-mails. In official communications, however, letters continue to be as important as ever. Almost always, a letter contains information meant for the addressee. In our day-to-day life, a letter brings to us information about somebody's birth, passing an examination, getting an appointment, fixing of marriage, travel abroad, death, and so on.

M. ***Office files*** : All decisions, big or small, taken by the government, governing body of an academic body, industrial enterprise, a research institution, a society, and so on are recorded in files. A service book (also a file) of an employee maintaining the papers relating to his/her appointment, promotion to the next higher grade, fixation of salary, report about his/her performance by his/her seniors, retirement, pension and so on is an important source of information about that person. Similarly, information regarding the establishment, running, closure, etc. of a ministry or department of a government, an industrial organization, an academic body, a society, or any other non-government organization, is also recorded in files. Hence, they are also important sources of information. The archives maintain important files and every effort is made to preserve each and every file, as files are such entities that have no copies or duplicates.

N. ***Computer files*** **:** A computer file is a collection of records or programs stored under a single filename. For computerization of a library catalogue, we create a record for each and every book in a computer. All these records are stored in a computer under a single name. The collection of these records constitutes a file and the name given to it is called filename. A digitized form of a book, a periodical, a thesis, etc. can be a computer file.

O. ***Databases*** **:** A database is a collection of cross-referenced files so designed as to retrieve information from a number of angles. A large number of indexing and abstracting services of the world have created their own databases, which can be searched from any part of the world on payment basis to retrieve necessary information. There are a number of vendors that possess plenty of online databases. Obtaining the password from the vendor one can search all these databases from a single access point.

P. ***Video Recordings*** **:** A video recording sound, colorful pictures, and animation. Many documentary films recorded in videotapes are excellent sources of information. Here, one not only gets the narration, but also the relevant pictures along with animation. This has a much better impact on the minds of the students and other viewers. The TV channels like Discovery and National Geographic are highly popular in as much as their shows are primarily based on video recordings.

2. *Secondary Sources* : Secondary sources of information are those which are either compiled from or refer to primary sources of information. The original information having been casually modified selected or reorganized so as to serve a definite purpose for group of users. Such sources contain information arranged and organized on the basis of some definite plan. These contain organized repackaged knowledge rather than new knowledge. Information given in primary sources is made available in a more convenient form. Due to their very nature, secondary sources are more easily and widely available than primary sources. These not only provide digested information but also serve as bibliographical key to primary sources of information. The primary sources are the first to appear, these are followed by secondary sources. It is difficult to find information from primary sources directly. Therefore, one should consult the secondary sources in the first instance, which will lead one to specific primary sources.

Kinds of Secondary Sources

"According to Bonn" has divided the secondary sources into three types which are as below:

1. Index Type
   - Index
   - Bibliography
   - Indexing periodicals
   - Abstracting Periodicals
2. Survey Type
   - Review
   - Treatise
   - Monograph
3. Reference Type
   - Encyclopedia

- Dictionary
- Hand book, Manual
- Critical Tables

Some important secondary sources are given below:

A. Monographs : A monograph is a scholarly piece of writing in form of an essay or book on a specific, often limited subject. It is a book that stands on its own rather than being part of a series. According to The National Research Council (NRC), a monograph is a specialized scientific book. Monographs are written by specialists for the benefit of other specialists and demand the highest standards of scholarship. Most monographic manuscripts are critically reviewed and edited resulting in books that are expected to have a reasonably long shelf life. Monographs serve as an important means for conveying basic background information, such as a narrative description of a disease, path-physiology, diagnostic techniques and common therapeutic regimes etc. This trend remains true today, whether the monograph is in the print or electronic format. Monographs can be located using bibliographies that list references of books with detailed bibliographic information (author, title, year of publication, publisher and date of publication). Bibliographies serve as tools for verification, location and selection of monographs. Today, many print sources for monographs are now in electronic formats. To locate monographs in a library collection requires using the library catalog and most libraries now have Online Public Access Catalog (OPAC). A good example is the National Library of Medicine LOCATOR plus.

B. Reviews (Survey Type) : A review is a survey of the primary literature. It aims to digest and correlate the literature over a given period. It also indicates the development and trends in the field concerned. It may appear as a collection of papers on regular basis (annual or quarterly or monthly) or in the form of an article in a periodical. A review provides background information to a new problem in a suitable form and serves as a key to literature. List of references given in a review can serve as first rate bibliography of the concerned subject for a period covered by it, e.g. *Annual review of biochemistry* (1932) Palo Alto: Annual Reviews. Annual.

C. Treatises : A Treatise is a comprehensive compilation or summary of information on a subject. A treatise on a subject provides enough information to a person to acquire basic knowledge, so essential for carrying out advanced research. It also provides facts, along with discussion. The fact may include physical constants methods of preparation and purification of compounds etc. Usually, it is limited to a broad field. Due to the very nature, these become out of date within a short period of time i.e. *Treatise on the calculus of finite differences (1960). 4th Ed. New York: Chelsa.*

D. Reference Books : (Also considered tertiary Sources) Reference works, which contain the desired information itself, are considered secondary sources of information. These include encyclopedias, dictionaries, handbooks, tables, formularies etc. these form an important part of secondary sources of information. The sources of ready reference books are as follows:

- ***Dictionaries* :** A dictionary is a book, which deals with words of a language or of some special subjects, authors, etc. Thus a dictionary is a wordbook. Although a dictionary is supposed to deal with words but often it may go beyond this. i.e. *Webster's third new international dictionary of English language* unabridged with seven language dictionary (1966).
- ***Encyclopedias (Also considered tertiary)* :** An encyclopedia is a book giving information on all branches of knowledge or a specific subject. It is an ideal book, which deals with concepts. An encyclopedia

is a storehouse of knowledge giving all information of significance. However, it is best used for finding answers to background questions related to general information and self-education. One often turns to encyclopedias for one's everyday information requirements. This is also true of scientists and technologists. i.e. *Encyclopedia Americana (1976). New York: Grolier. 30 vols.*

- ***Handbook*** **:** A handbook is a compilation of miscellaneous information in a compact and handy form. It contains data, procedures, and principles, including tables, graphs, diagrams and illustrations. Scientists and technologists use handbooks in their fields rather frequently i.e. *Britain, (1948/49) an official handbook. London: stationary office, annual.*
- ***Tables*** **:** Many of the handbooks contain data in the form of tables. Some of the handbooks devote substantial portion of the work to tables as compared with text. Tables are convent form to present data. There are extremely useful in Science i.e. *Tables of contents and numerical data (1947). Oxford: Pergamum Press. Vol. 1.*
- ***Manuals*** **:** In common practice, a manual is an instruction book, which instructs how to do something by means of specific and clear directions i.e. *Greenly, R.S. (1974). Professional Investor's Manual. London: Greenly.*
- ***Catalogues*** **:** A library catalogue as you know is a systematic list of books, periodicals, etc. possessed by a library or a set of libraries. Many libraries of the world bring out their catalogues in printed form. Some of the catalogues are really voluminous; for example, The British Library General Catalogue of Printed Books to 1975 is in 360 volumes. The Catalog of Books represented by Library of Congress printed cards

issued up to 31 July 1942 is in 167 volumes. The catalogue holds bibliographic information about millions and millions of books emanated from all over the world.

E. Text Books (Other than Fiction and Autobiography) : A textbook is a book of instruction. Its Primary aim is not to impart information about a specific subject but to enable one to develop proper understanding of the subject. Presentation is extremely important and it is prepared to serve a particular level of readership. It cannot be comprehensive. Often presentation is colorful and attractive, giving plenty of illustrations and diagrams. A good textbook takes into consideration the method of teaching and level of readership. It is revised keeping in view new developments and changing methodology of teaching. There is a difference of opinion about the place of text books as tertiary sources i.e. *Text Book of Crop Production, by P.C. Rahaja.*

F. Translations : Translations are an important part of secondary sources. Their characteristics are the same as those of primary or secondary or tertiary sources from which these are translated. Many of the authors of research papers prefer to cite original sources rather than translations.

G. Biographical words : A biography is a description or account of someone's life and the times, which is usually published in the form of a book or an essay, or in some other form, such as a film. An autobiography (auto meaning "self", giving "self-biography") is a biography of a person's life written or told by that same person. A biography is more than a list of impersonal facts (education, work, relationship and death), it also portrays the subject's experience of those events. Unlike a profile or curriculum vitae (resume), a biography presents the subject's story, highlighting various aspects of his or her life, including intimate details of experiences, and may include as analysis of the subject's personality.

H. Literary criticism : It is the study, evaluation and interpretation of literature. Modern Literary criticism is often informed by literary theory, which is the philosophical discussion of its methods and goals. Though the two activities are closely related, literary critics are not always, and have not always been, theorists.

I. Indexing Periodicals : An Indexing Periodical is a regularly issued compilation of titles of articles that appear in current primary source journals. Generally, titles of new books pamphlets etc. are also included. An index to a publication contains an alphabetical list of names, topics, places, formulate, titles of any significant items referring to material presented in the main part of the work. These items are arranged chronologically, geographically or in some other way. An indexing periodical is a regularly issued compilation of titles of articles that appear in current primary source journals, generally titles of new books, pamphlets are also included. i.e. *Reader's guide to periodical literature (1905). New York: Wilson. Vol.1.*

J. Abstracting Periodicals : Abstracts appear in different formats. The best known format for abstracting services is periodical. An abstracting periodical "is a regularly issued compilation of concise summaries of (I) significant articles (often in a very limited subject field) that appear in current primary sources journals and (II) important new research monographs, reports, patents and other primary source publication in that field."(Bonne, 1971). An Abstracting Periodical serves as an index, a tool for retrieval of information on a specific subject. However indexing periodicals are earlier to appear than abstracting periodicals.

K. Indexes : An Index to a work contains an alphabetical list of names, topics, places, formulae, titles of any significant item referring to material presented in the main part of the work. Sometimes, these items may be arranged chronologically, geographically or in some other way. A well compiled index adds to usefulness of a work i.e. *Index of Economic Journals* (1961-62).

L. Bibliographies : A bibliography is an organized list of primary or other sources relating to a given subject or person. It is usually arranged alphabetically by author or chronologically or topic wise. It may be comprehensive or selective. Sometimes it may be provided with annotations. It may be published as a part of a larger work or as a separate work. The basic aim of a bibliography is to assist the users in locating the existence of or identifying a book or any other material which may be interest to him. A well prepared bibliography provides a definite coverage of documents over a period of time within specified limits. Thus, it also serves the purpose of retrospective searching of literature, i.e. *Griffith, Dudley David (1955), Bibliography of Chaucer, 1908-53.* Seattle: University of Washington Press.

3. Tertiary Sources

This is the most problematic category of all. However, people rarely expected to differentiate between secondary and tertiary sources. Materials in which the information from secondary sources has been digested- reformatted and condensed, to put it into a convenient, easy to read form. Sources which are once removed in time from secondary sources and works which index, organize and compile citations to, and show you how to use, secondary sources.

Tertiary sources of information contain information distilled and collected from primary and secondary sources. The primary function of tertiary sources of information is to aid the searcher of information in the use of primary and secondary sources of information. Most of these sources do not contain subject knowledge. Due to increase in literature, tertiary sources are becoming increasingly important. Out of various kinds of sources, tertiary sources are the last to appear.

Type of Tertiary Sources

1. Bibliography of Bibliographies
2. Directories
3. Yearbooks
4. Guide to literature
5. List of research in progress
6. Guide to professional organizations
7. List of indexing and abstracting services
8. Almanacs
9. Union Catalogues

A. Bibliography of Bibliographies : Grant list when indexes secondary sources, then it comes in the form of tertiary source. This is called a list of bibliographies like World bibliography of Bibliographies by Besterman, T.

The lists of bibliographies direct readers to useful bibliographies through subject, individual, places, etc. The bibliographies referred to may be in the form of separately published book or part of the book or part of a periodical article or some other types of documents. Bibliography of bibliographies is highly selective in nature. These are of various types such as:

- Current bibliography of bibliographies
- Retrospective bibliography of bibliographies
- Guides to reference books
- Current bibliography of bibliographies

B. Directories : A directory lists names of persons, institutions or organizations of a particular area. A directory may include very brief information such as the name, address and the telephone number as we normally see in a telephone directory. At times, a directory contains lot more information. For example, Directory of Scientific Research Institutions in India. It provides among others the following information about an institution: name, name of the head, history, address, names of the divisions and divisional heads, field stations, objectives/functions, areas of research, achievements, special facilities, library and information services, other activities, and publications. Some directories are published annually, and others at regular or irregular intervals. Of course, there are directories that published only once.

C. Year book : A yearbook, as the name suggests appears annually, and updates information every year. Yearbooks are of various types and they can be categorized as; general and subject-oriented, national, regional and international. The Statesman's Yearbook, The Europa World Yearbook, Britannica Book of the Year, etc. fall under the category of general yearbooks. However, each one has its own distinctive characteristics. For example, Part I of The Statesman's Yearbook deals with international organizations, and Part II with the countries of the world in alphabetical order. Information given under each country comprises among others history, territory and population, social statistics, climate, constitution and government, administration, international relations, economy, energy and natural resources, industry, international trade, communications, social institutions, culture, and diplomatic representations. As we have general yearbooks, so also we have subject yearbooks. The yearbooks portray the development in the particular subject during the preceding year. Regional yearbooks usually cover a particular region.

According to ALA Glossary, "A yearbook is an annual volume of current information in descriptive and statistical form, sometimes limited to a special field".

D. Almanacs : By definition, an almanac is 'an annual calendar containing important dates and statistical information such as astronomical data'. The various almanacs published in our country provide data in chronological order of all the days of the year. Under each date the information given includes among others the date according to Indian calendars such as Sambat, Christian calendar, Muslim calendar, name of the day i.e. Sunday, time of sunrise, and sunset, day of the lunar fortnight i.e. ekadashi, purnima, zodiac sign, auspicious time, inauspicious time, specific time for various religious works like marriage, mundane, religious event of the day i.e. Good Friday, Lakshmi Puja, astronomical event i.e. lunar eclipse, solar eclipse if it falls on the day.

International almanacs like Whitaker's Almanac (1868) and Information Please Almanac (1947) are more like yearbooks than almanacs. For example Whitaker's Almanac 2002 provides up-to-date information about government and social structure of the United Kingdom and the rest of the world. In addition, it brings together a wide range of facts, figures and directory information. Only a small portion of the book is devoted to astronomical data like the time of sunrise, sunset, moonrise, moonset, lunar and solar eclipse, etc.

E. Union Catalogues : Union catalogue is a combined catalogue of holdings of books or periodicals or both mentioning location, edition, number of copies by accession numbers, volumes, etc. of a number of homogeneous or heterogeneous participating libraries covering library materials in all fields or limited by subject or form of material arranged by subject, or author or in chronological order maintained by a National Library, large reference library or a national bibliographical center.

4. Non-documentary sources

Non documentary sources of information form a substantial part of communication especially in science and technology. User's studies have underlined importance of such sources. These sources provide information which other sources do not.

There are two kinds of sources:

A. Formal Sources

- Research Organization
- Societies
- Industries
- Govt. department
- Universities
- Consultants

B. Informal Sources

- Conversation with colleges
- Visitors
- Attendance at Professional Meetings.

REFERENCES

1. Bonn, George S. (1971). Literature of Science and Technology. McGraw Hill Encyclopedia of Science and Technology 7, 614.
2. Dhiman, Anil K. & Yashoda Rani (2005). Learn Information and Reference Sources and Services. New Delhi: Ess Publication.
3. Hutchins, Margaret (1974). Introduction to reference work (p.10-15). Chicago: American Library Association.
4. Kragh, Helge (1989). An Introduction to the historiography of science. Cambridge University Press.
5. Krishan Kumar. Reference Services. 5th Ed. (P.115-127). New Delhi: Vikas Publishing
6. *Wong, CJ.* "LibGuides: Research Help: Types of Sources". *Libguides.merrimack.edu.* Retrieved 2017-04-25.

12
Popular And Scholarly Literature

INTRODUCTION

Popular literature includes those writings intended for the masses and those that find favour with large audiences. It can be distinguished from artistic literature in that it is designed primarily to entertain. Popular literature, unlike high literature, generally does not seek a high degree of formal beauty or subtlety and is not intended to endure. The growth of popular literature has paralleled the spread of literacy through education and has been facilitated by technological developments in printing. With the Industrial Revolution, works of literature, which were previously produced for consumption by small, well-educated elites, became accessible to large sections and even majorities of the members of a population.

Popular literature appears in magazines and newspapers. The covers are often glossy or eye-catching, and can be purchased at bookshops or newsstands. These sources are geared toward a broad, general audience, and the articles are reviewed by professional staff editors. Journalists cover news and current events in a field, write profiles of people, places, or events, and express political opinions.

SOME EXAMPLES OF POPULAR LITERATURE

- The New York Times
- Newsweek
- National Geographic
- Psychology Today
- Natural History
- The Nation
- New Republic
- Science News

SCHOLARLY LITERATURE

Scholarly literature is written by researchers who are experts in their field. People who write for academic journals are employed by colleges, universities, or other institutions of education or research. They submit articles to the editors of the journals, who decide whether or not to publish the article. The most prestigious academic journals subject articles to the peer-review process. This means that, before an article is accepted for publication, it is reviewed by several experts in the field, who suggest possible changes, and recommend to the editor of the journal whether or not to publish the article.

SOME EXAMPLES OF ACADEMIC JOURNALS

- Journal of American History
- Psychological Review
- Nature
- Annals of the National Academy of Science
- James Joyce Quarterly
- Journal of the American Musicological Society

Contents	*Popular*	*Scholarly Literature*
Purpose	To entertain the reader, to sell the products of their advertisers, and/or promote a viewpoint.	To report on original research or experimentation in order to make such information available to the rest of the scholarly community.
Language	Articles are usually very short, written in simple language and designed to meet a minimal education level. There is generally little depth to the articles' content.	The language of scholarly journals is that of the discipline covered. It assumes some scholarly background on the part of the reader.
Generally	Popular periodicals come in various formats, but they are usually glossy with colorful, flashy covers and photos intended to entice the readers and buyers at newsstand.	Scholarly journals generally have a sober, serious look. The articles contain mostly text, with many graphs and charts, but few photos.
Cite	Popular magazines rarely cite sources. The information is often second or third hand and the original source is sometimes obscure.	Scholarly journals always cite their sources in the form of footnotes or bibliographies.
Written	Articles are written by staff member or free lance writers.	Articles are written by a scholar in the field or by someone who has done research in the field.
Audience	General public, the interested non specialist.	Scholars, researchers and students.
Author	Author is frequently a journalist paid to write articles, may or may not have subject expertise.	Author's credentials are provided, usually a scholar or specialist with subject expertise.
Paging	Each issue begins with page 1.	Page numbers are generally consecutive throughout the volume.
Layout and Orga-	Informal, may include non-standard formatting.	Structured, includes the article abstract, goals and

nization	May not present supporting evidence or a conclusion.	objectives, methodology, results (evidence), discussion, conclusion, conclusion, and bibliography.

REFERENCES

1. https://www.libraries.rutgers.edu/scholarly_articles.

13

Web Based Information Sources

INTRODUCTION

Library collection management has changed dramatically in the past decade. The wide spread use of new technology in the publication of information through the Internet and WWW meant that libraries must begin to develop web based information collections. This created a massive shift in the generation of information, its publication and dissemination of electronic information.

Gradually the concept of library has changed very fast due to the impact of information communication technologies. Libraries not only possessed printed collection but also possessed digital collections. They have moved from print based environment to electronic environment. As the information environment changed rapidly there is wide spread availability of electronic resources in libraries. Dissemination of information at low cost and high speed that could not be obtained through paper has been achieved through electronic means. This resulted in the emergence of consortia that enabled libraries to have electronic access to professional literature included research journals, abstracts, review publications data bases in science and technology, social sciences and humanities. Online access to data bases enabled user to retrieve relevant and latest information with minimum time.

The different electronic formats that communicate information are OPAC'S online data bases, web databases, e-books, e-journals/ magazines, e-thesis and dissertations, e-reference sources, e-learning materials, e-research reports and e-newspapers. Thus electronic resources have become the vital part of university library collection in 21st century.

MEANING OF WEB BASED INFORMATION RESOURCES

Web based information resources is one of the emerging environments in libraries & Information communication in the competitive services. Web based information resources usually consist of e-books, e-Journals, articles, newspaper, thesis, dissertation, databases and CD-ROMs, which are likely to be the alternative to the print media. Familiarity with use of web based information resources in the libraries for rapid development is necessary and important.

DEFINITION

Web based information resources are those electronic formats that deliver a collection of data, be it a text referring to full text basis, e-journals, e-references, other multimedia products and numerical, graphical or time based, as commercially available that has been published.

SOME EXAMPLES OF WEB BASED INFORMATION RESOURCES

- E-Journals
- E-Reference Sources
- Subject Gateways
- Institutional Repositories
- Digital Libraries

1. E-JOURNALS

E-journals have become an important tool for scientists, research scholars and faculty members over the last few years. E-journals and journals article databases now form a large part of periodical collection of university libraries. E-journals are also available from other sources, including subject repositories, institutional repositories, author wed sited, and open access journals. Scholars, who are affiliated with universities that have substantial electronic collections and internet infrastructure, have the potential to access more journals and scholarly articles than ever before. This unprecedented access is true in many nations with developed infrastructure, but little is known about how reading patterns may differ among academics in different nations.

MEANING OF E-JOURNALS

E-Journals mean that they are originally published only in electronic format on the Internet.

DEFINITIONS

According to ALA Glossary of Library and Information Science journal is "A periodical specially one containing scholarly articles and/or disseminating current information on research and development in a particular subject field".

According to Webster's Third New International Dictionary of English Language, "Journal is a periodical publication, especially dealing with matters of current interest; often used of official or semi official publications of special groups.

Harrods's Glossary defines a journal as "A newspaper or periodical. Particularly a periodical issued by a society or institution and containing news, proceedings, transactions and report work carried out in a particular field".

Ashcroft and Langdon defines an electronic journal as "A journal, including indexing and abstracting services, provided by any electronic means, e.g. Internet, CD-ROM, although not necessarily exclusively by electronic means".

HISTORY AND GROWTH OF E-JOURNALS

The historical evolution of electronic journal has been traced to a 1960 UNESCO report that advocated use of computer technology to help the problems of traditional journal publishing.

Mental Workload, dealing with human-machine interactions in complex systems, has been identified as the first full-fledged electronic journal. It was issued in 1980 at the New Jersey Institute of Technology and funded by the National Science Foundation. Mental workload was referred, edited, and copyrighted the same as a print journal. In 1980s under the project, Birmingham Loughborough Electronic Network Development (BLEND) a journal entitled Computer Human Factors was produced, it was designed to accept, referee, edit, and archive articles electronically. The BLEND project resulted in two issues of Computer Human Factors, each containing two referred articles. However, both the mental workload and Computer Human Factors failed and their failure illustrated the importance of "human factors" (i.e., although the electronic medium allowed more rapid editing and refereeing, there were still "human delays in getting down to work"). In 1987, Syracuse University's e-journal New Horizons in Adult Education appeared inconspicuously. The BITNET (A U.S. University network founded in 1981) that started internet distribution of New Horizons in Adult Education and a handful of other e-journals produced at universities in the late 1980s and early 1990s attracted few students and scholars. Several electronic journals which began publication in 1990 included Public Access Computer Systems Review, Journal of the

International academy of Hospitality Research, Postmodern Culture, Current Cities etc.

Developments during the early 1990s testify to the burgeoning interest in electronic journals. The first meeting of the Association of Electronic Scholarly Journals took Place in October 1990 at North Carolina State University VPIEJ-L, an online discussion group devoted to electronic journals, was founded in the mid-1990s at the Virginia Polytechnic Institute and state University. Also during the early 1990s, some seminars or conferences devoted to electronic journals were organized. Typical examples include a seminar at Bond University in May 1992, sponsored by the Australian Serials Interest Group and the Australian Council of Libraries and Information Services, or the International Conference on Referred Electronic Journals, held at the University of Manitoba in Winnipeg, Manitoba, Canada, during October 1993. By the late 1990s, too many conferences to enumerate had been on the topic of electronic journals (Nisonger, 2004).

The mid-1990s witnessed the major trend in which the commercial and university presses offer simultaneously electronic versions of their established print journals. The commercial interest in e-journals started with the invention of World Wide Web and the release of Mosaic browser in 1993. However, by mid-I990s Elsevier, Wiley, and Springer started piloting e-journal systems. One of Springer's early tests, Red Sage was a partnership with university of California, San Francisco and Bell Laboratories. It featured an online alert system to send articles to users based on their profiled keywords, as a selective dissemination of information (SDI alert). The web was still in its infancy and accessible mostly through university networks. Every academic institution m was not wired and graphics could not be displayed with the sharpness comparable with the print publication. As a result of this uncertainty, many publishers provided free access to the online equivalent of journals held by libraries in print. University presses were interested in experimenting with the new medium. John Hopkins created project MUSE in 1995, seeing the promise off web even at that early stage. Users of project MUSE started to access files from their own work stations with multiple simultaneous accesses. The project MUSE innovators also recognized that the web would soon offer the ability to provide more content than the print medium- Moreover, full searching and enhanced graphics would make the e-versions more useful and popular. Not to be overlooked are the cataloguing advancement of this period. Despite a dramatic growth in e-journals both academic and commercial, without a gateway to them they would remain obscure. The first gateway built by libraries was Online Public Access Catalogue (OPAC). In 1995, the MARC 856 Electronic Location and Access field approved for use which resulted in rapid development of Web-based Catalogues. Thus in a short span of time, a deluge of e-journals was met by the tools to describe, organize and provide access to them in a traditional way. (Medeiros, 2009)

By 2000, e-journals became a normal part of the cataloguing workflow, yet new means of access were also being developed. Web developers were migrating manually coded web lists to databases that served alphabetical and subject arranged lists of e-journals to the web. Although web-based catalogues continued to evolve into more attractive system, their progress couldn't keep pace with the means available to web developers, which shifted preferred means of patron access to e-journals away from the catalogues. Database-driven website maintenance impacted the administration of e-journals that provided libraries a space to record internal notes about e-journal licensing terms. This effectively became the precursor to today's electronic resource management systems. Several publishers offered their journals through home-grown interfaces, and several others opted to outsource the hosting of their e-journals to interface platforms such as, High Wire Press, Meta Press and Ingenta Connect. More transient but nevertheless equally appealing access to e-journals for users came from aggregated collections such as EBSCO host, Gale Expanded Academic ASAP, and Pro Quest research Library. These entities provided the facility of federated searching across thousands of e-journals, yielding set of full text results. These services became common in late 1990's and currently are a staple of most academic library offerings.

CATEGORIES OF E-JOURNALS

Electronic journals can be grouped under the following broad three categories:

1. CD-ROM Journals : These are journals published on CD-ROM, may be bibliographical or full text. They vary in frequency and are distributed along with search software to access and print. Many publishers have started publishing some of their core journals on CDROMS. All journals and conference proceeding of IEEE and Elsevier's ADONIS, etc. are some of the best examples. CD-ROM journals are far more economical than online journals, because once they are acquired; the library can provide unlimited access to numerous users.

2. Networked E-Journals : These are electronic journals, available over networks, such as Internet, BITNET or any other commercial networks. Example of networked e-journals is e-newsletters, e-discussion lists, un-moderated bulletin boards, peer reviewed journals and popular magazines etc. Many of the networked e-journals are based on mailing list software, such as LISTSERV, List Proc etc.

3. Online Journals : These are paid journals that are available on "Cost-Per-Access" basis via online database such as Knight-Rider Information (ISI, Philadelphia), EBSCO Information services etc. Online databases provide access to a large number of bibliographic and full – text journals. Such databases have been found very useful for providing various types of library services. 'On-line' refers to the fact that searcher is in direct communication with the database. A search is conducted in a two way interaction between the searcher and with the computer. Online set up usually consists of a PC, modem, and STD line and subscribers password code (Thiruvarasu, 1998). Online services can be accessed locally from three major telecommunication carriers TYRNE, TELNET and UNINET. There are many other online services available apart from these three.

ADVANTAGES OF E-JOURNALS

- Speed of Production and Distribution
- Accessibility
- Subscription Costs
- Economical
- No Fear of Loss and Mutilation
- Multimedia Capabilities
- Internet and External links
- Seamless Access

LIMITATIONS OF E-JOURNALS

The following limitations are associated with the services of electronic journals, if subscribed in a library (Khan, 2012).

- Even though it is becoming cost effective, but initial investment is high. Special equipment (computer or printer) are required.
- Potential authors are reluctant to submit their papers in e-journals as scientist's main consideration in choosing a journal is its standard and reputation which is many times doubtful.

- Unless the system is not easy to use, contributors have no increase to change their normal pattern of publication.
- Uncomfortable for sustained reading on computer screen.
- Required technological support and compatibility of hardware may vary from one publication to another.
- Different formats have different pricing schemes, making their selection, use and organization increasingly difficult.
- They may take some time to display page images conveniently on computer screen.
- Involve legal copyright issues.
- The pricing scheme of some suppliers is very complicated and limiting and this might hinder libraries from utilizing e-journals.
- E-journals and articles are not physically present in the library.
- Often not included in indexing & abstracting services.
- Publishers change their day to day terms & conditions.
- Possibility of data manipulation by unauthorized persons.
- Lack of archiving and back files availability.
- Perishable citation: once printed, the details of paper journal remain constant. Thus, finding them again is easy. However websites change their URLs or frequently disappear altogether.

PROMINENT ONLINE DATABASES IN SCIENCE AND TECHNOLOGY

- Science Direct
- Springer Link
- Wiley-Blackwell

- Nature Publishing Group
- American Institute of Physics (AIP) Publishing
- American Chemical Society (ACS) Publications
- World Scientific Community
- Cambridge Journals Online
- Royal Society of Chemistry (RSC) Publishing
- MIT Press
- Scopus
- Web of Science

1. Science Direct : It is a leading full-text scientific database offering journal articles and book chapters from more than 2,500 peer-reviewed journals and more than 11,000 books. There are currently more than 11 million articles/chapters, a content base that is growing at a rate of almost 0.5 million additions per year. Science Direct is a part of Elsevier, which is the world's largest scientific, technical and medical information provider. Science Direct covers authoritative titles from the core scientific literature, including high-impact factor titles such as THE LANCET, Cell and Tetrahedron. The articles in Science Direct are broadly grouped in four main sections: Physical Sciences and Engineering, Life Sciences, Health Sciences, and Social Sciences and Humanities.

2. Springer Link : Springer Link is a leading global scientific, technical and medical publisher, providing researchers in academia, scientific institutions and corporate R & D departments with quality content via innovative information products and services. It is providing researchers with access to millions of scientific documents from journals, books, series, protocols and reference works. A total of around 7.5 million content items can be accessed from Springer Link. Springer believes it has the largest open access portfolio worldwide, with over 350 open access journals.

3. Wiley-Blackwell : Wiley's Scientific, Technical, Medical, and Scholarly (STMS) business, also known as Wiley-Blackwell, serves the world's research and scholarly communities, and is the largest publisher for professional and scholarly societies. Wiley-Blackwell's programs encompass journals, books, major reference works, databases, and laboratory manuals, offered in print and electronically. Wiley Online Library provide online access to a broad range of STMS content: over 4 million articles from 1,500 journals, 9,000+ books, and many reference works and databases.

4. Nature Publishing Group : Nature Publishing Group (NPG) is a publisher of high impact scientific and medical information in print and online. NPG publishes journals, online databases, and services across the life, physical, chemical and applied sciences and clinical medicine.

5. American Institute of Physics (AIP) Publishing : The American Institute of Physics (AIP) is a not-for-profit membership corporation created for the purpose of promoting the advancement and diffusion of the knowledge of physics and its application to human welfare. AIP Publishing LLC provides the global physical science community with a comprehensive collection of highly cited peer reviewed scientific information. Accessed by researchers at nearly 4,000 institutions worldwide, AIP Publishing's portfolio of 17 journals includes prestigious titles such as Applied Physics Letters, Journal of Applied Physics and The Journal of Chemical Physics, and the AIP Conference Proceedings series.

6. American Chemical Society (ACS) Publications : ACS is a congressionally chartered independent membership organization which represents professionals at all degree levels and in all fields of chemistry and sciences that involve chemistry. ACS Publications is the division of ACS provides the worldwide scientific community with a comprehensive collection of the most-cited, peer-reviewed journals in the chemical and related sciences. ACS Publications publishes more than 40 journals, Chemical & Engineering News, C& EN Archives, ACS Legacy Archives, and the ACS Symposium Series via its award-winning web-based platform. ACS journals are citations or Impact Factor in the seven chemistry categories as well as nine additional categories.

7. World Scientific Community : World Scientific Publishing Company was established in 1981, it is one of the leading scientific publishers in the world, and the largest international scientific publisher in the Asia-Pacific region. World Scientific publishes about 500 new titles a year and 120 journals in various fields. Many of its books are recommended texts adopted by renowned institutions such as Harvard University, California Institute of Technology, Stanford University and Princeton University.

8. Cambridge Journals Online : Cambridge Journals Online (CJO) is the online journals publishing service of Cambridge University Press. CJO hosts leading journals across multiple disciplinary collections of over 320 leading journals covering subjects including science and technology, medicine, and the humanities and social sciences.

9. Royal Society of Chemistry (RSC) Publishing : The RSC is the largest organization in Europe for advancing the chemical sciences. Supported by a worldwide network of members and an international publishing business, its' activities span education, conferences, science policy and the promotion of chemistry to the public. RSC publishing provides access to journals, books and databases linking over 1,121,413 chemical science articles and chapters. One can access the latest research of interest using the custom e-Alerts, RSS feeds and blogs or one can explore content using the quick and advanced searches. RSC provide access to the highest quality of integrated scientific research.

10. MIT Press : The MIT Press is the only university press in the United States whose list is based in science and technology. It publishes about 200 new books a year and over 30 journals.

11. Scopus : Scopus is the largest abstract and citation database of peer-reviewed research literature with more than 20,500 titles from more than 5,000 international publishers. It includes 49 million records, 78% with abstracts and over 5.3 million conference papers. It offers researchers a quick, easy and comprehensive resource to support their research needs in the scientific, technical, and medical and social sciences fields and arts and humanities.

12. Web of Science : It is the world's most trusted citation index covering the leading scholarly literature. It covers over 12,000 of the highest impact journals worldwide, including Open Access journals and over 150,000 conference proceedings. One can find current and retrospective coverage in the field of sciences, social sciences, arts, and humanities, with coverage to 1900.

Conclusion

Electronic journal open up many exciting opportunities and potentials for science and technological libraries in research and development institutions. This new service has a vast potential of providing a quality service. They possess many advantages and disadvantages. Librarians need to be able to identify and balance the factors that would make electronic journals a success or failure in their libraries. However in the context of shrinking budgets it is very essential to evaluate each e-journal so that the expenditure is justified economic prosperity has direct linkage with the growth of facilities for access to information. More and more libraries are redirecting their funds to offer free, direct on demand articles services to patrons. The technology has led to inevitable change in day-to-day working of libraries. To promote the use of e-journals in research and development in science and technological institutions, it is pertinent that libraries should improve their ICT infrastructure.

References

- Khan, Shajarul Islam. "Use of E-Journals by Students and Research Scholars in the Department of Botany of Aligarh Muslim University." Library Philosophy and Practice (2012). Web.
- Mederios, Norm. "Access Revolution: The Birth, Growth, and Supremacy of Electronic Journals as an Information Medium." E-Journals Access and Management. Ed Wayne Jones. New York: Routledge, 2009. 187-199. Print
- Nisonger, Thomas E. Management of Serial in Libraries. Colorado: Libraries Unlimited, 2004.Print.
- Thiruvarasu, S. "On-Line Database." Information Technology: Issues and Trends. Ed. B.Satyanarayana and V. Pulla Reddy. Cosmos: New Delhi: 1998. 55-78. Print.

2. E-REFERENCE SOURCES

Most of the reference sources are now available in electronic form. Some of the sources which were available in print form earlier are now available in electronic form only. Most of the material published today exists in computer readable form at some stage of its production process and making it in electronic form is easy.

Presently, most of the library users prefer to use electronic reference sources, because of the speed of searching, remote access and availability of these resources on the internet on 24/7 basis. Many libraries have a web page showing frequently used online reference works. It is observed that online sources most frequently used by the users are dictionaries (50%), followed by online periodicals, telephone directories and encyclopedias.

ADVANTAGES OF E-REFERENCE SOURCES

There are many advantages of E-Reference sources than their print counterparts:

- Electronic reference sources are more frequently updated than their print counterparts.
- They provide more search options.
- Provide access to wider range of information.
- Provide faster and easy access to information. This is particularly so in the case of indexing and abstracting periodicals, where back volumes are consolidated into single searchable database, search is easy and extremely fast.
- Online bibliographic databases provide linkages from citations to full text e-journals.
- Full-text data can be delivered instantly on the remote computer.
- Content can be delivered in multimedia format where text, video, and sound can be added.
- A print source can be used by one user at a time, whereas an online source can be accessed simultaneously by many users.
- An online electronic source can be accessed at any time and from any place where network exists.

EFFECTS OF E-REFERENCE SOURCES

It has been experienced that the reference sources and services are basically needed by the faculty and research scholars in university environment including colleges system in our country. Realizing, the importance of reference service, academic and research libraries globally create separate Reference Section duly supported with dedicated staff and collections based on the existence of financial resources. Similarly, currently under digital environment, libraries create separate web page in the main page under various heads like Virtual Reference Desk, FAQs, Ask the Librarian, Virtual Help Desk, Bulletin Board Service, E-Reference resources etc. Realizing this, the university library has created various, major links of e-reference sources for the benefit of the faculty and the students with the objective to provide access to various e-reference sources. Based on these reference sources, we are providing virtual reference services under Intranet and Internet environment.

INITIATIVES OF E-REFERENCE SOURCES

It is very much true that e-resources with specific reference to e-reference sources are fundamentally essential under digital are. There is strong need on the part of librarians and the top management of all institutions irrespective of their size and resources to build e-reference sources and also provide various e-reference services. The following major initiatives are required. These can be implemented in phased manner:

1. Web site of the Library

It is absolutely necessary for the librarians to make necessary arrangements for a comprehensive and interactive website exclusively for the library, integrating with the main website of an organization. The resources including e-reference sources need to be projected under Intranet and Internet environment depending upon the e-policy of respective institution. The domains of the website need to have recall value and professional web pages for each activity. It is also suggested that the websites for major libraries of the world need to be studied and reviewed first so that a good website is designed and developed for the users.

2. Identification of Related E-Reference Sources

It is necessary to identify e-reference sources useful to a specific organization. There is need to have a separate staff for digital library activities in the libraries. The staff can be assigned special task to prepare the list of e-reference sources both fee based as well as freely available e-reference sources which can be grouped and further sub grouped keeping in view of users and organizational interests.

3. Providing Related Hyperlinks

Currently, it is very easy to provide access to e-reference sources to users through simply providing hyper links in the website of a library. This can be done for both free and fee based e-reference sources. The university library of K.U.K has provided various hyper links to various important and useful e-reference sources in the website which are extensively used.

4. Periodic Presentation

There is great need to organize periodic presentations by the library staff at the doorsteps of users. This will help the users to know the existence of e-reference sources for their better and effective utilization. In this direction, the university library of K.U.K has taken various initiatives. Some of them are listed below:

- Organization of staff-users meets.
- Specialized presentations by e-resources vendors.
- Presentation by experts.
- Presentation by the librarian.
- E-announcements.

5. Developing Collaborations

There is an urgent need to develop constructive cooperation and collaborations among libraries at local, regional, national and international level to have more and more e-reference sources for the user's community for assisting them to achieve excellence in research, development and academic activities. It is nice to quote that Indian library especially colleges are actively participating to provide comprehensive and cost effective access solutions to e-sources.

FACTORS OF E-REFERENCE SOURCES

There is needed to keep the following factors in view while deciding to have e-reference sources for an institution:

- Continuous up-datation of hyperlinks.
- Continuous subscription to e-reference sources.
- Careful study of digital licensing provisions.
- To make provision for exchange of e-reprints for academic use.
- To ensure adequate on-line help and instructions.
- To provide adequate and frequent training to users and staff.
- To conduct periodic information literacy program.
- To provide training hand-outs to end users.
- To avoid duplication in the coverage of e-reference sources.
- To arrange trial for limited period.
- Loading of the software.
- Multiple authentications.

LIMITATIONS OF E-REFERENCE SOURCES

- Use of electronic reference sources requires expensive infrastructure, which must be acquired, maintained and upgraded. This covers computer hardware and software, Internet connection and subscription to databases.
- Electronic reference sources, despite being user friendly, require certain degree of computer literacy to get maximum benefit from them. This means libraries have to incur expenses to train their staff as well as their users to use these resources.
- Most of the publishers of e-reference books sell their products through license agreement, which imposes

certain restrictions on their usage.

- Reading from computer screen is strenuous. Most of the users prefer to take print out for reading.

EXAMPLES OF E-REFERENCE SOURCES

Now a good number of E-Reference sources are available on internet and CD-ROMs, some important reference sources are given below:

1. On Internet

Encyclopaedia Britannica Online : Encyclopaedia Britannica Online is the website of Encyclopaedia Britannica, Inc. and its Encyclopaedia Britannica, with more than 120,000 articles that are updated regularly. It has daily features, updates and links to news reports from The New York Times and the BBC. The 2010 edition of the Britannica was the last printed version and was sold until stock ran out in 2012. Roughly 60% of Encyclopaedia Britannica's revenue comes from online operations, of which around 15% comes from subscriptions to the consumer version of the website. Subscriptions are available on a yearly, monthly or weekly basis. Special subscription plans are offered to schools, colleges and libraries; such institutional subscribers constitute an important part of Britannica's business. Encyclopedia Britannica Online available by different Categories:

- Animals
- Art and Music
- Astronomy
- Biological Sciences
- Chemistry
- Countries of the World
- Earth and Geography
- Government, Law, and Politics

- Health and Medicine
- History
- Life and the Biosphere
- Literature
- Mathematics
- Philosophy
- Physics
- Plants
- Religion
- Society
- Sports and Recreation
- Technology

Roget's International Thesaurus Online : Roget's Thesaurus is a widely used English-language thesaurus, created in 1805 by Peter Mark Roget (1779-1869), British physician, natural theologian and lexicographer. It was released to the public on 29 April 1852. The original edition had 15,000 words, and each new edition has been larger. The Karpeles Manuscript Library Museum houses the original manuscript in its collection. Roget's Thesaurus is composed of six primary classes. Each class is composed of multiple divisions and then sections. This may be conceptualized as a tree containing over a thousand branches for individual "meaning clusters" or semantically linked words. Although these words are not strictly synonyms, they can be viewed as colors or connotations of a meaning or as a spectrum of a concept. One of the most general words is chosen to typify the spectrum as its headword, which labels the whole group. Roget's schema of classes and their subdivisions is based on the philosophical work of Leibniz (see Leibniz-Symbolic thought), itself following a long tradition of epistemological work starting with Aristotle.

Encyclopaedia Online : Encyclopaedia is a book or set of books giving information on all the fields of knowledge or on particular subject field with articles arranged alphabetically. A general Encylopaedia covers information on topics from every field of knowledge. Specialized or subject Encyclopaedia provides more detailed or technical information on specific area of knowledge such as science and technology, social sciences, humanities, or arts. Articles in an Encyclopaedia vary in length ranging from a paragraph to over hundred pages depending upon the topic covered, target audience and type of Encyclopaedia i.e., single volume or multivolume Encylopaedia.

Webster's Dictionary Online : Webster's Dictionary is any of the dictionaries edited by Noah Webster in the early nineteenth century, and numerous unrelated dictionaries that have adopted the Webster's name. "Webster's" has become a generalized trademark in the U.S. for dictionaries of the English language, and is widely used in English dictionary titles or even to dictionaries in general. The only modern dictionaries that trace their lineage to Noah Webster's are published by Merriam-Webster.

Almanacs Online : Almanacs online contain statistics and facts about countries, events, personalities, or subjects. Almanac resources have call numbers that begin with AY.

Newspapers Online : An online newspaper is the online version of a newspaper, either as a stand-alone publication or as the online version of a printed periodical. Going online created more opportunities for newspapers, such as competing with broadcast journalism in presenting breaking news in a timelier manner. The credibility and strong brand recognition of well established newspapers, and the close relationships they have with advertisers, are also seen by many in the newspaper industry as strengthening their chances of survival. The movement away from the printing process can also help decrease costs. Online newspapers, like printed newspapers, have legal restrictions regarding libel, privacy and copyright; also apply to online publications in most countries as in the UK. Also, the UK Data Protection Act applies to online newspapers and news pages. Up to 2014, the PCC ruled in the UK, but there was no clear distinction between authentic online newspapers and forums or blogs. In 2007, a ruling was passed to formally regulate UK-based online newspapers, news audio, and news video websites covering the responsibilities expected of them and to clear up what is, and what isn't, an online news publication. News reporters are being taught to shoot video and to write in the succinct manner necessary for internet news pages. Some newspapers have attempted to integrate the internet into every aspect of their operations, e.g., the writing of stories for both print and online, and classified advertisements appearing in both media, while other newspaper websites may be quite different from the corresponding printed newspaper.

2. CD-ROM Format

CD-ROM is another publishing medium falling under the economic category of electronic sources available in most of the Indian libraries. It is capable of containing enormous quantity of information. Most of the Indian libraries are using this medium these days to fulfill their users' requirements in an economic way. This form has been found to be economic, particularly when one and the same source is to be used by many users again and again. There is a long list of reference sources available on CD-ROMs, some of the important examples are given below:

1. Encyclopaedias
   - Academic American Encyclopedia
   - McGraw-Hill Encyclopedia of Science & Technology
   - New Encyclopaedia Britannica

2. Bibliographies:
   - BIP Plus
   - Books Out of Print Plus
   - Ulrich's International Periodicals Directory
3. Indexing/Abstracting Sources:
   - Cumulative Book Index
   - Library Literature
   - Library & Information Science Abstracts
4. Dictionaries:
   - McGraw-Hill Dictionary of Scientific & Technical Terms

References

- http://www.eb.com
- http://www.thesaurus.com
- http://www.encyclopaedia.com
- http://www.dictionary.com
- http://www.virtualref.com/libdocs
- http://www.newsrack.com
- http://www.samachar.com

3. SUBJECT GATEWAYS

The Internet became a major medium in the information world. It offers access to massive amount of information resources but the fact remains that it is still very hard for people to locate high quality information among the general chaos. In the past few years the issue of resource discovery on the Internet has been the focus of much work by many different communities. Subject gateways provide access to reliable and up-to-date web resources for all subjects, which have carefully chosen and quality checked by experts in their field.

HISTORY AND CURRENT STATUS

In the UK, the Joint Information Systems Committee (JISC) of the UK Higher Education Funding Councils funded the establishment of a series of subject gateways, the Access to Network Resources (ANR) projects, as part of the e-Lib (electronic libraries) programme. These gateways were:

- ADAM art and design
- CAIN conflict studies
- BIZ/ED business and economics
- EEVL engineering
- IHR-Info history
- OMNI biomedicine
- RUDI urban design
- SOSIG social sciences

Because of the nature of the funding authorities, these gateways were to concentrate on sites of relevance to users in UK higher education, and to favour, though by no means to restrict themselves to, UK sites. However, their significance extends beyond the UK context, because of the innovative nature of these gateways, with procedures for ensuring quality and consistency in the choice of resources for inclusion, and in organization and maintenance of the gateways themselves. These gateways are discussed generally by Kerrimiur, 1999, while Macleod, Kerr and Guyon, 1998, and discuss in detail the development of the EEVL engineering gateway.

Some, though not all, of these gateways use the ROADS software, the product of another ANR project, for creation and maintenance of a database of resource descriptions, and hence for creating selective subject gateways, and allowing cataloguing, searching and browsing of resources. Thus, although other subject gateways were set up in the UK and elsewhere, the e-Lib gateways very much set the standard for this kind of search aid. It was announced during early 1999 that, after the cessation of funding of the e-Lib gateway programme, that JISC would fund a new Resource Discovery Network in place of the existing e-Lib subject gateways, with an expanded remit, to provide services to users outside the academic community. This is discussed later.

MEANING OF SUBJECT GATEWAYS

A web based mechanism for accessing a collection of high quality, evaluated resources identified to support research in a particular subject discipline.

DEFINITIONS OF SUBJECT GATEWAYS

According to Koch, "Subject gateways are Internet services which support systematic resource discovery. They provide links to resources (documents, objects, sites or services), predominantly accessible via the Internet. The service is based on resource description."

"A subject gateway is a web site that provides searchable and browsable access to online resources focused around a specific subject. Subject gateways resource descriptions are usually created manually rather than being generated via an automated process. Because the resource entries are generated by hand they are usually superior to those available from a conventional web search engine."

"Subject gateways are online services and sites that provide search and browse catalogues of internet based resources. Subject gateways will typically focus on a related set of academic subject areas."

FEATURES OF GATEWAY

1. The host institutions of each gateway have a mandate to be information providers, but they are not required to be information creators.

2. Each gateway has a distinctive logo and a reflective name, thereby positioning them for a significant Web presence. Distinctive branding also bears fruit as a common recognition technique.
3. Each gateway has selected and utilized a standard metadata schema for describing the resources incorporated into the gateways. The metadata is applied by librarians or educators with experienced knowledge of the disciplines.
4. The resources in each gateway have all been selected according to predetermined criteria, published at each gateway site as part of a content coverage policy. A gatekeeper function, often a mix of computer and human intervention, ensures adherence to the selection criteria.
5. The coverage policies have made electronic resources, both 'born digital' and digitized, the highest priority for inclusion in the gateways; The resources are supported by similar architectures, based on distributed creation and maintenance of their metadata, with a centralized facility for access

WHY GATEWAY

Library web sites are becoming increasingly complex. Complexities in the form of links and services are profusion of print and electronic formats, duplication and the general web resources. When the content becomes massive the functions of the library web sites needs more restructuring. This complex environment has arisen from various factors including:

1. Innovative ways of providing information and services such as electronic resources, course specific, and library help pages and document delivery.
2. Complex library searches due to the cross functions

and links between the online catalog, journal aggregator databases, electronic resources etc.

3. The need to identify and present high quality free information resources on the web and distinguish those from library licensed material.
4. The increasing expectations of users for interfaces to lead directly, without undue hunting, to the information or service they need.

HOW TO USE SUBJECT GATEWAYS

Information is retrieved from subject gateway by browsing or searching by keyword - in exactly the same way you would in a classified directory. Again, it's important to remember that when you search a subject gateway you are not searching the resources themselves, but only the records created for that resource.

WHEN TO USE SUBJECT GATEWAYS

If you want general information in a specific subject area : A subject gateway performs best for general queries for the same reason a classified directory does - a very specific term is less likely to be included in a catalogue record.

If you want access to structured, high quality information : Classified directories, the resources subject gateways have been organized to enable structured browsing through subject hierarchies.

CHARCTERISTICS OF SUBJECT GATEWAY

Resources Selection : A human intermediary adds value by selecting appropriate internet resources, usually according to rigid selection criteria. Resources are usually selected for their quality, authority, accessibility, currency and subject relevance. Other selection criteria may also apply such as language or geographic coverage.

Resource Description : Selected resources are annotated by a human intermediary with a full description of the resource. The descriptions will be entered according to a predefined, structured metadata schema. The metadata is structured into separate field. This enables the resource to be easily identified and located. It also facilitates structured searching. The descriptions may contain information about the content, author, publisher or publication date of the resource.

Collection Maintenance : Regular maintenance of the collection occurs, including the removal of resources that are no longer appropriate, are superseded or contain data entry errors. Regular link checks may also be carried out. These procedures may be automated or carried out manually through human intervention. A policy will exist that details these procedures.

Subject Classification : A human intermediary uses a subject classification schema to index all resources. This facilitate subject browsing.

LIBRARY RELATED SUBJECT GATEWAYS

These library related gateways are:

BUBL Information Service : Subject coverage: General, including, arts, humanities, media & social sciences: A national information service for the higher education community. Includes an A-Z list of subject resources as well as links to e-journals and mailing lists. BUBL is a UK-based interactive information service which provides links to over 12,000 internet resources in a wide range of subject areas.

Design Library : Subject coverage: Design Links to industrial design, interaction design, graphic design, environmental design & design schools.

Digital Librarian : Subject coverage: General Annotated index of Internet resources.

EDWEB : Subject coverage: Education**:** The purpose of this hyper book is to explore the worlds of educational reform and information technology.

EELS : Engineering Electronic Library: subject coverage: Engineering, Physics, Mathematics, Energy Technology, Nuclear Technology, Light and Optical Technology, Computer Science, Polar Research, Cold Region Technology.

EEVL : Subject coverage: Engineering Edinburgh Engineering Virtual Library. Provides access to quality resources for engineering on the Internet.

PICK : Subject coverage: Librarianship and Information Science: A gateway to quality Librarianship and Information Science resources on the Internet.

References

- http://bubl.ac.uk/
- http://www.dh.umu.se/design_lib/design_library.html
- http://www.digital-librarian.com/
- http://eels.lub.lu.se/%20
- http://www.eevl.ac.uk/

4. INSTITUTIONAL REPOSITORIES

Institutional repository is a database with a set of services to capture, store, index, preserve and re-distributes a university's scholarly research in digital formats. Institutional repositories consist of formally organized and managed collections of digital contents generated by faculty, staff & students at an institution. The contents of these repositories can be available for integration with in campus library & course management systems, & can also be made available to colleagues and students at other institutions, as well as to the general public. When we use the term repositories today, we can be speaking about one of many different technologies that support the storage & distribution of digital contents, including:

- Collection based digital repositories managed by library professionals, either stand alone or aggregated.
- Course management systems and associated file stores.
- Collections of research data and report managed by academic departments.
- Student's academic portfolio systems.
- Institutional files storage systems.
- Digital asset management workflow systems.
- Web content management systems used by institutions or departments to store and stage web contents.

MEANING

An institutional repository is an archive for collecting, preserving, and disseminating digital copies of the intellectual output of an institution, particularly a research institution.

Institutionally Meaning : it means that an IR is the natural extension of history, research, prestige and impact of an institution or a group of institutions, as consortia.

A digital institutional repository could be any collection of digital material hosted, owned or controlled, or disseminated by a college or university, irrespective of purpose.

DEFINITIONS

According to Crow, "Digital collections capturing and preserving the intellectual output of a single or multi-university community."

According to Lynch, "Defines IRs in the following way: A university-based institutional repository is a set of services that a university offers to the members of its community for the management and dissemination of digital materials created by the institution and its community members. It is most essentially an organizational commitment to the stewardship of these digital materials, including long-term preservation where appropriate, as well as organization and access or distribution".

OBJECTIVES

The four main objectives for having an institutional repository are:

- To create global visibility for an institution's scholarly research.
- To collect content in a single location.
- To provide open access to institutional research output by self-archiving it.
- To store and preserve other institutional digital assets, including unpublished or otherwise easily lost ("grey") literature (for example, theses or technical reports).

INSTITUTIONAL REPOSITORY POLICY

Repositories now represent potentially rich sources of information, data, images, and valuable research results. The movement is new and the time it takes to plan, formulate policies, and bring Institutional communities to consensus can make it a slow process. Each institution defines its own policies dealing with access to and use of materials in Repositories. Not all materials can be made available freely. Copyrighted materials may carry a variety of restrictions. Nonexclusive publisher licenses would increase availability to these materials and place the publishers in the Open access arena. Some publishers permit authors to self-archive. Other publishers opt for exclusive licenses for a limited time, while still others will not allow any deviation from exclusive copyright. Some materials may be restricted to a small group of researchers or to people associated with the institution because they represent work in progress deemed proprietary or that may entail sponsor restrictions.

The key issues to be considered while developing Institutional Repositories are Institutional culture and consensus has to be discussed:

- The scope of the Repository as to type of publications to be part of Institutional Repository.
- The information content of the Repository.
- Access levels as to full text or abstract level/ access to type of users or privileges.
- Legal aspects i.e. copyright acts.
- Standards
- Sustainability and maintenance

The appropriate software and funding has to be taken into account before going for Institutional Repository projects at institution level. Institutional culture depends on how the organization is structured as well as how much collaboration and trust exists within an institution. In academic organizations, faculty belongs to departments, disciplines, and research groups. Academic competition may be fiercer in some universities than in corporations. In an internally competitive environment where cooperation and trust are not nurtured, building a Repository will become more difficult. Faculty will not contribute willingly to a central Repository unless they have been consulted and trust the process. Faculty need to be convinced that contributing to a Repository will enhance their reputations in their disciplines and result in wider dissemination of their work.

SOFTWARE FOR INSTITUTIONAL REPOSITORIES

1. ARNO : The ARNO project (Academic Research in the Netherlands Online) has developed software to support the implementation of Institutional Repositories and link them to distributed Repositories. The project is funded by IWI (Dutch acronym for: Innovation in Scientific Information Supply). Project participants are the University of

Amsterdam, Tilburg University and the University of Twente. The ARNO system was released for public use in December 2003. It has been in use at the universities of Tilburg, Amsterdam, Rotterdam, Twente and Maastricht.

2. CERN Document Server Software (CDSware) : The CERN Document Server Software (CDSware) was developed to support the CERN Document Server. The software is maintained and made publicly available by CERN and supports electronic preprint servers, online library catalogs, and other web-based document depository systems. CERN uses CDSware to manage over 450 collections of data, comprising over 620,000 bibliographic records and 250,000 full-text documents, including preprints, journal articles, books, and photographs. CDSware was built to handle very large Repositories holding disparate types of materials, including multimedia content catalogs, museum object descriptions, confidential and public sets of documents, etc.

3. DSpace : The DSpace software has been purpose built in collaboration between Hewlett Packard and MIT to offer IR services. It is specifically designed to manage diverse heterogeneous types of digital content. It offers interoperability via OAI-MHP (Open Archive Initiative – Metadata Harvesting Protocol – a software standard that allows specialized search engines to gather article metadata from compliant websites) and built-in support for Dublin Core metadata (Dublin Core is an agreed metadata standard used in library cataloguing and elsewhere, though other metadata schemes are possible). It uses persistent identifiers via the CNRI Handle system.

4. Eprints : The Eprints software has the largest and most broadly distributed installed base of any of the Repository software systems described here. Developed at the University of Southampton, the first version of the system was publicly released in late 2000. The project was originally sponsored by CogPrints, but is now supported by JISC as part of the Open Citation Project and by NSF. Eprints worldwide installed base affords an extensive support network for new implementations. The size of the installed base for Eprints suggests that an institution can get it up and running relatively quickly and with a minimum of technical expertise. The number of Eprints installations that have augmented the system's baseline capabilities for example, by integrating advanced search, extended metadata and other feature indicates that the system can be readily modified to meet local requirements.

5. Fedora : The Fedora digital object Repository management system is based on the Flexible Extensible Digital Object and Repository Architecture (Fedora). Fedora is one of a number of repository architectures that have been proposed over recent years for use in digital libraries. The Digital Library Research and Development Department at the University of Virginia Library interpreted the architecture and built a prototype that demonstrated the feasibility of the architecture with their large and diverse digital collections. In September 2001 the University of Virginia received a grant of US$ 1,000,000 from the Andrew W Mellon Foundation to enable the library, in collaboration with Cornell University, to build a sophisticated digital object repository system based on the Flexible Extensible Digital Object and Repository Architecture (FEDORA).

6. I-TOR : i-Tor (Tools and technologies for Open Repositories) was developed by the Innovative Technology-Applied (IT-A) section of Netherlands Institute for Scientific Information Services (Dutch acronym: NIWI). NIWI calls i-TOR "a web technology by which various types of information can be presented through a web interface," irrespective of where the data is stored or the format in which it is stored. It aims to implement a "data independent" Repository, where the content and the user interface function as two independent parts of the system. In essence, i-Tor acts as both an OAI service provider, able to harvest OAI compatible Repositories and other databases, and an OAI data provider. Because i-Tor is able to publish data from a variety of relational databases, file systems, and websites, the system allows institution considerable latitude in the way it organizes its Repository.

7. MyCoRe : MyCoRe grew out of the MILESS Project of the University of Essen. The MyCoRe system is now being developed by a consortium of universities to provide a core bundle of software tools to support digital libraries and archiving solutions. The bundle is designed to be configurable and adaptable to local requirements without the need for local programming efforts. In contrast to MILESS, which provides a hard-coded Qualified Dublin Core data model, the MyCoRe data model is completely configurable. Further, MyCoRe provides a sample application, based upon a "core" of functionality, which shows users how to build their own applications using metadata configuration files.

8. DARE : Digital Academic Repositories (DARE) is a collective initiative by the Dutch universities to make all their research results digitally accessible. It can be seen as a national level, albeit federally structured, Repository. Its programme of research projects is broadly similar to the JISC FAIR programme. The project was awarded 2 million Euros for the period 2003-2006 by the Dutch government. All participating institutions will adopt the same standards, while retaining their own responsibility in setting up and maintaining their own Repositories.

9. Greenstone Digital Library Software (GSDL) : The Greenstone Digital Library Software is internationally renowned Open source software for developing Institutional Repositories. It is promoted by the New Zealand Digital Library project research group at the University of Waikato, headed by Dr. I. H. Witten. The software is issued under the terms of GNU General Public License. Greenstone is supported by the UNESCO and Human Info NGO Belgium for spreading the benefits of this software to developing countries. It provides a way of building, maintaining and disseminating digital library collections, Opening up new possibilities for organizing information. Greenstone builds collections using popular and standard digital formats such as HTML, XML, PDF and other formats which include multimedia files. It is provided with effective full text searching and metadata based browsing facilities that are attractive and easy to use. It runs on a wide variety of platforms such as Windows, Linux and provides indexing, searching, browsing, metadata extraction and is OAI compliant.

INSTITUTIONAL REPOSITOTY PROJECTS

DSpace Project : The DSpace project at MIT was funded by Hewlett Packard to the tune to $1.8m, plus 3 FTE HP staff and $400k in systems equipment. The DSpace Federation is a group of institutions that are using DSpace software to build their own Repositories. The DSpace Federation Project is a one-year study which will begin the process of building a collaborative federation of institutions running DSpace. This group will test the adaptability of the system to a targeted group of institutions with varied needs. Federation Project members include Cambridge, Columbia, Cornell, Massachusetts Institute of Technology, Ohio State, Rochester, Toronto, and Washington (Smith, 2003).

RoMEO Project : The RoMEO Project (Rights Metadata for open archiving) was a JISC funded project at the University of Loughborough to investigate the rights issues surrounding the self-archiving of research in the UK community under the Open Archive Initiative Protocol for Metadata Harvesting (OAI-PMH). Through surveying the academic community it ascertained how give-away research literature and metadata was used and how it should be protected. From this work, the RoMEO project created a list of publishers' conditions for self-archiving. After negotiation with the RoMEO Project team and JISC, SHERPA developed the outcomes of this project into a database-driven searchable service and knowledge bank of information. SHERPA maintains the SHERPA/RoMEO listing, which details the rights given to authors by the major publishers of peer-reviewed academic journals. It is now possible to search for many publishers and find out what permissions are normally given as part of each copyright transfer agreement.

SHERPA Project : The SHERPA project (Securing a Hybrid Environment for Research Preservation and access) has been set up to encourage change in the scholarly communication process by creating Open-access Institutional e-print Repositories for the dissemination of research findings. The outcomes of the project will be advice on the building and maintenance of IRs, guidelines on IPR and copyright issues, and advocacy material to publicize an institution's Repository (Hubbard & Pinfield, 2003).

TARDis Project : The TARDis project (Targeting Academic Research for Dissemination and Disclosure), run by Southampton University and is planning to develop a multidisciplinary Institutional e-print archive and assess and evaluate the activity within a library-led infrastructure. It is designed to tackle head-on the major problem faced by IRs, namely the lack of participation by faculty: "TARDIS will investigate and report on strategies to overcome the technical, cultural and academic barriers, which currently restrict the development and particularly the acquisition of content of Institutional e-Print archives. It will develop a working model of a multidisciplinary Institutional archive." The project runs from August 2002 until July 2004. The TARDis Project has now come to an end. There will be no further major updates to this site but it will be maintained until at least 2008. All project materials will be deposited into the University of Southampton Research Repository. The TARDis Project has now evolved into a University funded service, maintained by the Southampton University Library in partnership with the Information Systems Service and the School of Electronic and Computer Science.

DAEDALUS : DAEDALUS is a project concerned with the establishment of a range of OAI-PMH-compliant digital collections at the University of Glasgow. These will include e-prints (both published and peer reviewed academic papers, and pre-prints and grey literature), theses, resource-finding aids and Institutional documents. It runs until July 2005.

Caltech : Caltech's CODA (Collection of Open Digital Archives) Repository was established in 2001. It currently consists of some 11 archives with a further six listed as in development. The system allows document counts and a wide range of access statistics to be viewed by any user. The following table lists the active archives, their numbers of records and the total number of document accesses since launch. The vast majority of the content appears to be grey literature: theses & dissertations, technical reports and conference presentations.

E-Scholarship : The California Digital Library (CDL) eScholarship Repository, announced in April 2002, illustrates the continuum between digital libraries broadly conceived and Institutional Repositories. The CDL launched the eScholarship Repository, a web site and a suite of digital support services, to distribute academic research and working papers of University of California faculty. E-Scholarship uses the OAI metadata harvesting protocol to provide interoperability. The CDL initiative includes a suite of digital services to store and disseminate faculty research in digital formats. The CDL system uses the web-based are press (vendor) system to manage paper submission, processing, and dissemination. Additionally, the system also supports a topical alerting service that alerts users to new content in their specified areas of interest. There are about 2450 e-prints (both pre-prints and post-prints), mostly in the social sciences, mainly economics and related areas (e.g. transportation). The stated policy is to accept "journals, peer-reviewed series, working papers, discussion papers series, and other electronic forms of scholarship". Most of the documents we viewed were working papers. Content is stored as PDF only (but the system will accept and convert Word, RTF etc. into PDF).

CARL : The CARL Institutional Repositories Pilot Project is an initiative to implement Institutional Repositories at several Canadian research libraries. The project, which is spearheaded by the Canadian Association of Research Libraries, was launched in September 2002 and has 12 libraries participating. The Repositories will be searchable using one interface and freely accessible to anyone with an Internet connection. The ultimate vision is to have a number of robust and interoperable archives containing Canadian scholarly output that will form a part of a larger global system of Repositories.

Utrecht : DISPUTE, the Institutional Repository of the University of Utrecht was originally scheduled for release at the end of 2002. The site is currently (in early 2004) in a preliminary state and states variously that the final site will be available in October 2003 (sic) or by the end of 2003 (sic). All this suggests the going has not been as easy as was originally envisaged. At present there appears to be about 400-500 math and 40-50 physics e-prints, plus some other documents and theses. Several of the e-prints we viewed were scanned from published literature (e.g. Physical Review). The site also appears more a portal to a disaggregated collection of resources than a single IR.

ARNO : The Academic Research in the Netherlands Online (ARNO) project, run from September 2000 until

September 2002, sought to design and implement university digital archive servers to preserve the academic output (including research reports, pre-prints, theses and dissertations, and articles published in regular scholarly journals) of member institutions. The project's goal was to make the Repository freely accessible via OAI interoperability standards. The project was being implemented by the library staffs of the University of Twente, the University of Amsterdam, and Tilburg University.

References

- *Crow, R. (2002). Case for institutional repositories: a SPARC position paper.* Association of Research Libraries. Retrieved April, 2017 from http://www.arl.org/sparc/ir/ir.html
- *Lynch, Clifford. (2003). Institutional Repositories: Essential Infrastructure for Scholarship in the Digital Age ARL; 226; 2003; pp. 1-7.* Retrieved May 21, 2017, from www.arl.org/newsltr/

5. DIGITAL LIBRARIES

A digital library is a collection of documents in organized electronic form, available on the Internet or on CD-ROM (compact-disk read-only memory) disks. Digital libraries can vary immensely in size and scope, and can be maintained by individuals or organizations . The digital content may be stored locally, or accessed remotely via computer networks. These information retrieval systems are able to exchange information with each other through interoperability and sustainability (Lanagan, 2012).

MEANING OF DIGITAL LIBRARY

A digital library, or digital collection, is an online database of digital objects that can include text, still images, audio, video, or other digital media formats. Depending on the library, a user may be able to access magazine articles, books, papers, images, sound files, and videos.

USE OF TERM

The first published use of the term may have been in a 1988 report to the Corporation for National Research Initiatives. The term was first popularized by the NSF/DARPA/NASA Digital Libraries Initiative in 1994. Bush, 1945 created a vision based on experience "Digital library".

DEFINITIONS

According to Shiri (2003), "Organizations that provide the resources, including the specialized staff, to select, structure, offer intellectual access to, interpret, distribute, preserve the integrity of, and ensure the persistence over time of collections of digital works so that they are readily available for use by a defined community or set of communities.

DELOS Digital Library Reference Model defines a digital library as, "An organization, which might be virtual, that comprehensively collects, manages and preserves for the long term rich digital content, and offers to its user communities specialized functionality on that content, of measurable quality and according to codified policies.

According to Lynch (1994), "digital Libraries provide users with coherent success to a very large, organized repository of information and knowledge.

On the basis of the above definitions, I come to the conclusion that digital library is a library in which collections are stored in digital formats and accessible by computers. The content may be stored locally, or accessed remotely.

FUNCTION OF DIGITAL LIBRARY

- Access to large amounts of information to users wherever they are and whenever they need it.
- Access to primary information sources.
- Support multimedia content along with text

- Network accessibility on Intranet and Internet
- User-friendly interface
- Hypertext links for navigation
- Client-server architecture
- Advanced search and retrieval.
- Integration with other digital libraries.

PURPOSE OF DIGITAL LIBRARY

- Expedite the systematic development of procedures to collect, store, and organize, information in digital form.
- Promote efficient delivery of information economically to all users.
- Encourage co-operative efforts in research resource, computing, and communication networks.
- Strengthen communication and collaboration between and among educational institutions.
- Take leadership role in the generation and dissemination of knowledge

ADVANTAGES OF DIGITAL LIBRARY

No physical boundary : The user of a digital library need not to go to the library physically; people from all over the world can gain access to the same information, as long as an Internet connection is available.

Round the clock availability : A major advantage of digital libraries is that people can gain access 24/7 to the information.

Multiple accesses : The same resources can be used simultaneously by a number of institutions and patrons. This may not be the case for copyrighted material: a library may have a license for "lending out" only one copy at a time; this is achieved with a system of digital rights management where a resource can become inaccessible after expiration of the lending period or after the lender chooses to make it inaccessible (equivalent to returning the resource).

Information retrieval : The user is able to use any search term (word, phrase, title, name and subject) to search the entire collection. Digital libraries can provide very user-friendly interfaces, giving click able access to its resources.

Preservation and conservation : Digitization is not a long-term preservation solution for physical collections, but does succeed in providing access copies for materials that would otherwise fall to degradation from repeated use. Digitized collections and born-digital objects pose many preservation and conservation concerns that analog materials do not. Please see the following "Problems" section of this page for examples.

Space : Whereas traditional libraries are limited by storage space, digital libraries have the potential to store much more information; simply because digital information requires very little physical space to contain them and media storage technologies are more affordable than ever before.

Added value : Certain characteristics of objects, primarily the quality of images, may be improved. Digitization can enhance legibility and remove visible flaws such as stains and discoloration (Gert, 2012).

LIMITATION OF DIGITAL LIBRARY

Cost Limitation : To establish a digital system in the traditional Library system is costlier in initial stage.

Skill person : If we want to work in digital system we need skill person in respect of working and maintaining

Law effect : In today some people wants to secure their publications, matters etc. that why they copyright their publications. Whenever a user will try to copy some matters, he will suffer from copyright law. There are some other laws like cyber law, which affect the digital library system.

Effect of Technology : In today advancement becomes in the both area like soft ware and hardware. The digital library wholly dependent on telecommunication and computer. As new technology comes in the market the digital system should change or adopt that technology.

Security problem : When our digital system is connected to Internet the major problem is the security to prevent the unauthorized access and to prevent the information from virus is the major task in digital system.

DEFERENCE OF TRADITIONAL & DIGITAL LIBRARY

Traditional Libraries	*Digital Library*
Print collection	All resources in digital form.
Stable, with slow evolution	Dynamic and ephemeral
Individual objects not directly linked with each other.	Multi-media and fractal objects
Flat structure with minimal contextual metadata	Scaffolding of data structures and richer contextual metadata.
Scholarly content with validation process	More than scholarly content with various validation processes
Limited access points and centralized management	Unlimited access points, distributed collections and access control
The physical and logical organization correlated.	The physical and logical organization may be virtually
One way interactions	Dynamic real-time dialogue
Free and universal access.	Free as well as fee based.

ARCHITECTURE OF DIGITAL LIBRARY SYSTEM

Digital library system represents the richness and wealth of information which provides the unsophisticated users with flexible access to rich and complicated information. The key components of digital library system are represented in the following chart.

User interfaces : Both the pilot and the prototype have two user interfaces: one for the users of the library, the other for the librarians and system administrators who manage the collections. Each user interface is in two parts. A standard Internet browser is used for the actual interactions with the user. This can be Netscape Navigator, Microsoft's Internet Explorer. The browser connects to client services, which provide intermediary functions between the browser and the other parts of the system. The client services allow the user to decide where to search and what to retrieve; they interpret information structured as digital objects; they negotiate terms and conditions, manage relationships between digital objects, remember the state of the interaction, and convert among the protocols used by the various parts of the system.

Repository : Repositories store and manage digital objects and other information. A large digital library may have many repositories of various types, including modern repositories, legacy databases, and Web servers. The interface to this repository is called the repository access protocol (RAP). Features of RAP are explicit recognition of rights and permissions that need to be satisfied before a client can access a digital object, support for a very general range of dissemination's of digital objects, and an open architecture with well defined interfaces.

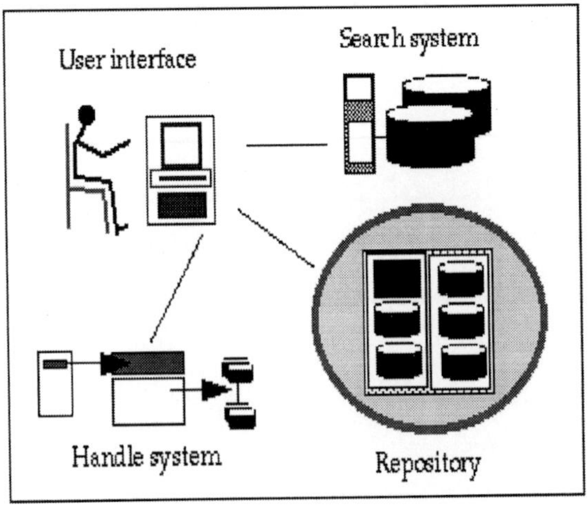

Handle system : Handles are general purpose identifiers that can be used to identify Internet resources, such as digital objects, over long periods of time and to manage materials stored in any repository or database. When used with the repository, the handle system receives as input a handle for a digital object and returns the identifier of the repository where the object is stored.

Search system : The design of the digital library system assumes that there will be many indexes and catalogues that can be searched to discover information before retrieving it from a repository. These indexes may be independently managed and support a wide range of protocols (Jange, 2001).

REFERENCES

- Gert, J. (2000). Selection for Preservation in the Digital Age. *Library Resources & Technical Services* 44(2): 97-104.
- Jange, Suresh. (2001). Digital libraries: An overview.1-3. Retrieved June, 2017 from *http://www.eprints.rclis.org/4975/1/Digital-Library-overview.pdf*
- Lanagan, J. & Smeaton, A. F., (2012). Video digital libraries: contributive and decentralized. International Journal on Digital Libraries 12 (4): 159–178.
- *Witten, I. H. & Bainbridge, D. N. (2009). How to Build a Digital Library. Morgan Kaufman.*

14

Study of International Encyclopedia of Social Sciences

INTRODUCTION

The International Encyclopedia of the Social Sciences was first published in 1968 and was edited by David L. Sills and Robert K. Merton. It contains seventeen volumes and thousands of entries written by scholars around the world. The 2nd edition is composed entirely of new articles. It was published in 2008 and edited by William A. Darity, Jr., an American economist. Though the 1968 Encyclopedia was initially intended to "complement, not supplant" MacMillan's earlier, fifteen-volume Encyclopaedia of the Social Sciences, which had been published from 1930 to 1967 and was edited by American economists Edwin Robert Anderson Seligman and Alvin Saunders Johnson, it effectively replaced the earlier Encyclopaedia, in practice (Cavin, 1969).

The entirely new International Encyclopedia of the Social Sciences covers scholarship and fields that have emerged and matured since the publication of the original international edition. Like its predecessors, the set meets the needs of high school and college students, researchers inside and outside academia, and lay readers in public libraries. The new set highlights the expanding influence of economics in social science research and features nearly 3,000 entirely new articles and important biographies contributed by thousands of scholars (including several Nobel prize winners) from around the world on a wide array of global topics, including: achievement testing, censorship, personality measurement, aging, income distribution, foreign aid (political and economic aspects), food (world problems, consumption patterns), cultural adaptation, comparative health-care systems, terrorism, political correctness, agricultural innovation, legislation of morality, sexual violence and exploitation, white collar crime.

FEATURES

- 2,990 articles contributed by a team of international scholars, including hundreds of entries covering the increasingly influential fields of economics and statistics.
- Written for researchers inside and outside academia; perfect for advanced high school and college students as well as teachers, lay readers and professionals
- Also available in eBook format, providing full search capabilities 24/7 access; no special readers of hardware required

REFERENCE

- Cavin, James P. (1969). The International Encyclopedia of the Social Sciences: A Review Article. American Journal of Agricultural Economics 51(2): 268–278.

15

International Encyclopedia of Social and Behavioural Sciences

INTRODUCTION

The International Encyclopedia of the Social & Behavioral Sciences, originally edited by Neil J. Smelser and Paul B. Baltes, is a 26-volume work published by Elsevier. It has some 4,000 signed articles (commissioned by around 50 subject editors), and includes 150 biographical entries, 122,400 entries, and an extensive hierarchical subject index. It is also available in online editions. Contemporary Psychology described the work as "the largest corpus of knowledge about the social and behavioral sciences in existence. It was first published in 2001, with a 2nd edition published in 2015. The second edition is edited by James D. Wright.

FEATURES

- Provides authoritative, foundational, interdisciplinary knowledge across the wide range of behavioral and social sciences fields
- Discusses history, current trends and future directions
- Topics are cross-referenced with related topics and each article highlights further reading

SUBJECT CLASSIFICATION

Contents include the following broad Subject Classification:

1. Overarching Topics : Institutions and infrastructure, History of the social sciences and the behavioral sciences, Ethics of research and applications, Biographies, Integrative concepts and issues.

2. Methodology : Statistics, Mathematics and computer sciences, Logic of inquiry and research design.

3. Disciplines : Anthropology, Demography, Economics, Education, History, Linguistics. Philosophy, Political science, Clinical psychology and applied psychology, Cognitive psychology and cognitive science, Developmental psychology, social psychology, personality psychology and motivational psychology, Sociology.

4. Intersecting Fields : Evolutionary sciences, Genetics, behavior and society, Behavioral neuroscience and cognitive neuroscience, Psychiatry, Health, Gender studies, Religious studies, Expressive forms, Environmental sciences/ ecological sciences, Science and technology studies, Area studies and international studies.

5. Applications : Organizational studies and management studies, Media studies and commercial applications, Urban studies and Urban planning, Public policy, Modern cultural concerns.

REFERENCE

- International Encyclopedia of the Social & Behavioral Sciences. Ed. 2

16

International Bibliography of the Social Sciences

INTRODUCTION

The International Bibliography of the Social Sciences (IBSS) is a bibliography for social science and interdisciplinary research. The database focuses on the social science disciplines of anthropology, economics, politics and sociology, and related interdisciplinary subjects, such as development studies, human geography and environment and gender studies. It was established in 1951 and prepared by the Fondation Nationale des Sciences Politiques in Paris. Production was transferred to the London School of Economics in 1989, and then to ProQuest in 2010.

HISTORY

IBSS was established in 1951 by the International Committee for Social Science Information and Documentation, a non-governmental organization recognized by UNESCO. From 1951 to 1989 it was prepared at the

Fondation Nationale des Sciences Politiques in Paris and produced in four printed volumes: Economics, Political Science, Anthropology and Sociology. From 1989 to 2010 it was produced at the British Library of Political and Economic Science of the London School of Economics, with the help of funds from the Economic and Social Research Council (ESRC) from 1995 to 2009. It was purchased by ProQuest in January 2010, and production moved to Pro-Quest's UK headquarters in July that year. In 2016, production was transferred yet again, this time to Louisville, Kentucky.

It was made available in electronic format via CD-ROM in 1993; it became available online in 1995.

COVERAGE

IBSS includes approximately 2.7 million references to journal articles, books, reviews and selected chapters and is growing at the rate of about 100,000 items per year. Over 2800 current journals are regularly indexed, as well as 1415 ceased titles. Coverage extends from the present back to 1951. It also includes records for about 400,000 books, including 60,000 individual book chapters -7,000 books are added each year. There is considerable international coverage; about 50% of the titles included are published outside the US or the UK, with about half of those in English and half in other languages. About three-quarters of the current journal articles have abstracts.

AVAILABILITY

The online database is available to institutional subscribers through the Pro-Quest database. It is not available to individual subscribers. Print volumes are published annually by Routledge. In the UK, the Economic and Social Research Council has paid for access by members of UK higher and further education institutions, ESRC-recognized research institutes and central government departments since 1955.

ONLINE FORMAT

Searches can be carried out by keyword, author or journal; results can be printed, emailed, saved or downloaded into a bibliographic management software package. The database is updated weekly, and users can set up email alerts or RSS feeds of the new records added. A range of user guides and tutorials are available via the IBSS website. There are links to the full text of articles for those in individual institutions that subscribe to them.

REFERENCES

1. The International Committee for Social Science Information and Documentation, ICSSD; partner in the MOST Programmes.
2. ProQuest acquires IBSS". *Pro-Quest. 14 January 2010.* Retrieved 13 January 2017.

17
Social Sciences Citation Index

INTRODUCTION

The Social Sciences Citation Index in Web of Science Core Collection is a carefully selected and evaluated collection delivers to users the most influential scientific research information from the 20th century. With the addition of Century of Social Sciences, SSCI delivers comprehensive back file and cited reference data from 1900 to 2009.The world itself changed dramatically during the first half of the 20th century, and the published research during this period of time is reflective of these great changes. The ability to search an entire century of information in one place, across 55 disciplines of the social sciences, is simply invaluable resource for academic study at all levels.

DATABASE COVERS

The SSCI citation database covers some 3,000 of the world's leading academic journals in the social sciences across more than 55 disciplines. It is made available online through the Web of Science service for a fee. The database records which articles are cited by other articles.

COMPREHENSIVE COVERAGE

- 6.4 Million Records in the social sciences.
- Only Web of Science Core Collection has social sciences coverage, 1900 to 1955, Century of Social Sciences.
- A collection of some of the oldest, and most prestigious journals in their respective fields
- Full bibliographic and cited reference data for journals in disciplines such as: communication, education, geography, history & philosophy of the social sciences, law, political science, public health, social issues & sociology.
- Various national perspectives in the fields of anthropology and geography.
- The economics collection includes the Journal of Political Economy, one of the oldest and most prestigious journals in its field.
- Full integration with Web of Science.

CENTURY OF SOCIAL SCIENCE

1900 to 1955 : Century of Social Sciences delivers comprehensive back file and cited reference data from 1900 to 1955. Combined with existing Web of Science Core Collection back-files, this carefully selected and evaluated collection delivers to users the most influential scientific research information from the 20th century.

The world itself changed dramatically during the first half of the 20th century, and the published research during this period of time is reflective of these great changes.

- Coverage of over 300 journals in the social sciences back to 1900
- A collection of some of the oldest, and most prestigious journals in their respective fields
- Extensive coverage of the high impact psychology

journals, including 5 titles associated with Sigmund Freud

- Full bibliographic and cited reference data for journals in disciplines such as: communication, education, geography, history & philosophy of the social sciences, law, political science, public health, social issues & sociology
- Various national perspectives in the fields of anthropology and geography
- The economics collection includes the Journal of Political Economy, one of the oldest and most prestigious journals in its field
- Full integration with Web of Science

CRITICISM

Philip Altbach has criticized the Social Sciences Citation Index of favoring English language journals generally and American journals specifically, while greatly under representing journals in non-English languages. In 2004, economists Daniel B. Klein and Eric Chiang conducted a survey of the Social Sciences Citation Index and identified a bias against free market oriented research. In addition to an ideological bias, Klein and Chiang also identified several methodological deficiencies that encouraged the over-counting of citations, and they argue that the Social Sciences Citation Index does a poor job reflecting the relevance and accuracy of articles.

REFERENCES

- Altbach, Philip *(2005). Academic Challenges: The American Professoriate in Comparative Perspective, Dortrecht; Springer. 147–165.*
- Daniel, Klein & Eric, Chiang (2004). The Social Science Citation Index: A Black Box with an ideological bias, *ECON Journal Watch* 1(1), 134-165.

18
International Political Science Abstracts

INTRODUCTION

International Political Science Abstracts/ Documentation Politique Internationale (IPSA) is a bimonthly peer-reviewed academic journal that covers political science. The editors-in-chief are Paul J. Godt (American University of Paris) and Serge Hutig (Fondation Nationale des Sciences Politiques). The journal was established in 1951 and is published by Sage Publications on behalf of the International Political Science Association (IPSA).

International Political Science Abstracts (IPSA), produced since 1951 by the International Political Science Association, is the authoritative global standard in support of scholarly research in political science and proximate disciplines. This resource tool provides abstracts of virtually all the relevant articles published in journals (and yearbooks) around the world, helping researchers and students efficiently locate and exploit the latest in the professional literature.

INDEXING AND ABSTRACTING

The journal is abstracted and indexed in:

- Academic Search
- International Bibliography of Periodical Literature in the Humanities and Social Sciences
- International Bibliography of the Social Sciences
- Scopus
- Sociological Abstracts
- Worldwide Political Science Abstracts

TOPICS INCLUDE

- Method & Theory
- Political thinkers and ideas
- Political & Administrative Institutions
- Political processes (Public opinion, attitudes, parties, forces, groups, and elections)
- International Relations
- National & Area Studies

SELECTION GUIDELINES

- Scholarly studies are chosen preferably to informative articles; only exceptionally are unsigned contributions, official texts and popular articles indicated.
- The major journals in the field are covered in full (for articles and substantial research notes); less important journals, journals in related disciplines and general interest periodicals are covered selectively.
- Translations and re-publications of articles already abstracted are mentioned only exceptionally.
- The editors seek to avoid abstracting redundant articles.
- Studies produced in countries where political science

is not well developed, or about countries on which information is scarce, are treated less selectively.

Each issue contains a Subject Index (in English), cumulative for all previous issues of the same annual volume. The final issue of each annual volume contains also an Author index.

STRUCTURE

- Political Science: Method & Theory
- Political thinkers and ideas
- Governmental & Administrative Institutions
- Political Process: Public opinion, attitudes, parties, forces, groups et elections
- International Relations
- National & Area Studies
- Book Reviews
- Edited Volumes

ANNUAL SUBSCRIPTION

Non-Members of IPSA : Please visit the SAGE Publications Website

Members of IPSA : Associate members (institutions) pay a substantially lower rate: US$ 556 only (instead of US$ 1112). Individual members: US$ 102 only (instead of US$ 204).

ELECTRONIC DATABASE

The International Political Science Abstracts Database contains nearly 400,000 abstracts at the end of 2017 and adds some 8,000 each year. It is published online by EBSCO with data since inception (1951), by Ovid Technologies with data since 1989. Both publishers grant a 50 percent discount to subscribers in developing countries and Eastern Europe.

REFERENCES

- http://www.bl.uk/eresources/images/ipsa.pdf
- https://www.ipsa.org/publications/abstracts

19

Psychological Abstracts

INTRODUCTION

A brief history of Psychological Abstracts is presented, and the development of this index over its nearly one-hundred year history is described. The various concerns and problems of both the publisher and users of the psychological literature are reported, and present and future solutions are discussed.

HISTORY OF PSYCHOLOGICAL ABSTRACTS

Founded in 1927, Psychological Abstracts contains non-evaluative summary abstracts of literature in the field of psychology and related disciplines, which are grouped into 22 major classification categories. It includes summaries of technical reports as well as journal articles and books. Each edition is collected into a cumulative volume every six months, with an index listing both the volume's contents and the national and international journals in which the abstracted literature appear. These journals are cited within the volume by codes listed in each monthly issue. A table of contents near the beginning of each issue guides readers to broad general areas that they may wish to investigate, while the subject indexes in the cumulative volumes refers them to articles on a particular topic.

In addition to research articles, Psychological Abstracts features theoretical discussions and reviews of other investigations, and also contains an author index for readers who would like to follow up their research by studying additional articles or books by a given author.

PUBLICITY

Monthly journal published by the American Psychological Association (United States).

CD-ROM Database

- PsycLIT®, the CD-ROM version of Psychological Abstracts, became available in 1993, and is used by many academic and large public libraries.
- PsycLIT®, a two-CD set which is updated quarterly, includes over 670,000 records.
- PsycLIT® indexes and abstracts articles dating from 1973 from 1,300 professional journals. The database also indexes and abstracts books and book chapters dating from 1987.

REFERENCES

- http://psychology.jrank.org/pages/511/Psychological-Abstracts.html

20
Bibliography of Doctoral Dissertations

INTRODUCTION

Presents trend of doctoral research activities undertaken in social sciences and humanities across the institutes of higher education in India. The research is based on the secondary data compiled from the bibliography of doctoral dissertations, published on an annual basis by the Association of Indian Universities in India, in the field of social sciences and humanities.

A bibliography of doctoral dissertations in social science and humanities is a list of all of the sources you have used (whether referenced or not) in the process of researching your work. In general, a bibliography should include:

- The authors' names.
- The titles of the works.
- The Guide of the works.

- The names and locations of the university that published your copies of the sources.
- The dates your copies were published.
- The page numbers of your sources (if they are part of multi-source volumes).

21

Statistical Abstracts India

INTRODUCTION

The present Statistical Abstract is the fourth in a series brought out by this Directorate on the basis of secondary data sources. The Uniqueness of Statistical Abstract is that it contains time series data on various socio-economic parameters and serves as an effective quantitative tool for reaching to logical conclusions in the context of planning and public policy making.

HISTORY

The foundation of the statistical system in India was laid down by the British administration. The Provincial Governments were required to publish the relevant statistics in their annual administration reports. They, in turn, depended upon the district offices. These statistics covered a wide range of subjects. The forms for this information were later made uniform, and the first Statistical Abstract of British India (1840-1865) was based on such information provided by the Provinces. One of the notable contributions was the publication, in the first half of the nineteenth century, of District Gazetteers. Several Commissions and Committees appointed by the Government of India for studies of specific fields also recommended that the Provinces should create institutions to collect statistics in the relevant fields. Thus, the Indian Industrial Commission (1916-1918) recommended that a Department of Industries should be created in the Provinces, with representatives throughout the Province to collect information on industries. Later the Royal Commission on Agriculture in India (1924-1925) pointed out that not only should the Provinces be self-sufficient in the field of statistics, but also that there should be a large Central Organization. Later, the Famine Enquiry Commission (1945) suggested the appointment of qualified Statistical Officers at Provincial Headquarters to assist the Director of Agriculture.

AREA

The Statistical Abstract India has included broad subjects:

- Population,
- Data on different sectors of the economy,
- Namely,
- Agriculture,
- Industry and Infrastructure sector,
- Economic indicators like Gross state domestic product & per capita income,
- Level & pattern of household consumer expenditure,
- Poverty,
- Prices etc.

REFERENCES

- http://mospi.nic.in/141-historical-perspective

Unit-III

INSTITUTIONAL SOURCES

22

Information Generation & Dissemination Institutional Resources

INTRODUCTION

Recognizing the need of research in social sciences, Government of India has initiated various programmes which include the setting up of ICSSR, ICWA, Indian Institute of management-Ahmedabad, Indian Institute of Public Administration, National Council for Applied Economic Research, TISS, UNESCO, ICHR, London School of Economics and Political Science, Social Science Research Council as the major institution. The target users for the Government are all institutions engaged in the generation and dissemination of knowledge in various areas, such as research laboratories, universities and other institutions of higher learning, including professional institutions. Government of India has already connected over 1669 institutions under various categories throughout the country. There are several other institutions both governmental and nongovernmental and other professional organizations that are involved in the promotion of various social science disciplines. These institutions are either mission-oriented or discipline oriented.

The Indian Council of Social Science Research are recognized major subjects i.e. Economics including Commerce; Education; Management & Business administration; Political science including International relations; Psychology; Public Administration and Sociology including Social work and Criminology.

The Social Science has information generation & dissemination resources are given below:

- ICSSR
- ICWA
- Indian Institute of management, Ahmedabad
- Indian Institute of Public Administration
- National Council for Applied Economic Research
- TISS
- UNESCO
- ICHR
- London School of Economics and Political Science
- Social Science Research Council

1. ICSSR (INDIAN COUNCIL OF SOCIAL SCIENCE RESEARCH)

HISTORY

The Indian Council of Social Science Research (ICSSR)

is the national body overseeing research in the social sciences in India. It was established in New Delhi in 1969 by the Government of India to promote research in social sciences in the country. ICSSR has developed ICSSR Data Service to serve as a national data service for promoting powerful research environment through sharing and reuse of data among social science community in India.

OBJECTIVES

The first and foremost objective of this portal is to provide seamless and integrated access to a wide range of datasets generated by the Ministry of Statistics and Programme Implementation (MOSPI), New Delhi, social science institutions under direct purview of ICSSR and other Government organization, to researchers who are looking for high quality social and economic research datasets with following aims and objectives.

- To serve as a national data service for promoting powerful research environment through sharing and reuse of data among social science community in India.
- To acquire, process, organize, preserve and host research data and its metadata along with ETL (Extract, Transform and Load) facilities of raw data in social sciences and related domains collected from diverse sources for easy sharing and access.
- To facilitate online submission, access, search, browse, discovery, conversion, analysis and visualization of data through intuitive interfaces.
- To impart training and spread awareness about benefits of data sharing and reuse amongst social science research community in India.
- Interact, cooperate and collaborate with other national and international data services and repositories for data and resource sharing and improved management of data services.

- Review the progress of social science research and give advice to its users.
- Sponsor social science research programmes and projects and administer grants to institutions and individuals for research in social sciences.
- Institute and administer scholarships and fellowships for research in social sciences.
- Indicate areas in which social science research is to be promoted and adopt special measures for development of research in neglected or new areas.
- Give financial support to institutions, associations, and journals engaged in social science research.
- Arrange for technical training in research methodology and to provide guidance for research.
- Co-ordinate research activities and encourage progrmmes for interdisciplinary research.
- Develop and support centers for documentation services and supply of data.
- Organize, sponsor, and finance seminars, workshops and study groups.
- Undertake publication and assist publication of journals and books in social sciences.

PROGRAMME AND SERVICES

1. Fellowships

Four categories of fellowships are offered / awarded to scholars who are at various levels in their profession:

National Fellowships are offered to eminent retired socials scientists, who have made outstanding contribution to research in their respective fields, to enable them to continue their academic work and research.

Senior Fellowships are awarded to social scientists between the age group of 45-70 years, who have done Ph D and have quality research work, publications and papers in professional journals to their credit. Besides, civil servants, journalists and social workers for their academic interests are also considered.

Post-Doctoral Fellowships are awarded to scholars, below the age of 45 years, who have shown significant competence in research work, have completed their Ph.D. at the time of their application and desire to work on approved research themes at institutions of excellence under the guidance of senior social scientists.

Doctoral Fellowships are open to doctoral students, preferably below the age of 40 years, who have a Master's degree from a recognized university with a first or second class and are registered for a doctoral degree in social sciences.

2. Research Projects

Promotion of Research in Social Sciences is one of the major activities of ICSSR. Research grants is direct financial support to research projects taken up by social scientists in addition to their normal duties in an honorary capacity. ICSSR provides grants to scholars to conduct research in various fields of social sciences which have a theoretical, conceptual, and methodological or policy orientation on the subject of their choice. The research projects may belong to any of the prescribed social science disciplines or may be interdisciplinary in nature. The specific objectives of the programme are: a) to support high quality independent programme of research; b) to provide opportunities for training of future researchers; c) to contribute to the development of elaboration of new theoretical or methodological approaches to research; d) to maintain and sustain varies disciplinary research activities; e) to foster and promote collaborative, multidisciplinary research activities among researchers in the social sciences; and f) to facilitate communication of research outputs both within and beyond the academic community as well as to provide inputs to administrators and policy makers.

Two categories of Research projects: First, Major and Minor Research Projects and secondly Research Programmes, formerly known as Research Projects Responsive and Research Projects Sponsored respectively. As per the guidelines proposals are invited, scrutinized, processed and awarded every year.

3. International Collaboration

The International Collaboration Programme of the ICSSR provides an opportunity to both Indian and foreign scholars in the field of social sciences to interact and research. It has been envisaged to promote academic links among the social scientists in India and abroad. The Council is one of the implementing agencies of the social science component of the Cultural Exchange Agreements (CEPs) and Educational Exchange Programmes (EEPs) signed between the Government of India and the governments of other countries.

4. Training and Capacity Building

A basic requirement for high quality research in Social Sciences is the training in the science and art of doing research. While the philosophical basis of Social Science research is common to social sciences generally, different subjects have evolved their own theoretical frameworks and procedures/techniques of research. However, scholars engaging themselves in interdisciplinary or multi-disciplinary research need to familiarize themselves with the research strategies of disciplines other than in which they are trained. Moreover, from the stage of research problem to the ultimate reporting and publication of the findings, there are several aspects in which a good researcher has to refine his skills.

Therefore, the ICSSR funds and sponsors Research Methodology and Capacity Building Programmes in Universities and Research Institutes:

The ICSSR Training and Capacity Programme (TCB) provides grants to the social science faculties for organizing research methodology and capacity building programme for young researchers and junior faculties in various social science disciplines as under:

- Sociology and Social Anthropology
- Political Science / Public Administration
- Economics
- International Studies
- Social Geography and Population Studies
- Commerce and Management
- Social Psychology
- Education
- Social Linguistics / Socio-Cultural Studies
- Law / International Law
- National Security & Strategic Studies
- Other allied Social Science disciplines (Library Science, Social Work, Media Studies, Modern Social History, Health Studies, Gender Studies, Environmental Studies, Diaspora Studies, Area Studies, Sanskrit-Society & Culture etc.) to promote interdisciplinary and multidisciplinary research.

5. Research Survey & Publication

- Publication grant/subsidy for publication of doctoral thesis/ research report/ papers presented in seminars/conferences etc.
- Grant-In-Aid for Supporting Professional Associations/ Organizations of Social Scientists for their Development.

v Grant-In-Aid for Professional Associations/ Organizations of Social Scientists including Universities, Colleges and Research Institutes for Publication/ Running of their Research Journal(s).

6. Data Archives

7. Social Science Documentation Centre (NASSDOC)

National Social Science Documentation Centre (NASSDOC), was established in 1970 as a Division of the ICSSR with the objective to provide library and information support services to researchers in social sciences; those working in academic institutions, autonomous research organizations, policy making, planning and research units of government departments, business and industry etc. NASSDOC also provides guidance to libraries of ICSSR Regional Centres and ICSSR supported Research Institutes. Meeting the challenges posed by technology driven world, it exemplifies the use of digital environment for creating, applying and utilizing information with its automated library collection, WEBOPAC, online databases/e-resources etc. It has effectively attained itself to the web enabled information and is marching ahead.

RESEARCH INSTITUTE

Research Institutes and Regional Centres Division (RI&RC) provides maintenance and development grants to Research Institutes and maintains Regional Centres in different regions of the country. The Research Institutes are of all India character-outside the scope of the University Grants Commission (UGC). The main objectives are:

- Dispersal of talent from more developed to less developed regions, especially, to areas where social science research are under developed; and
- Development of quality of research and interdisciplinary research in social sciences in order to improve the social science inputs into development.

The Council is at present assisting 30-research-institutesand 6 Regional Centres in different regions in India.

REGIONAL CENTRES

The ICSSR has six Regional Centres. Their location and coverage are as follows:

Eastern Regional Centre, Kolkata covering Bihar, Orissa, West Bengal and Jharkhand, and the Union Territory of Andaman and Nicobar Islands.

North-Eastern Regional Centre, Shillong covering Arunachal Pradesh, Assam, Manipur, Tripura, Meghalaya, Mizoram, Nagaland and Sikkim.

Northern Regional Centre, New Delhi covering Delhi, Madhya Pradesh, Rajasthan Uttar Pradesh, Chattisgarh and Uttranchal.

Southern Regional Centre, Hyderabad covering Andhra Pradesh, Karnataka, Kerala, Tamil Nadu, and the Union Territories of Lakshadweep and Pondicherry.

Western Regional Centre, Mumbai covering Gujarat, Maharashtra, Goa and the Union Territories of Daman and Diu, Dadra and Nagar Haveli.

North-Western Regional Centre, Chandigarh covering Haryana, Himachal Pradesh, Jammu & Kashmir, Punjab, and the Union Territory of Chandigarh.

LIBRARY SERVICE

- Bibliography on Demand and Literature Search Services
- E-resources for ICSSR Research Institutes and Regional Centres
- E-Resources available at NASSDOC
- Continuing Education Programme
- Current Awareness Service / Research Information Series

- Document Delivery / Inter-Library Loan / Reprography Service
- Professional Skill Development and Networking
- In-House Databases/Publications
- ICSSR Sales and Distribution Unit
- Online Public Access Catalogue (OPAC)
- Current Journals (Print + Online)

LIBRARY MEMBERSHIP

ICSSR-NASSDOC library's membership is open to the following categories of readers:

Official Members : These include ICSSR Council Members/ senior officials of the ICSSR secretariat and regular professional staff of the ICSSR (i.e. Research Assistants/Documentation Assistants and above). They are entitled to borrow books from the library for 15 days.

Consulting Members : Consultation facility is extended to academicians, research scholars, students and members of general public that may include retired persons and other categories of readers. Consultation membership fee is Rs. 300 per annum (minimum Rs. 50 for one month).

Borrowing Members : Borrowing facility is extended to social scientists, academicians, students and general readers who are registered as members of the library. Books are issued against a security deposit of Rs.1000/- per book. Maximum of two books can be issued to individual members at a time.

Institutional Members : Institutional membership is also available against a payment of Rs. 6000 for one year. Five (5) books can be borrowed by an institutional member for a period of one month.

Guest Members : There is no fee for guest readers who want to consult the library for a day or two. They are issued a guest card for the day.

COUNCIL

'Council' is the **Governing Council** and highest decision-making body of the ICSSR. It consists of twenty-six members including the Chairman and the Member-Secretary. The Chairman along with eighteen social scientists is nominated by the Government of India. In addition, there are six representatives of the Government of India including one each from the Department of Education, Ministry of Social Welfare and Ministry of Finance. The term of the Chairman, Member-Secretary is normally of three years. Similarly, the term of office of all other nominees is generally of three years. The meeting of the Council, as per the Memorandum Of Association (MOA), should be held at such time as may be determined by the Chairman who may convene the ordinary general meeting whenever he thinks fit. However, the Council should ordinarily hold at least two ordinary general meetings every year. Ten members of the Council present shall form the quorum in every meeting of the Council (for further details, please see Memorandum of Association. Important committees of the ICSSR are the Policy, Planning and Administration Committee (PPAC) and the Research Committee (RC).

Policy, Planning and Administration Committee (PPAC)

The Rules contained in the MOA provide for the formation of the Committee. It states that there shall be a Policy, Planning and Administration Committee which shall look after, subject to Rules and Regulations and Orders of the Council, the policies, plans, administration and financial affairs of the council. PPAC consists of the Chairman, the Member-Secretary and not less than five or more than nine members appointed by the Council at the Annual General Meeting. The term of the Committee shall be one year from the date of the AGM in which it is constituted. However, the

Committee once constituted shall continue in office until another PPAC is constituted. By convention, representatives of the Department of Education and Finance, Govt. of India are always appointed to the PPAC. Every meeting of the Committee shall be presided by the Chairman and in its absence, by a member chosen by the members present at the meeting. The Committee shall meet at least three times a year at such time as the Chairman may decide. Five members shall constitute a quorum.

The Research Projects Committee (Research Committee) of the Council shall scrutinize the sanctioning of grants-in-aid to research projects and other research proposals for financial assistance submitted to the Council or sponsored by the Council subject to Rules and regulations and orders of the council. The Committee consists of the Chairman, the Member-Secretary and not less than five or more than twelve members appointed by the Council at the Annual General Meeting (not more than three of the members may be persons who are not members of the Council).The term of the Research Committee shall be for one year from the date of the AGM on which it is constituted. However, a Research Committee once constituted shall continue in office until another Research Committee is constituted. The committee shall meet at least three times a year. A minimum of five members constitute a quorum.

REFERENCES

- https://www.icssr.org

2. ICWA (INDIAN COUNCIL OF WORLD AFFAIRS)

HISTORY OF THE COUNCIL

The Indian Council of World Affairs was established in 1943 by a group of Indian intellectuals as a think tank. It was registered as a non-official, non-political and non-profit organization under the Registration of Societies Act 1860.

By an Act of Parliament in 2001, the Indian Council of World Affairs has been declared an institution of national importance. The Vice President of India is the ex-officio President of ICWA. It is devoted exclusively for the study of international relations and foreign affairs. Historic international conferences like 'Asian Relations Conference' in 1947 under the leadership of freedom fighter Sarojini Naidu and 'United Nations and the New World Order' in 1994 have been held by this think tank in which world renowned dignitaries addressed huge gatherings of intellectuals. Scores of conferences, meetings and panel discussions have been organized by the Council in its elegant building called "Sapru House".

The first Prime Minister of independent India, late Pandit Jawaharlal Nehru, the architect of India's foreign policy, was a regular visitor to Sapru House to confer with noted scholars, intellectuals and academics. In 2009, an initiative was taken to commemorate the 'Asian Relations Conference' and a conference titled "Emerging China: Prospects for Partnerships in Asia" was organized. It was addressed by 25 foreign scholars from 15 countries and was attended by academics, diplomats and policymakers.

Spread over two acres of land in the heart of New Delhi, Sapru House has lush green lawns with high quality infrastructure. The present building was inaugurated by Pandit Jawaharlal Nehru in May 1955. It is named after the eminent Indian Jurist and intellectual, Sir Tej Bahadur Sapru, the founder President of the Council. A number of renowned and prestigious Indian think tanks and organizations like the "Institute for Defence Studies and Analyses" (IDSA), "School of International Studies" (which was later merged with the famous Jawaharlal Nehru University), "Children's Film Society of India" and the "Press Institute of India" were established in this building. The Council has a state of the art Auditorium with a seating capacity of 380 persons. It has a separate Conference Room and a Conference Hall where panel discussions and seminars are held regularly. International personalities come and address meetings at Sapru House on regular basis.

THE OBJECTIVE OF THE COUNCIL

The Indian Council of World Affairs Act, 2001 lays down the objectives of the ICWA. Section 13 of the Act lists the objectives as:

- To promote the study of Indian and international affairs so as to develop a body of informed opinion on international matters.
- To promote India's relations with other countries through study, research, discussions, lectures, exchange of ideas and information with other organizations within and outside India engaged in similar activities.
- To serve as a clearing house of information and knowledge regarding world affairs.
- To publish books, periodicals, journals, reviews, papers, pamphlets and other literature on subjects covered under clauses (a) & (b).
- To establish contacts with organizations promoting objects mentioned in this section.
- To arrange conferences and seminars to discuss and study the Indian policy towards international affairs.
- To undertake such other activities for the promotion of ideas and attainment of the above mentioned objects.

RESEARCH WORK

The ICWA research faculty comprises of Director (Research), fifteen Research Fellows and three Research Interns. The focus of research at ICWA is on the political, economic and security developments in India's immediate and extended neighborhood. The faculty members also follow trends and development in Asia, Africa, Europe, and the United States. The Research Fellows contribute, Issue briefs, Policy Briefs, Viewpoints on regular basis which are published on the ICWA website. The Sapru House Papers that are designed to provide in-depth analysis of key foreign policy issues to stimulate debate and discussions. Besides, books by the research faculty are also published. The ICWA Fellows actively participate in international conferences both in India and abroad, contribute papers to Indian and foreign scholarly journals, and take part in workshops, lectures, and seminars. The above activities are resulting in academic networking, promoting synergy in multi-disciplinary research and in expanding ICWA's research capacity and profile.

ICWA Library (Sapru House Library)

ICWA Library was inaugurated by Pt. Jawaharlal Nehru as the premier collection of documents on international relations in India. One of India's finest and most coveted research libraries; the Indian Council of World Affairs' Library is located in the heart of New Delhi. It is well equipped on international affairs and allied streams including political history and developments in India.

Functioning since 1955, the Library is a treasure trove of more than 141,000 volumes of books, thousands of them rare, bound periodicals, rare maps, microfiches and about one million press clippings in digital format with special reference to international relations, international law and international economy. It offers a congenial atmosphere with a reader-cultured approach in a serene and calm environment. It subscribes to 67 national and international research journals, receives 164 journals on exchange/gratis basis. Library subscribes 12 national daily newspapers. Library has more than 35 thousand periodicals in bound form. Newspaper files of *the Hindu* (Madras) from 1933 to

1979, *the Times of India* (Bombay) from 1945 to1975 and *the Times of India* (New Delhi) from 1969 to 2004 are also preserved beside stray volumes of *The Asian Age, The Economic Times, The Financial Times (London), The International Herald Tribune, The Nation (Lahore), The Pakistan Times and The Japan Times (Tokyo)* News.

LIBRARY SERVICES

Online Resources Services

Web OPAC

Bibliographic Service : Bibliographies on specific topics are provided to the Institute's researchers on request.

Current Awareness Services : New books are kept on display for a week and bibliographic details are notified to ICWA researchers.

Reference Service : Information is collected from the library and internet resources against specific requests from the Institute's researchers.

Selective Dissemination of Information (SDI) : SDI is provided to ICWA researchers in their specific areas of research.

Photocopy : Photocopying at nominal charges.

DELNET Online : Provides access to DELNET Union Catalogues and other Databases to Member-Libraries

JSTOR

Project MUSE : Project MUSE is a leading provider of digital humanities and social sciences content; since 1995, its electronic journal collections have supported a wide array of research needs at academic, public, special, and school libraries worldwide. MUSE books and journals, from leading university presses and scholarly societies, are fully integrated for search and discovery.

Special Collection Services

Heritage of Diplomacy" is a bouquet of books written by ambassadors and senior diplomats. This special collection is available in the Indian Council of World Affairs library. Anecdotes, memoirs, short stories, autobiographical accounts and relations of India with other countries looked through the prism of our Ambassadors are some of the highlights of this collection.

Newspaper files of the Hindu (Madras) from 1933 to 1979, the Times of India (Bombay) from 1945 to1975 and the Times of India (New Delhi) from 1969 to 2004 are also preserved beside stray volumes of The Asian Age, The Economic Times, The Financial Times (London), The International Herald Tribune, The Nation (Lahore), The Pakistan Times and The Japan Times (Tokyo) News.

United Nations & European Union Section : The ICWA Library is a repository for the United Nations and European Union documents, periodicals and its other publications. The library has almost all the UN documents since 1945. Important among them are Security Council and General Assembly debates and their Resolutions. The access to these documents is free of charge. Similarly, the Library has almost all the publications of the European Union documents under a repository scheme.

PUBLICATION

India Quarterly

India Quarterly is a peer reviewed journal of international affairs. When launched in 1945, its focus was primarily on India and Asia. However, as India's an interest have expanded so too has the mandate of the journal to include submissions on varied themes that are likely to impact India's global interests.

- Sapru House Papers
- Heritage of diplomacy
- Oral history project
- ICWA guest column
- Shod lekh

ICWA COMMITTEES

- Programme Committee
- Finance Committee
- Research Committee
- Library Committee
- Web Committee
- Web Committee

CSCAP-INDIA COMMITTEE

- Annual Report
- Annual Account
- ICWA Act
- Budget
- MoUs
- Sexual Harassment of Women

REFERENCES

- https://icwa.in/index.html
- https://icwa.in/libraryonline.html

3. IIMA (INDIAN INSTITUTE OF MANAGEMENT-AHMEDABAD)

INTRODUCTION

The decade following independence in 1947 was witness to a surge of innovative ideas to build a fledgling independent nation into a model democratic state committed to growth with equity. The establishment of the Indian Institute of Management Ahmedabad (IIMA) was the outcome of one such innovative initiative. Led by space scientist Dr. Vikram Sarabhai and an eminent industrialist and philanthropist Shri Kasturbhai Lalbhai, and proactively supported by the then Chief Minister of Gujarat, Dr. Jivraj Mehta, a group of enlightened individuals set up IIMA in 1961. This group ably wove together a coalition of five actors - the governments at the centre and the state, local industrialists, the Ford Foundation and the Harvard Business School, to establish the foundations of the Institute.

IIMA was set up as an institution that would be managed by a Society, the IIMA Society, created under the Societies Act. The Institute was to be run by a Board of Governors, constituted by the IIMA Society; the Board would have representation from all the relevant constituencies so as to reflect the multifarious needs of a developing nation. IIMA was therefore conceived as a Board-managed institution, free from the exclusive control of any one constituency. Thus, operational freedom is an integral part of the DNA of IIMA.

Thus, created and nurtured as an institute of management and not just as a business school, IIMA has produced numerous leader-managers for the business and public sectors who, with their dreams, aspirations and vision, have shaped their organizational, economic and social contexts. In this educational journey IIMA has been led by its commitment to:

- Hosting faculty who have distinguished themselves as teachers, researchers, consultants and policy shapers, and are constantly in touch with the world of practice.
- Developing innovative and appropriate curricula and pedagogy that are student-centred.
- Fostering research as a tool to extend the frontiers of knowledge, both applied and conceptual.

- Creating management scholars-teachers and researchers.
- Establishing infrastructure of high quality.

IIMA has been consistently ranked as the premier management school in the country by several national agencies. IIMA programmes are also ranked highly in several international rankings. In 2008, IIMA became the first management school in the country to be awarded EQUIS (European Quality Improvement System) accreditation by the EFMD (European Foundation for Management Development).

VISION AND STRATEGIC PRIORITIES

In accordance with its broader vision of 'educating leaders of enterprises', IIMA, in the recent past, has been following a three-pronged approach-connect, nurture, and grow.

IIMA is connecting with alumni, corporate, researchers, and the local community by reaching out to them proactively. We seek to nurture a high-performance work environment by supporting a climate of autonomy, stretch, and team work amongst our faculty members, staff and students. And we are growing our capacity, in a thoughtful and strategic manner, so as to have an impact commensurate with our ambition and to ensure that we continuously improve the quality of our people and our learning.

CAMPUS

The IIMA campus is situated across 106 acres in Vastrapur, Ahmedabad. The campus houses the academic blocks, faculty offices, student and faculty accommodation, the Dr. Vikram Sarabhai Library, the R.J. Mathai Auditorium, the Louis Kahn Plaza, the International Management Development Centre, the Kasturbhai Lalbhai Management Development Centre, the Centre for Innovation,

Incubation and Entrepreneurship, sport facilities, several food outlets and merchandise stores

AWARDS & HONOURS

IIMA attracts students who are not just proficient academically but are also talented in many other ways. Some of the awards that recognize outstanding academic and non-academic achievements include the following:

The Kollengode V. Srinivas Award : Instituted by the parents of the late Kollengode V. Srinivas to recognize the all-round performance of an outstanding student and honour the memory of Srinivas's association with the Institute.

The S. Umapathy Prize : Instituted by the brother of the late S. Umapathy to recognize the academic excellence of a student and honour the memory of Umapathy's association with the Institute.

The S. K. Seth Memorial Award : Instituted by Mrs. Shanti Seth in memory of her husband, the late Sri S. K. Seth, the first librarian of the Institute.

The Academic Merit Award : Presented by The Institute and Nestle India Ltd. It carries a certificate of merit and a cash award.

IFCI and Chaudhary-Padmanabhan-Pant Award: Presented for the best Thesis Proposal.

Travel Awards : Presented for participation in international conferences.

Long Service Award : Presented to retiring employees with a record of long service in the Institute.

The Sajeev Sirpal Academic and Creativity Excellence Award : Instituted in memory of Shri Sajeev Sirpal (PGP 1984) by Kanaka Sirpal (PGP 1984) and friends to recognize excellence in academics and creativity among participants of the PGP.

The "Late Shri B. V. Doshi Memorial Entrepreneurship Assistance" : Instituted in the memory of Shri B.V. Doshi by his grandson Mr. Sahil Doshi, Ivory Rose, to recognize graduating students from the PGP or PGP-FABM batches exhibiting entrepreneurial spiri.

The Smt. J Nagamma Memorial Award : Instituted in memory of Smt. J Nagamma by her son Mr. Pramod Kunju (PGP 1999). This award is meant to recognize excellence in academics of a PGP student who has obtained highest CGPA at the end of the first year.

Outstanding Sportsperson Award : This award recognizes excellence in sports.

The IIMA Alumni VVEF Outstanding Researcher Award : Instituted by the Vidya Vardhini Education Foundation, a Section 25 Company run by IIMA alumni. Every year, the Award goes to one faculty member who has contributed significantly to research.

The Marti Mannariah Gurunath Outstanding Teacher Award : Instituted by Prof Marti Subrahmanyam (1967-69), Professor at Stern School of Business, in memory of his father Mr. Mannariah Gurunath. Every year, the Award goes to one faculty member who has taught the batches graduating in that convocation.

ACADEMIC PROGRAMMES

- Fellow Programme in Management (FPM)
- Post Graduate Programme in Management (PGP)
- Post Graduate Programme in Food and Agri-business Management (PGP-FABM)
- Post Graduate Programme in Management for Executives (PGPX)
- Faculty Development Programme (FDP)
- Armed Forces Programme (AFP)
- ePost Graduate Programme (ePGP)

- Executive Education Programmes (EEP)

NICMAN

National Information Centre on Management has been set up at the Indian Institute of Management, Ahmedabad, initially sponsored by the National Information System for Science & Technology (NISSAT), Department of Scientific & Industrial Research, Government of India to provide efficient information services on management and its related disciplines at the national level. The centre was formally inaugurated in 1996 to serve as a national information facility for dissemination of business and management information.

LIBRARY

The Vikram Sarabhai Library (VSL) is named after Dr. Vikram Sarabhai, world renowned physicist and founding Director of IIMA. It was set up in 1962 and is one of the best management libraries in Asia. The library is open 24x7. Our mission is to facilitate convenient and user friendly access to current, global and relevant information by identifying, acquiring, organizing and retrieving information in various formats (print & non print) to serve the information needs of the academic fraternity of IIMA to meet their teaching, research, consulting, training and learning requirements.

The strength of the library is its digital collection of 100+ databases, accessible from any networked computer within the campus, which provides scholarly, company and industry information. The library provides specialized tools like EBSCO Discovery, journal title search (A to Z), remote login (restricted to internal users) and institutional repository searching. Recently the Library has introduced Kindle E-Book Readers Borrowing Service and it is in great demand among the library users.

LIBRARY SERVICES

1. Research Help : If you need any help regarding your project/research like; collecting data, acquiring research papers, etc. you may submit a form or drop an email at reference@iima.ac.in

2. RemoteXS Facility : This facility enables users (faculties and students) to access library online resources when they are off campus. Click here to know how to avail this facility.

3. Purchase/Subscription Request : want to suggest new books/Journals/database to the library, log in and fill the form.

4. Inter Library Loan Service : Documents which are not available in the library can be requested by filling the form.

5. Reservation Policy : The faculty & students can reserve the item/s which is issued to others. Whenever the item/s is/are returned, the user will get an auto email. They can also reserve the book/s which is available in the library. In such cases, the staff will collect the book/s from the stack area and keep it at the circulation counter. The same will be conveyed to the faculty by email. In both the cases, the reserved items should be collected within 2 days, else the reservation will stand cancelled and the item will be issued to other immediate member. Reserve/Hold the book/s through the online catalogue, using "Place hold" option.

6. Photocopy Facility : For Black and White copy: INR 1/- (A4 size) and INR 2/- (A3 size). For Color copy: INR 10/-(A4 size) and INR 15/- (A3 size). The charges are applicable for printing/photocopy of articles, book chapters, etc. The library has facility of photocopy where you have to login to use the photocopier.

7. Book Drop Box Facility : The book drop box has been placed at the entrance of the underpass from the new campus near the AXIS Bank ATM. This is to facilitate easy return of issued library books by just dropping the books inside the drop box instead of coming physically to the library to return the book. The Library will arrange to collect the books daily at 5 p.m. The user will get a confirmation mail from library circulation once the book is returned in the library software.

8. Kindle E-Book Reader : The Vikram Sarabhai Library offers "Kindle e-book Reader Lending Service" to encourage and support paperless reading. Presently twenty E-Book Readers, Kindle Paper White & Kindle Voyage along with Kindle unlimited eBook package* are available for 15-day loan.

9. Online Payments : The Vikram Sarabhai Library accepts online payments (Minimum Rs. 5/-) for various purposes through Credit card/Debit card/Net banking. Please select the relevant payment purpose from the list given below:

Library Service	*Online Payment URL*
Photocopy/Printing Charges	[Pay]
Fine/Overdue Charges	[Pay]
Lost Books Charges	[Pay]
Membership Charges	[Pay]

You can track your payment using track payments.

10. Document delivery service : The Vikram Sarabhai Library is introducing a new service from June 6, 2018 for library users in the New Campus, wherein we will deliver the library books that you need at the Material Distribution Centre, PGPX Office, New Campus between 2.00 pm and 4.00 pm daily (except on Saturdays, Sundays and Public Holidays). Please note that the books that are put on hold (opt for the pickup location as New Campus) before 12.00 noon will be delivered on the same day between 2.00 pm and 4.00 pm. For books that are put on hold after 12.00

noon, they will be delivered on the next day at the new campus. The books have to be picked up within two working days, after which the books will be transferred back to the main library.

11. Online Chat Service : The Vikram Sarabhai Library is introducing a new service "Online Chat Service" (Tawk.to) to serve the library users in a better way and also for providing immediate and quick reference services to the user community. The service would help users to obtain the primary level information about the library services and resources in the chat mode. We are starting this service from today and initially the service would be available from 9.00 am to 8.00 pm on all days except for weekends and public holidays.

12. OPAC Services

13. E-Resource Services

EVENTS

Confluence : Confluence is the annual international management symposium hosted by IIM Ahmedabad. This event was started in 1999. The primary events at Confluence include master plan, the business plan competition; a business quiz event; a business simulation event and a business strategy simulation event.

Chaos : Chaos is the annual cultural festival of IIMA. Its yearly editions have been centred on themes like diversity, colour or going green. The cultural festivities draws foot falls of around 50,000 visitors from Ahmedabad over four days and participation from institutes across the country. ProNites are especially a huge success with a large number of top class artists coming and performing on one stage.

Insight : Insight is the annual market research festival of IIMA and is one of the oldest events organized by the institute.

ConneXions : ConneXions is the event for the PGPX program at IIMA. It is a knowledge summit that epitomizes the vibrancy and buzz of a business school.

REFERENCES

- https://www.iima.ac.in/web/about-iima/home/about-iima
- https://en.wikipedia.org/wiki/Indian_Institute_of_Management_Ahmedabad

4. IIPA (INDIAN INSTITUTE OF PUBLIC ADMINISTRATION)

HISTORY

Public Administration has always implied Government when 'public' actually means community or people. In the post-colonial, post-independence paradigm of the early 1950s, Public Administration really meant providing service to the people by the State apparatus using the ground rules of justice, ethics and fair-play. This was the intention of the visionary Pandit Jawaharlal Nehru when he established the Indian Institute of Public Administration on March 29, 1954 based on the recommendations of a survey carried out in 1953 by Prof. Paul H. Appleby, Dean, Maxwell School of Citizenship and Public Affairs, Syracuse University and a Consultant with the Ford Foundation invited to advice on the subject, by the Government of India.

As the Institute's first President for a decade, Prime Minister Nehru placed great emphasis on 'de-colonial sing' the mind-set of administration, making it more people-oriented. And he placed a great responsibility on the IIPA to enhance the frontiers of knowledge in public policy and governance through applied research and education as well as training of administrators to serve the people of India. Enhancing leadership and managerial qualities on the one hand and developing a service-orientation on the other are the thrust areas of the Institute's education and training activities. Its faculty is involved with research work mainly to simplify procedures and suggest policy changes to ensure improved delivery of public services.

As India globalizes under growing media glare, her administration and governance have to change with the times and respond to the high expectations of a society where the demographic pre-ponderance of youth, the increasing struggles of urban and rural India, the development-sustainability conflict and the continuing problems of poverty related malnutrition together throw up challenges that require great resilience in administration and delivery. IIPA takes the reality of Governance in transition into consideration in all its skill-development, research and knowledge management activities.

OBJECTIVES

- To promote and provide for the study of Public Administration and economic and political science with special reference to public administration and the machinery of government and educational purposes incidental thereto.
- To undertake, organize and facilitate study courses, conferences and lectures and research in matters relating to public administration and the machinery of government.
- To undertake and provide for the publication of journals and of research papers and books to impart training in and promote the study of public administration.
- To establish and maintain libraries and information services to facilitate the study of public administration and spreading information in regard thereto.
- To constitute or cause to be constituted Regional Branches at convenient centers in India to promote the objects of the society.

- To cooperate with approved institutions and bodies for the purposes of helping the cause of public administration

ACTIVITIES

Activities : Through six decades of experience in research, training and rendering policy advice, conferences and seminars, case studies and publications, the IIPA has made significant contribution to public administration at the Union, State and Local levels. The Institute has a distinguished faculty in the areas of public administration, political science, economics, finance, law and justice, management, behavioural science, rural studies, urban studies, sociology, policy science, environment, e-governance and information and communication technology.

Research : The Institute undertakes research in a large number of diverse areas that include economic and social policies, legal framework for administration at various levels, procedural and organizational change in government, citizen-centric administration, effective development of urban and rural areas, disaster management, consumer protection and welfare, poverty alleviation and gender studies. It specializes in policy evaluations, service delivery and impact analysis studies. At any point of time around 30 research studies are on-going.

Training and Educational Programmes : The Institute conducts around 90-100 short and long-term learning programmes aimed at capacity enhancement of civil servants, defence officers, technocrats and executives of public sector undertakings (PSUs) currently. These programmes are either fee-based or sponsored by the Government. It designs customized programmes for other organizations. Its flagship training initiatives include a ten-month Advanced Professional Programme in Public Administration (APPPA) that is sponsored by Department of Personnel and Training

(DoPT). This multi-faceted programme for senior officers of the Central Government was started in 1975 and is now in its 39th year. The Institute nurtures close academic association with universities, research centres, training institutions and government departments. Another important sponsorship is the series of managerial skill-development engagements for senior scientists supported by the Department of Science and Technology. Customised programmes for private sector industry especially in areas of their interface with Government at all levels and activating knowledge centres in Ministries and State Governments are new initiatives. The Institute also organizes a number of international training programmes for participants from developing and developed.

Policy Advice : IIPA undertakes a large number of assignments for Government, Public Sector Undertakings and multilateral, bilateral and other international agencies on a wide range of policy related areas. The Institute's faculties serve on a large number of Committees constituted by Union, State and Local Governments, Planning Commission, Cabinet Secretariat, as well as expert groups constituted by international agencies and thereby contribute to the task of nation building.

Conferences/Workshops/Seminars : The Institute organizes conferences/seminars/ workshops on contemporary themes and public policy issues with a view to bring together practising administrators and academia to evolve policy inputs for good governance.

Dissemination of Information : The Institute has enriched the literature on Public Administration through a large number of serials and monographs besides research studies, proceedings of seminars /conferences and lectures, etc. The Institute publishes five periodicals regularly:

- Indian Journal of Public Administration (IJPA, Quarterly, published since 1955).

- Lok Prashasan (Hindi, six-monthly, published since 2009)
- Nagarlok (Quarterly, published since 1969)
- Documentation in Public Administration (DPA, Quarterly, published since 1973).
- IIPA Newsletter (Monthly, published since 1955)

So far IIPA has published about 400 books, monographs, reports, working papers, and compendiums in spheres of governance and public administration.

NETWORK AND COLLABORATION

With a membership over 11,000 including about 100 overseas, the IIPA has a nation-wide network of 23 regional branches and 44 local branches, which provide exchange of ideas on current trends and practice in public administration to public servants, academics and students.

The Institute is one of the founder members of the Eastern Regional Organization for Public Administration (EROPA). It works in association with the universities, industry associations advanced research institutes, training centers and government departments in India. The Institute also collaborates with the Ecole National d' Administration, France, Korea Institute of Public Administration, Government of Mauritius, Government of Argentina, the Bangladesh Public Administration Training Centre (BPATC), Party School of the Central Committee of the Communist Party, People's Republic of China. Of late there are new windows of cooperation opening with Vietnam, the GIZ and the Potsdam University of Germany.

INSTITUTIONAL REQUIREMENTS

- The nominations for the courses sponsored by Department of Personnel and Training (DOP&T) and conducted by the Institute are invited by the Department of Personnel and Training, Ministry of

Personnel, Public Grievances and Pensions, Government of India.

- Nominations for the fee-based courses of the Institute and courses organized by its twelve centres are invited by the Institute in respect of each programme. The participant/s should report for training only after getting confirmation by the Institute that their nomination has been accepted.
- Institute rules require that course fees are sent through Demand Drafts, drawn in favour of the Director, Indian Institute of Public Administration, New Delhi, which should invariably be sent in advance along with the nomination/s for the concerned programme/s.
- Most training programmes are meant for in-service personnel only, viz., Officers from Central Ministries/ Departments including Armed Forces; State Governments; Public Sector/State Enterprises and Departments of Local Self Governments and faculty of universities, colleges and institutes.
- IIPA also conducts workshops, skill-development interaction and seminars for Civil Society and the public on topical Governance related issues. Certificates of participation are invariably given at the end of all programmes.
- For further information about training activities/ course, write to the respective Programme Coordinator(s), the Coordinator (Training) or the Deputy Registrar (Academic Services), IIPA, Indraprastha Estate, Ring Road, New Delhi-110002.

ACADEMIC CENTRES

The academic interaction between the faculty members of the institute is facilitated through the academic centres of the institute. The Institute has following nine centres:

- Centre for economic analysis and financial management
- Centre for management studies, public enterprises and behavioural studies
- Centre for public policy, planning and development studies
- Centre for rural development administration & Panchayati Raj
- Centre for urban studies
- Centre for consumer studies
- Centre for learning in ICT & e-governance
- Centre for climate change, environment and drought administration
- Centre for ethical governance and social justice

LIBRARY

The IIPA Library is one of the major social science resources in India. It has a collection of about 215909 volumes of books and periodicals and receives 327 current periodicals. As on March 31, 2015 the computerized library database has 121819 records relating to books and 107874 records relating to periodical articles.

The collection is particularly rich in the areas of public administration, management sciences, economics, planning and development, political science, sociology, rural and urban studies, gender studies and environmental sciences. The Public Document Section of the Library which contains Census of India publications, reports of various committees and commissions appointed by the Central and State Governments, National Sample Survey reports, annual reports of various ministries and departments of the Government of India, and select publications of international organizations, is acknowledged to be one of the richest collections in the country.

LIBRARY SERVICES

- Current awareness services
- Book Alert
- Article Alerts, and weekly Current Contents and News Alert to keep its readers informed of the incoming documents.
- Subject bibliographies available on demand.
- Web OPAC
- Photocopying Services
- Audio/Video collection: The Library has over 500 CD's on various aspects related to Public administration in general.
- Thesis/dissertation Services
- Monographs, Reports, Working Papers Services.
- **Institutional Repository of IIPA :** This Digital Repository is showcasing the research output and published resources of the Institute. The resources are represented in the communities created for various types, such as – Annual General Body Meetings-Presidential Addresses, Faculty Publications, Rare Books, Annual Reports, Special Reports, Thematic Papers, and Working Papers and like. It also includes Theses and dissertations submitted by APPPA participants for their M.Phil degree.
- **I-Portal Services**
  - — Digital Library Services
  - — Open Access e-resources
  - — World bank
  - — PAIRS
  - — PAN

REFERENCES

- http://www.iipa.org.in
- http://www.iipa.org.in/library.html

5. NCAER (NATIONAL COUNCIL FOR APPLIED ECONOMIC RESEARCH)

HISTORY

NCAER's roots lie in Prime Minister Nehru's early vision of a newly-independent India needing independent institutions as sounding boards for the government and the private sector. Remarkably for its time, NCAER was started in 1956 as a public-private partnership, both catering to and funded by government and private industry. NCAER's first Governing Body included the entire Cabinet of economic Ministers and the leading lights of the private sector, including names like C. D. Deshmukh, J.R.D. Tata, John Mathai, and Asoka Mehta. The Ford Foundation provided strong financial support in the early years, combined with support from the Finance Ministry and Tata Sons.

On October 31, 1959, Prime Minister Pandit Jawaharlal Nehru laid the foundation stone for the current iconic campus designed by Harvard-trained architect, A. P. Kanvinde. In doing so, he laid the foundation a unique research institution that has stood the test of time in its service to the nation. More than five decades later on July 27, 2013, Prime Minister Dr Manmohan Singh laid the foundation stone for the new NCAER India Centre that will come up on this campus as part of the physical rejuvenation of NCAER.

MISSION & VISION

Established in 1956, NCAER is India's oldest and largest independent, non-profit, economic policy research institute. Six decades in the life of a nation is a long time. It is even longer in the life of an institution. But the promise of NCAER-to ask the right questions, gather good evidence, analyse it well, and share the results widely-has endured. India has achieved much, and much remains undone. As the economy has changed, so too has NCAER, to continue to help understand India's rapid economic and social transformation. As newer and more complex economic challenges emerge, NCAER will have to do more to keep its promise. To do this well, that is NCAER's promise renewed.

NCAER ACTIVITIES

NCAER has done pioneering research work in areas of applied economics with an emphasis on policy analysis and application of modern quantitative techniques to development issues, regional development and planning, household income, consumption, savings and energy.

- Develop policy reports for clients.
- To examine domestic agricultural market structures, policy, linkages between agricultural price policy and poverty and the role of the Panchayats in fostering sustainable development.
- Track key sectors of the economy for subscribers.
- Forecast the economic outlook.
- Conduct, design and analyse surveys that illuminate public policy issues as well as assist private sector decisions.
- Disseminate research findings.

RESEARCH AREAS ACTIVITIES

NCAER's work falls into four thematic areas:

1. Growth, Trade, and Economic Policy

- Assessments of the current state of the economy.
- Short term forecasts through computable general equilibrium models.

- Medium term forecasts through econometric models.
- Monitoring of cyclical patterns in key variables that affect industrial, financial and international trade activity.
- Quarterly review.

2. Investment Climate, Physical and Economic Infrastructure

- Policy issues relevant to industry, infrastructure and international economic cooperation.
- Sectoral studies that evaluate the competitiveness of industry.
- Impact of economic liberalization on infrastructure development.
- Conduct of sample survey and statistical analysis of data for different types of research studies.
- Market information survey of households (MISH).
- Tracking consumer demographics and consumption patterns across product categories.

3. Agriculture, Rural Development and Resource Management

- Reforms in the agricultural sector and agreement on agriculture (AoA) under the WTO.
- Price policy and public distribution system (PDS).
- Land consolidation, fragmentation and optimal land use plans.
- Rural infrastructure and agro processing.
- Irrigation and watershed management.
- Changing food baskets and their impact on production patterns.

4. Household Behaviour, Poverty, Human Development, Informality and Gender

- Evaluation of poverty and employment focus on informal sector employment.
- Sectoral studies in population and demographic transition.
- Morbidity and health economics.
- Economics of education.
- Gender studies.

The focus of NCAER's work in these areas is on generating and analyzing empirical evidence to support and inform policy choices. It is also one of a handful of think tanks globally that combine rigorous analysis and policy outreach with deep data collection capabilities, especially for household surveys.

DATA

1. National Surveys

National surveys collect data for the entire country: both the constituent states and union territories. Unlike the Census of India, which enumerates every household unit in the country, the national surveys pick samples of households from each state so that the final sample is representative of the entire country. Besides the government, NCAER is the only other organization in India conducting national surveys.

- NCAER-National Data Innovation Centre (NDIC)
- India Human Development Survey (IHDS)
- Additional Rural Incomes Survey (ARIS)/Rural Economic & Demographic Survey (REDS).

2. Consumer Surveys

Consumer surveys measure consumer behaviour with a focus on consumption of market goods. These surveys are important both for profit-making organizations, who use the data to improve marketing strategies, and for those involved in policy design. Evaluating the expenditure patterns of consumers can help a government understand by identifying social sectors that need additional attention.

- National Survey of Household Income and Expenditure (NSHIE)/Market Information Survey of Households (MISH).

3. Sector Data

Any economy is an aggregation of different sectors. To understand the interactions between these sectors within the economy, NCAER partners with institutions to collect data for a wide range of sectors like agriculture, fisheries, handlooms, housing, ICT, inland waterways, youth readership and business expectations.

- Handloom Census
- Quarterly Business Expectations Survey

SPONSORS & PARTNERS

NCAER collaborates extensively with a diverse range of partners from the government, the private sector, non-profits and inter-governmental agencies on projects, seminars conferences and publications both nationally and internationally.

NCAER is a part of the network of 49 think tanks in 22 countries that are receiving core funding through competitive, multi-year institutional grants from the global, multi-donor, Think Tank Initiative. Other than links in India, NCAER also has global links with major think-tanks and universities including the Brookings Institution, the National Bureau of Economic Research, the Pew Research Center, Columbia University, the University of Maryland, various US universities; the London School of Economics and Oxford University in England; the New Economic School in Moscow;

Tsinghua University in Beijing, China; Australian National University, Monash University, and ACIAR in Australia; and the Fung Global Institute in Hong Kong. NCAER has links in South Asia with the Institute of Policy Studies, Colombo; the Pakistan Institute of Development Economics, Islamabad; and the Bangladesh Institute of Development Studies and the Centre for Policy Dialogue in Dhaka. A full list of NCAER's partners is given below:

- Administrator, Universal Service Obligation Fund, Department of Telecommunications, Government of India
- Agricultural And Processed Food Export Development Authority, New Delhi
- All India Artisans And Craft Workers Welfare Association
- ASSOCHAM, New Delhi
- Australian Centre for International Agricultural Research, Canberra
- Bearing Point Global Operations, New Delhi
- British High Commission, New Delhi
- Chronic Poverty Research Centre, IIPA, New Delhi
- CITI Bank, India
- Competition Commission of India
- Defence Research and Development Organization, Ministry of Defence, Government of India
- Delhi Development Authority, New Delhi
- Department for International Development, UK
- Department of Secondary Education, Government of India
- DFID-HTS Development Ltd., UK
- Embassy of Japan, New Delhi
- EU-INDIA Economic Cross Cultural Programme, European Commission

- German Development Corporation
- Harvard University
- HDFC Bank, India
- Hindustan Aeronautics Limited
- Indian Council of Agricultural Research
- Inland Waterways Authority of India
- International Food Policy Research Institute, USA
- Japan External Trade Organization
- Maruti Udyog Ltd.
- MAX New York Life Insurance Co. Ltd.
- Mckinsey Knowledge Centre Pvt. Ltd.
- Ministry of Commerce & Industry, Government of India
- Ministry of Commerce, Government of India
- Ministry of Communications and Information Technology, Government of India
- Ministry of Environment and Forests, Government of India
- Ministry of Finance, Government of India
- Ministry of Food and Consumer Affairs, Government of India
- Ministry of Human Resource Development, Government of India
- Ministry of New and Renewable Energy, Government of India
- Ministry of Panchayati Raj, Government of India
- Ministry of Small Scale Industry, Government of India
- Narmada Valley Development Authority, Madhya Pradesh
- National Aids Control Organization
- National Cooperative Development Corporation

- National Informatics Center, Department of Information Technology, Government of India
- National Institute of Advanced Studies, India
- National Institute of Health and Human Development, USA
- Petroleum Federation of India
- Petroleum Planning and Analysis Cell, Ministry of Petroleum, Government of India
- Planning Commission, Government of India
- Reserve Bank of India
- Royal Norwegian Embassy, New Delhi
- Sab-Miller, India
- State Bank of India
- Task Force on Interlinking of Rivers
- Tata Sons, India
- The Neil D. Levine Institute of International Relations and Commerce, State University of New York
- The World Bank
- United Nations Development Programme (UNDP)

EVENTS

- Release of NCAER-State Investment Potential Index: The 2018 N-SIPI
- The Impact of Groundwater Accessibility on the Performance of Firms
- Environmental Catastrophes and Mitigation Policies in a Multi-region World
- The India Policy Forum 2018

NCAER LIBRARY

The NCAER Library is one of India's premier research libraries in applied economics. Set up in 1956 when NCAER was established, the library has provided solid research support for almost 60 years to NCAER's researchers and to policy makers, researchers, consultants, students and others from all over India and overseas. The NCAER Library's physical collections include approximately 28,000 printed volumes and over 34,000 Government of India and state government official reports,15,000 other documents, and an increasing collection of resources in electronic format. NCAER subscribes to more than 270 serial and periodical titles. It also provides access to multiple online databases. NCAER's collection of Indian economics documents and economic data, going back to soon after India's independence, is unparalleled in its depth and breadth.

The library subscribes to about 250 journals and databases like PROWESS, Capex, Indiastat.com, India Trades and Agriwatch. Access to e-journals and back-filed collections through Science Direct and J-store are also available. NCAER is a depository library for the Asian Development Bank, the IMF, and the United Nations. The library has continued to provide excellent indexing services through our quarterly publication Artha Suchi, which now has more than 30,000 bibliographical references.

Libraries are experiencing major shifts in the way information is stored and accessed, creating immense new digital opportunities. Digital preservation will be critical to provide access to some of our irreplaceable collections. Digitization will be a priority agenda for the library in the years ahead, particularly for the 1,300 or so unique reports in the library that constitute a formidable intellectual property and need protection and preservation.

LIBRARY SERVICES

The NCAER Library provides a variety of services to researchers at the Council and those who visit the library for research purposes. The services provided by the library include.

- Bibliographic service
- Reference service
- Photocopy service
- Resource sharing and Inter library loan
- Recent additions
- Current awareness services in economics
- Artha Suchi- an index to Indian Economic Literature
- E-Resources

NCAER PUBLICATION

- India Policy Forum 2016-17
- MARGIN The Journal of Applied Economic Research
- Margin 2006

REFERENCES

- http://demo.ncaer.org/index.aspx
- http://www.ncaer.org/index.php

6. TISS (TATA INSTITUTE OF SOCIAL SCIENCE)

HISTORY

The Tata Institute of Social Sciences (TISS) was established in 1936, as the Sir Dorabji Tata Graduate School of Social Work. The first school of social work in India, TISS was a pioneering effort with the objective of Social Welfare through academic excellence, a characteristic of the Sir Dorabji Tata Trust (SDTT). Its establishment was the result of the decision of the Trustees of the SDTT to accept Dr. Clifford Manshardt's vision of a post-graduate school of social work of national stature that would engage in a continuous study of Indian social issues and problems and impart education in social work to meet the emerging need for trained human power. This subsequently influenced the direction of social work education and social research in

India. In 1944, the Sir Dorabji Tata Graduate School of Social Work was renamed as the Tata Institute of Social Sciences. The year 1964 was an important landmark in the history of the Institute, when it was declared Deemed to be a University under Section 3 of the University Grants Commission Act (UGC), 1956.

Since then, TISS has been expanding continuously in terms of educational programmes and infrastructure. While responding to the changing needs of the social and educational system in the country, the Institute has gone far beyond the initial concern of social work education. Thus, what started as a small institution offering a post-graduate diploma in Social Work grew into Deemed to be a University and as a result, diversified its activities. Since its inception in 1936, the Tata Institute of Social Sciences has never limited itself to the mandate of a conventional university; rather, it has worked for the promotion of sustainable, equitable and participatory development, social welfare and social justice through: Value-based professional education for social work and other human service professions; Social research and dissemination of socially relevant knowledge; Social intervention through training and field action projects; Contribution to social and welfare policy and programme formulation at state, national and international levels; and Professional response to national calamities, through relief, rehabilitation and disaster management. Over the years, the Institute has, among other thrusts, made a significant contribution to policy, planning, action strategies and human resource development, in several areas, ranging from sustainable rural and urban development to education, health, communal harmony, human rights and industrial relations. In all cases, the focus has been on the disadvantaged and marginalised sections of society, such as organised and unorganised labour, women, children, Dalits, and tribals.

Today, the TISS is a Government of India Institution and has earned recognition as an Institution of Repute from different Ministries of the Government of India, various State Governments, international agencies such as the United Nations, and the non-government sector, both national and international. This is due to the academic freedom leading to a positive work ethos and creativity in the Institute, strong linkages among education, research, field action and dissemination and the social commitment and responsiveness to varying social needs.

VISION

- Create Dignity of Labour and create career channels for people to the top managements of corporate and services.
- Create a new work ethic based society to transform India to a developed industrial and economic powerhouse generating patents, inventions and innovations.
- Enable the socially, economically and physically disadvantaged and the elderly to develop/utilize competency up to their full physical and motor abilities and potential.
- To be an institute of national excellence providing competency development and gainful employability to 5% of India's aggregate demand for skilled labour and another 15% through catalyzing and 'spread' effects.

MISSION

The Mission of TISS-SVE is to transform unemployable youth into a professional level technician in a world class plant or service facility in two years. TISS will design and adopt a scaled up and technology enabled models in order to address the vast needs of skilled manpower in our Country.

TISS LIBRARY (SIR DORABJI TATA MEMORIAL LIBRARY)

Sir Dorabji Tata Memorial Library at TISS has been consistently making efforts to develop a strong collection of learning resources and to provide a human moderated access to knowledge. In its quest for excellence, library has achieved many milestones. Indian Library Association, New Delhi, conferred it with *"ILA - Dr. L. M. Padhya Best University Library Award"* for the year 2008, for the best practices being followed in the university library administration and for its excellent services. At individual levels also, library team members have been conferred with awards, fellowships, etc. Ever since the commencement of academic restructuring in 2004, library has enhanced its collection extensively. More than 25,000 new books have been added to the collection as library did an extensive collection development exercise considering the new programmes being introduced by the institute. Currently, it holds about 123,000 books in principle domains of social sciences. Journals subscription base (including e-Journals), which was 2835 in 2007 has gone up to 10,298 journals in 2015.

To support institutes mission, Library has always strived hard to achieve equity and inclusion in higher education. "Cyber Library" has been established to undertake the social responsibility of providing access to computers and Internet facility to the students coming from economically weaker sections. To make learning resources available to visually challenged students, library started a centre with assistive technologies "M K Tata Centre for the Visually Challenged". Library has made major developments in terms of integrating ICT in library and information services. Several digitization activities, digital literacy and awareness programmes are being carried out continuously. Institutional repository has been set up. Along with UGC INFONET, library also spends considerable amounts to subscribe online databases/e-journals, needed for the institute academic programmes.

In order to share and exchange expertise, library has established several national and international collaborations. Major institutions with which library has collaboration are London School Of Economics Library, UK, Mahasarakham University, Thailand, International Federation of Library Association (IFLA, The Hague, Netherlands). Library is active in capacity building and outreach activities. It has conducted several national and international workshops, conferences and training programmes. As part of academic restructuring, library started to work on its academic programmes in 2008. In 2010, PG Diploma in Digital Library was launched, followed by Masters and PhD Programmes in 2012. All these academic programmes are being offered through its *"Centre for Library and Information Management Studies"*

SDTM LIBRARY VISION

Provide essential and specialized information support to users by procuring and organizing information resources, providing human and technologically moderated access to knowledge and aiding users to identify, locate, obtain and evaluate information.

SDTM LIBRARY OBJECTIVES

- Provide high quality library and information services to support institute's expansion, in terms of new programmes/research thrust areas and additional students across four campuses.
- Develop library and information services to provide continuing high quality support for teaching and learning.
- Develop library and information services to provide continuing high quality support for research and consultancy at institute and in the wider social science

community.

- Manage and focus resources to deliver priorities and develop library staff within a culture of innovation and service improvement.

TISS LIBRARY HISTORY

TISS Library established along with the institute way back in 1936 is one of the leading social science libraries in the country. The library was named as "Sir Dorabji Tata Memorial Library" on 3rd May, 2002 in the memory of late Sir Dorabjii Tata. It is geared to meet the academic and research information needs of the user community. It provides a helpful environment for intellectual enquiry by providing user-focused services to obtain and evaluate scholarly information and knowledge. Since the library specializes in the field of applied social sciences, it has become most sought after library for the social scientists in India. It is a unique Knowledge Centre, which offers essential and specialized information resources and services to meet the growing information needs by:

TISS LIBRARY RESOURCES & SERVICES

- Developing user-based resources.
- Organizing information resources.
- Providing human and technologically moderated access to information.
- Facilitating users to identify, locate, obtain and evaluate information.
- Book bank Services
- New Arrivals services
- Cyber Services
- MK Tata Centre for the Visually Challenged Services
- Document Delivery Service
- Inter Library Loan Services

- Photocopying/Printing Services
- Scanning Services
- OPAC Services
- Thesis & Dissertation Services
- Conduct Orientation/awareness programs for specific research areas about e-resources
- Referral Services from other institutes and universities in India and abroad
- Research tools Services
- Literature Search services
- Citing and Referencing services
- Endnote services
- Writing for Publication services
- E-Journals and Online Databases.
- E-Resources under UGC-INFONET Digital Consortium:
  - Project Muse (389 journals)
  - Wiley Inter Science (503 journals)
  - Oxford University Press (202 journals)
  - JSTOR (729 journals)
  - Springer Link (1236 journals)
  - Taylor & Francis (1076 journals)
  - Cambridge Journals Online (279 journals)
  - JCCC (Gateway Portal)
  - ISID (Industrial Development Bibliographic Database)

TRAINING FACILITIES

Training: "Information and Digital Literacy: Tools for Research": Digital and Information Literacy are integral skills as much of the information we access is in digital format. It is the ability to use digital technology and tools to locate, evaluate, use and create information. Following Training programmes are being offered to develop the capacity of students and scholars in research skills.

Current Awareness: Keeping your research Up-to-date using Web 2.0 tools: RSS Feeds, Feed Readers, Setting up subject interest alerts in databases, Citation Alerts, Conference Alerts, Publisher's eTOC services. Networking with Professionals in the same research area. Increasing your productivity by making the most of web 2.0.

Effective Literature Searching for your research (Programme Specific): Explore bibliographic databases, subject specific databases, e-journals, Data Sets and library catalogue to pool all resources needed for your Project work/ Thesis.

Citing and Referencing Guide: Introduction to Citing and Referencing, Citing Web resources, Referencing Styles: Harvard, APA, Chicago Manual Styles.

Endnote: Getting Started: Introduction, Accessing Endnote, Creating Libraries, Referencing and selecting styles, Exercises. Working with to create in-text citations, footnotes and bibliographies, editing and reformatting word, Exercises.

Zotero, Citations Management: Collect, organize, cite, and share your research sources.

Copy Right and not Copy Cat: Good Academic Practice when writing your thesis.

Student Guide to Plagiarism: Accessing Urkund, Submitting work to Urkund, Urkund originality Reports, Interpreting Urkund originality Report, Further Links and resources.

Copyright: Introduction, Copyright Laws, Educational Copying, Copyright Licenses, Copyright and Internet.

Writing for Publication: Publication Types, Identify journals for publishing, Impact factor and H Index, Peer

Review/Referee process, Citation Databases: Web of Science, JCCC.

Getting Noticed : The databases that help you choose where to publish.

Library Induction : Layout, Services, resource location, Organization of resources, Online Catalogue, Cyber Library, MK Tata Centre, Help points, etc.

DIGITAL LIBRARY

Institutional Repository (ETD) : SDTM Library has set up an institutional repository and archiving facility for the TISS community, using the DSpace open source software developed at the MIT libraries & Hewlett-Packard. This service enables the Institute community to archive their preprints & post prints and other scholarly publications. In keeping with the objectives of the open access movement, TISS has established this service to facilitate the institute researchers in self archiving and long-term preservation of their scholarly publications, provide easy access to these publications worldwide and improve impact of their research.

Digitization Rojects : *The Indian Journal of Social Work* (IJSW) is a pioneering publication of the social work profession in India, published by the Tata Institute of Social Sciences. The IJSW is published every January, April, July and October, and has entered its 69th year of uninterrupted publishing, a record in journal publishing. The first issue of the IJSW was published in June 1940. SDTM Library took the mammoth task of digitizing the journal since 1940. The database includes all the articles, book reviews and notes published in Indian Journal of Social Work from Vol.1-69 (1940-2008). All the articles are in PDF format. A search interface has been provided using Greenstone Digital Library software. Full text Access **IJSW** on Intranet.

Sociological Bulletin is the official journal of the Indian Sociological Society, started in the year 1952. The collection includes all the full text articles published in the journal "Sociological Bulletin" from 1952-2006. It is published thrice a year: January-April, May-August, and September-December. The digitization work has been carried out at Sir Dorabji Tata Memorial Library, Tata Institute of Social Sciences, Mumbai. There are more than 600 research articles available in the collection. The CD of the Sociological Bulletin was officially launched at 33rd All India Sociological Conference held at Dept. of Sociology, Karnataka University, Dharwad (Karnataka State), 29-30 November to 1st December, 2007. There was an overwhelming response for the CD among the participants of the conference.

Parsee Literature : 150 years old Parsee literature of 10,000 pages has been digitized and made it available for the reference in CD-ROM format. The literature was in Gujarati script and the language was Parsee. Entire 32 volumes have been accommodated in THREE CDs.

CAMPUSES

- Mumbai
- Tuljapur
- Hyderabad
- Guwaha

ACADEMICS

Schools and Centres : 21 School and 45 centres.

Teaching Programmes : Masters Programmes, Doctoral Programmes, Bachelors Programmes, Short Term Programmes, Online Programmes, Open & Distance Learning (ODL) Programmes.

International Relations Office (IRO) : The International Relations Office (IRO) was established in the year 2006 as the International Students' Office (ISO) to facilitate mutually beneficial international academic exchange and collaboration between TISS and foreign Universities/Institutions. Since its inception, IRO has worked pro-actively to establish International partnerships by assisting/ facilitating drawing up of MoUs/ agreements between TISS and International institutions as well as developing proposals for collaboration, and providing the necessary administrative institutional support to operationalizing these partnerships and collaborations. It is important to note that, TISS is one of the few Indian Universities that has a full-fledged International Relations Office (IRO) that offers support and active engagement for Internationalizing Higher Education.

COLLABORATIONS

The TISS has over the years build bridges with many Universities across the world. We have signed MoUs and/or have developed linkage with some prestigious international Universities.

Collaboration with International Federation of Red Cross and Crescent Societies (IFRC) : The International Federation of Red Cross and Crescent Societies (IFRC) and the Tata Institute for Social Sciences (TISS) have established an on-line Certificate Course on Disaster Management. This initiative is in line with IFRC's Strategy 2020, Strategic Aim 1: "Save lives, protect livelihoods, and strengthen recovery from disasters and crises" and TISS's commitment to excellence in disaster management education. The programme provides an on line learning platform through the blend of academic excellence and practical experiences. It reaches individuals from various backgrounds. Having a diverse set of participants across the globe, the course aims to bridge the gap between theoretical approach to emergency management and practical approach to reduce vulnerabilities and building resilience. It is of 22 credits and broadly covers 8 modules over a period of 12 months. The assessment method includes assignments, quiz and discussion forum. Also, there is a component of supervised and graded term paper and field practicum of one month in the final module.

- Collaboration with Universities in USA:
  - University of Chicago, Chicago, USA.
  - James Maidson University, Virginia, USA.
  - University of South Carolina, Columbia, USA.
  - George Warren Brown School of School Work, St. Louis, USA.
  - The New School, New York, USA.
  - Wells College, Aurora, New York, USA.
  - University of Delaware, Delaware, USA.
  - Tulane University, New Orleans, USA.
  - University of Utah, Salt Lake City, USA.
  - Yeshiva University, USA.
  - University of Nebraska for establishing a Global Consortium for Education in Family Studies.
- Collaboration with Universities in Europe
  - Roskilde University, Denmark.
  - Foundation Nationale Des Sciences Politiques, Paris, France.
  - Institute d" Etudes Politiques de Lille, Lille, France.
  - London School of Economics, London.
  - Management Centre Innsbruck, Innsbruck, Austria.
  - Tampere University, Finland.
  - Muenster University, Germany.
  - University of Hertfordshire, UK.
  - University of Leuven, Belgium - Otto-von-Guericke-University, Magdeburg, Germany.

  - Partner with 12 European Universities under the Erasmus Mundus, viz. Lund University, Sweden (Lead/ Coordinating university), Albert-Ludwigs-University of Freiburg, Germany, Freie University at Berlin, Germany, International Institute for Geo-information Science and Earth Observation, The Netherlands, Karolinska Institute, Sweden, Norwegian University of Science and Technology, Norway, Politecnico di Milano, Italy, University of Amsterdam, The Netherlands, University of Deusto, Spain, University of Leuven, Belgium, University Pierre and Marie Curie, France, Vilnius University, Lithuania.

- Collaboration with Universities in Australia
  - University of Sydney, University of Western Australia, and Griffith University- On 'Institutions for Food Security: Global Lessons from Rural India'.
  - Charles Stuart University, Australia.
  - Victoria University, Australia.
- Collaboration with Universities in other countries
  - York University, Canada.
  - Critical Edge Alliance - An alliance of progressive Universities in USA, Denmark, Brazil, Columbia, Morocco and India.

REFERENCES

- http://www.tiss.edu
- http://library.tiss.edu

7. UNESCO (UNITED NATIONS EDUCATIONAL, SCIENTIFIC AND CULTURAL ORGANIZATION)

HISTORY

As early as 1942, in wartime, the governments of the European countries, which were confronting Nazi Germany and its allies, met in the United Kingdom for the Conference of Allied Ministers of Education (CAME). The Second World War was far from over, yet those countries were looking for ways and means to reconstruct their systems of education once peace was restored. Very quickly, the project gained momentum and soon took on a universal note. New governments, including that of the United States, decided to join in. Upon the proposal of CAME, a United Nations Conference for the establishment of an educational and cultural organization (ECO/CONF) was convened in London from 1 to 16 November 1945. Scarcely had the war ended when the conference opened. It gathered together the representatives of forty-four countries who decided to create an organization that would embody a genuine culture of peace. In their eyes, the new organization must establish the "intellectual and moral solidarity of mankind" and, in so doing, prevent the outbreak of another world war.

At the end of the conference, thirty-seven countries founded the United Nations Educational, Scientific and Cultural Organization. The Constitution of UNESCO, signed on 16 November 1945, came into force on 4 November 1946 after ratification by twenty countries: Australia, Brazil, Canada, China, Czechoslovakia, Denmark, Dominican Republic, Egypt, France, Greece, India, Lebanon, Mexico, New Zealand, Norway, Saudi Arabia, South Africa, Turkey, United Kingdom and United States. The first session of the General Conference of UNESCO was held in Paris from 19 November to 10 December 1946 with the participation of representatives from 30 governments entitled to vote.

VISION

Political and economic arrangements of governments are not enough to secure the lasting and sincere support of the peoples. Peace must be founded upon dialogue and mutual understanding. Peace must be built upon the intellectual and moral solidarity of humanity.

In this spirit, UNESCO develops educational tools to help people live as global citizens free of hate and intolerance. UNESCO works so that each child and citizen has access to quality education. By promoting cultural heritage and the equal dignity of all cultures, UNESCO strengthens bonds among nations. UNESCO fosters scientific programmes and policies as platforms for development and cooperation. UNESCO stands up for freedom of expression, as a fundamental right and a key condition for democracy and development. Serving as a laboratory of ideas, UNESCO helps countries adopt international standards and manages programmes that foster the free flow of ideas and knowledge sharing.

UNESCO's founding vision was born in response to a world war that was marked by racist and anti-Semitic violence. Seventy years on and many liberation struggles later, UNESCO's mandate is as relevant as ever. Cultural diversity is under attack and new forms of intolerance, rejection of scientific facts and threats to freedom of expression challenge peace and human rights. In response, UNESCO's duty remains to reaffirm the humanist missions of education, science and culture.

MILESTONES

16 November 1945 : representatives of 37 countries meet in London to sign UNESCO's Constitution which comes into force on November 4, 1946 after ratification by 20 signatories.

1948 : UNESCO recommends that Member States make free primary education compulsory and universal.

1952 : An intergovernmental conference convened by UNESCO adopts the Universal Copyright Convention. In the decades following World War II, the Convention served to extend copyright protection to numerous states not then party to the Berne Convention for the Protection of Literary and Artistic Works (1886).

1956 : The Republic of South Africa withdraws from UNESCO claiming that some of the Organization's publications amount to "interference" in the country's "racial problems". The state rejoins the Organization in 1994 under the leadership of Nelson Mandela.

1958 : Inauguration of UNESCO's permanent Headquarters in Paris designed by Marcel Breuer (US), Pier-Luigi Nervi (Italy) and Bernard Zehrfuss (France).

v **1960**: Launching of the Nubia Campaign in Egypt to move the Great Temple of Abu Simbel to keep it from being swamped by the Nile after construction of the Aswan Dam. During the 20-year campaign, 22 monuments and architectural complexes are relocated. This is the first and largest in a series of campaigns including Moenjodaro (Pakistan), Fez (Morocco), Kathmandu (Nepal), Borobudur (Indonesia) and the Acropolis (Greece).

1968 : UNESCO organizes the first intergovernmental conference aimed at reconciling the environment and development, now known as "sustainable development". This led to the creation of UNESCO's Man and the Biosphere Programme.

1972 : The Convention concerning the Protection of the World Cultural and Natural Heritage is adopted. The World Heritage Committee is established in 1976 and the first sites are inscribed on the World Heritage List in 1978.

1974 : H.H. Pope Paul VI awards the John XXIII Peace Prize to UNESCO.

1975 : The United Nations University is established in Tokyo under the auspices of the UN and UNESCO.

1978 : UNESCO adopts the Declaration on Race and Racial Prejudice. Subsequent reports on the issue by the Director-General serve to discredit and dismiss the pseudo-scientific foundations of racism.

1980 : The first two volumes of UNESCO's General History of Africa are published. Similar series focus on other regions, notably Central Asia and the Caribbean.

1984 : The United States withdraws from the Organization citing disagreement over management and other issues. The United Kingdom and Singapore withdraw in 1985. The Organization's budget drops considerably.

1990 : The World Conference on Education for All, in Jomtien, Thailand, launches a global movement to provide basic education for all children, youth and adults. Held ten years later in Dakar, Senegal, the World Education Forum commits governments to achieving basic education for all by 2015.

1992 : Creation of the Memory of the World programme to protect irreplaceable library treasures and archive collections. It includes sound recordings, film, videotape, newsprint, photographs or digital documents.

1997 : The United Kingdom returns to UNESCO.

1998 : The Universal Declaration on the Human Genome and Human Rights, developed and adopted by UNESCO in 1997, is endorsed by the UN.

2001 : UNESCO Universal Declaration on Cultural Diversity is adopted by the General Conference.

2003 : The United States of America returns to UNESCO.

2005 : Brunei Darussalam becomes UNESCO's 191st Member State.

2007 : Montenegro and Singapore join UNESCO, bringing the number of Member States to 193.

2008 : The 1,700 year-old Aksum obelisk, taken to Rome by Mussolini's troops in 1937, is reinstalled in its original location in northern Ethiopia.

2009 : General Conference elects Irina Bokova of Bulgaria to be UNESCO's tenth Director-General and the first woman to occupy the post.

2011 : South Sudan and Palestine become UNESCO's 194th and 195th members.

OBJECTIVES AND FUNCTIONS

The following objectives and functions are given below:

- To promote intellectual co-operation and mutual understanding of peoples through all means of mass communication.
- To give fresh impulse to popular education and to the spread of culture.
- To maintain, increase and diffuse knowledge.
- To encourage scientific research and training.
- To apply sciences to ensure human development and the rational management of natural resources.
- To provide a platform for dialogue and participation of members of the Forum to promote and strengthen the processes of democratization, the rule of law and respect for human rights in Africa and the Arab region.
- To help strengthen Arab-African relations and promote cooperation at the legislative, institutional, business, academic and civil society organizations levels.
- To strengthen the conditions necessary for peace in both regions, given that conflict is incompatible with

democracy and human rights and reduces all possibility for their development.

- To establish and/or strengthen existing research networks, undertake research and studies, disseminate the findings, organize dialogues and debates, and formulate policy recommendations, strategies and plans of action in the fields of democracy and human rights.
- To promote and undertake advocacy and ensure the participation of the Forum members to raise awareness and effective participation and engagement of the citizens, political actors and other decision-makers in the activities of the Forum and national processes.
- To encourage policy-makers to promote the participation of women in political, legislative, social, economic and cultural processes.
- To promote youth participation in political, legislative, social, economic and cultural processes.
- To support and strengthen, through partnerships and networks, the contribution of civil society organizations in promoting democracy and respect for human rights.
- To encourage and foster implementation of the Forum's recommendations, resolutions, strategies and plans of action through national ownership, integration and/or adoption of national legislations, strategies, plans of action and other national systems, and to monitor implementation.
- To promote advocacy activities that support the implementation of regional and international instruments and decisions in the fields of democracy and human rights, and that support existing mechanisms and national institutions.
- To establish a sound communication programme at the Forum to disseminate all the Forum's outputs and

activities through different media and IT channels.

- To take any other measures conducive towards the promotion of democracy and human rights in Africa and the Arab region.

ACTIVITIES

UNESCO implements its activities through the five programme areas:

1. Education
2. Natural sciences
3. Social and human sciences
4. Culture
5. Communication and Information

MAIN ACTIVITIES

UNESCO

- Coordination of the Joint Programme
- Support national institutions to safeguard cultural heritage and promote cultural diversity.
- Promote mentorship programmes in handicrafts and performing arts.
- Support the establishment of a national Living Human Treasures system.
- Promote the establishment of a Seal of Excellence for Cambodian cultural products.
- Promote the establishment of provincial Cultural Centres.

UNDP

- Identify promising cultural products and services with high participation of women for improved commercialization.

- Develop and support implementation of sales and marketing strategies of selected cultural products.
- Build capacity of local NGO partners in the field in the area of sales and marketing.
- Strengthen market linkages between producers and buyers of selected products.
- Identify challenges in the implementation of trade-related law and help coordinate market responses, in order to facilitate sales and promotion of cultural products at grassroots level.
- Support training in trade-related legislation for producer groups and civil society organizations.
- Promote establishment of provincial public-private consultations.

FAO

- Identify potential products and producers in ethnic minority areas.
- Facilitate the formation of producer groups and provide support in organization and management.
- Support the groups by providing training on production skills, management and networks.
- Support product development using available natural resources.

ILO

- Identify existing and potential groups and associations of artists and producers.
- Develop and deliver training in financial literacy and basic business skills.
- Support market linkages by addressing key bottlenecks in value chains.
- Support providers to identify and develop business

development services that are appropriate to the target indigenous groups.

- Train trainers to facilitate basic business development services for member-based producer organizations.

UNESCO LIBRARY

The UNESCO Library, created in 1946, is a special library whose "main purpose is to serve" members of the Secretariat by providing them with the library materials and information needed for the execution of the Organization's programmes, as defined by the representatives of UNESCO's Member States in the General Conference.

Ever since 1946, UNESCO librarians have been developing a collection of research and reference materials on subjects pertinent to the work of the Organization. As one of the United Nations system libraries, the UNESCO Library collection contains practically all publications issued by UNESCO or under its auspices, as well as a selection of scholarly titles devoted to the areas covered by UNESCO programmes: education, culture, natural sciences, social and human sciences, communication and information. The collection offers an overview of the Organization's current and past activities and programmes as recorded in publications and other resources. It is a unique comprehensive source for research on the United Nations Educational, Scientific and Cultural Organization (UNESCO).

LIBRARY SERVICES

- Wi-Fi access Services.
- Six user terminals.
- Photocopy Services.
- Microfiche reader/printer Services.
- Reference desk Services.
- Open access to reference titles and daily press Services.

- Access to the UNESCO Archives Services.
- Wheelchair accessible Services.
- Sending photocopies and PDF files of articles and book chapters Services.
- Providing help in using the catalogue and e-resources Services.
- Compiling literature lists on request Services.
- Loan of books and periodicals Services.
- Ordering of publications Services.
- UNESDOC@lerts, enabling you to receive e-alerts about new issues of electronic publications.
- E-resources databases Services.
- Bibliographies Services.
- Training Services.
- Selective dissemination of information Services.
- Searching on internet Services.
- Searching database(s): UNESDOC/UNESBIB.
- Indexing & Abstracting Services.
- Institutional Repository.
- Referral service.
- Library orientation and Bibliographic instruction.
- Extension service.
- Translation Services.

UNESCO PUBLICATION

- Community Media Sustainability Policy
- World Trends in Freedom of Expression and Media Development
- Youth and Violent Extremism on Social
- Survey on Privacy in Media
- Terrorism and the Media: A Handbook

- Principles for governing the Internet
- Countering online hate speech
- Building digital safety for journalism
- World trends in freedom of expression
- Teaching journalism for sustainable
- The Communication and Information
- Pressing for Freedom: 20 years of World
- Freedom of Expression Toolkit
- Freedom of connection, freedom
- Global survey on Internet privacy
- Conflict-sensitive reporting: state of the art

REFERENCES

- https://en.unesco.org
- http://www.unesco.org/library/about1.html

8. ICHR (INDIAN COUNCIL OF HISTORICAL RESEARCH)

HISTORY

The Indian Council of Historical Research (ICHR) is autonomous organizations under Ministry of Human Resources Development (MHRD), Government of India duly registered, vide Registration No. S 5339 dated 7th March 1972 under Societies Registration Act (Act. xxi of 1860) being an Act for registration of Literacy, Scientific and Charitable Societies.

The Ministry of Education & Social Welfare (now Ministry of Human Resource Development), Govt. of India, on 27th March 1972 founded the Indian Council of Historical Research (ICHR) on the recommendation of a Working Group set up by the Govt. of India in December 1971 comprising Professor R.S. Sharma, Patna University (Chairman); Professor Satish Chandra, Jawaharlal Nehru University;

Professor Tapan Ray Chaudhuri, Delhi University; Dr. S.N. Prasad, Director National Archives; Shri J. Veeraraghvan, Director (Internal Finance), Ministry of Education and Social Welfare; and Smt. S. Doraiswami, Deputy Education Adviser, Ministry of Education and Social Welfare.

AIMS & OBJECTIVES

The primary objective of the Indian Council of Historical Research is to promote and give direction to historical research and to encourage and foster objective and scientific writing of history. Enhancing the academic standard of the output of ICHR activities has been foremost objective in our agenda. The aims & objectives of the Council as laid down in the Memorandum of Association are as follows:

- To foster objective and scientific writing of history such as will inculcate an informed appreciation of the country's national and cultural heritage.
- To review the progress of historical research from time to time and indicate neglected or new areas where research needs to be specially promoted.
- To sponsor historical research programmes and assist institutions and organisations engaged in historical research.
- To provide technical assistance for the formulation of historical research programme by individuals or institutions and to support institutional arrangements for training in research methodology.
- To develop and support centres for documentation and reference service on historical research.
- To maintain a National Register of research workers in history and their fields of specialization.
- To initiate measures, in cooperation with State Archives and Regional Record Survey Committees, for the location, survey, listing and 'preservation of historical

material in private custody or in institutions lacking the necessary facilities.

- To indicate periodically areas and topics on which historical re-search is to be promoted and adopt special measures for the development of research in neglected or new areas of historical research such as economic and social history, historical geography, history of science and technology, history of arts, etc.
- To coordinate research activities in the field of historical research.
- To act as a clearing house of ideas and information on historical research in India and abroad.
- To organize, sponsor and support seminars, workshops, and conferences for the promotion and utilization of historical research.
- To promote publications of historical research of a high standard and to undertake publication of digests, periodicals and journals devoted to such research.
- To encourage the production of popular literature this would foster an objective understanding of India's cultural heritage.
- To undertake the compilation and publication of source material such as would facilitate historical research and historical writing;
- To institute and administer scholarships and fellowships for historical research.
- To develop a body of talented young historians and to identify and encourage research talent, encourage the young teachers in universities and other research organizations.
- To advise the Government of India on all such matters pertaining to historical research and training in history methodology as may be referred to it from time to time,

including co-operational arrangements in historical research and training facilities with foreign academic bodies.

- To enter into arrangements with the Government of India, State Governments and other public or private organizations or individuals for furtherance of its objectives, for implementation of its programmes and for securing and accepting endowments, grants-in aid, donations or gifts on mutually agreed terms and conditions.
- To acquire by gift, purchase, lease or otherwise any property, movable or immovable, which may be necessary or convenient for the purposes of the Council and to construct, alter and maintain any building or buildings for the purposes of the Council.
- To draw, make, accept, endorse, discount and negotiate Government of India and other promissory notes, bills of exchange or other negotiable instruments.
- To invest the funds of the Council in such securities or in such manner as may from time to time be determined be the Governing Body and, from time to time, to sell or transfer such investments.
- To take over and acquire by purchase, gift or otherwise from Government and other public bodies or private individuals, movable and immovable properties or other funds together with any attendant obligations and engagements not inconsistent with the objects of the Council.
- To sell. transfer, lease or otherwise dispose of any movable or immovable property of the Council; and
- Generally to take all such measures as may be found necessary from time to time to promote historical research and its utilization in the country.

FUNCTIONS

- To provide fellowships and financial assistance to the young teachers in colleges, Universities and registered research organizations, as well as to senior scholars who might need financial support.
- To bring historians together by providing financial assistance for holding symposia, seminars, workshops, etc for exchanging views related to history.
- To provide publication subsidy to the seminars, congress proceedings and journals so that these publications may reach to researchers and scholars.
- To publish a biannual Journal - the Indian Historical Review, and another journal Itihas in Hindi.
- To maintain a large and expanding Library-cum-Documentation Centre with facility of DELNET and J-STOR at the Headquarters at New Delhi, exclusively for researchers and scholars.
- To maintain three Regional Centres namely ICHR North-East Regional Centre (Guwahati), ICHR Southern Regional Centre (Bangalore) and ICHR Western Regional Centre (Pune) which also maintain Library-cum-Documentation Units enriched with research materials for the benefit of scholars and students of their respective regions and take such other measures as the Council considers appropriate in order to implement the stated objectives of the Indian Council of Historical Research.
- As envisaged in Para 2(q) of Memorandum of Association (MOA) 1972, the Council advises the Government of India on all such matters pertaining to historical research and training in history methodology as may be referred to it from time to time, including co-operational arrangements in historical research and training facilities with foreign academic bodies.

MISION

The importance of giving a proper direction to historical research and of encouraging and fostering objective and scientific writing of history is being increasingly recognized in the country. The subject gains not only form the point of view of national integration but also from that of the need to inculcate a healthy respect for our cultural heritage without encouraging a blind acceptance of superstition, obscurantism and revivalism.

It is equally important to promote application of historical method to the study of the social sciences and the humanities, so that an inter-disciplinary approach is achieved in an understanding of these subjects. The development and adoption of new historical methods have a bearing not only for the study of history but in improving and updating techniques and methods of social sciences and humanities as a whole. Indian Council of Historical Research is an autonomous body registered under the Societies Registration Act would help in achieving these objectives and in enunciating and implementing a national policy of historical research.

The frame-work within which the body works as follows:

- The Indian Council of Historical Research is consisting mainly of eminent historians of the Country.
- The Council covers history in its broader aspect including the history of art, literature and philosophy and allied subjects such as archaeology, numismatics, epigraphy and the historical study of manuscripts. It also promotes the study of any subject with a strong historical bias and content.
- The Council assists to promote scientific research in history and also associates with universities and research institutes not only in India but also abroad.

GRANTS

There is no deadline for submitting applications for fellowships and Grants from the ICHR. These are received throughout the year. However the meetings of the Research Grant Committees are held at regular intervals, after the receipt of the expert opinions upon the submitted applications as to the viability of a research project and/or symposia on the convenience of its chairman. The details of the fellowships and grants made by the ICHR are:

- National Fellowship
- Gurukul Fellowship
- Senior Academic Fellowship
- Post Doctoral Fellowship
- Junior Research Fellowship
- Research Projects Grant
- Foreign Travel Grant
- Seminars/Workshops/Conferences Grant
- Contingency (Study- cum-Travel) Grant
- Publication Subsidy

ICHR LIBRARY

The ICHR Library and Documentation Centre is the knowledge hub of ICHR and is designed to support the research objectives of the various units of the organization and also to act as a national facility to support scholars and researchers from India and abroad. It is a unique library having collections mainly in the fields of, Ancient History, Medieval History, Modern History, Archaeology, Anthropology, Philosophy, Religion and other allied disciplines. Our mission is to acquire, organize and update the library collection to support the teaching-learning and research activities.

The Library of this centre is stored with books including

reference books, new arrivals of display both books & journals and along with reading room facilities is situated at the 3rd floor of this building. The Documentation Centre is situated at the 2nd floor of this building with Wi-Fi enabled environment and is consisted of the reports, conference proceedings, theses and dissertations and other valuable source documents This Centre subscribes to more than 100 national and international journals in print, many e-Journals and also subscribing Online databases from different publishers. Apart from these, the Documentation Centre has a good collection of microfilms and microfiches.

LIBRARY SERVICES

Passport Services : The visiting scholar should bring original and valid photo ID - Passport (Foreign Scholars), and University issued ID (Indian Scholars) for easy access of services.

Photocopy Services : Photocopyi ıg (black & white as well as colour) facility shall be available on payment basis (to be notified from time to time) as per the provisions of the Copyright Act with special permission of the Librarian/ Incharge.

Microfilm/Microfiche Services: Microfilm/Microfiche readers have been provided for use of the scholars.

Inter-Library Loan : Material from other libraries may be obtained on Inter-Library Loan basis, if possible.

Computer Services : Scholars shall also be allowed to use computer terminals for accessing library information and other databases. They can also bring their own laptops for use in the library.

Print copies of microfilm : Scholars shall have the facility to get print copies of microfilm/microfiche after obtaining permission from the Deputy Director (Documentation) on payment basis (to be notified from time to time) under provisions of the Copyright Act/Restrictions placed in it.

- Online Databases
  - DELNET
  - JSTOR
  - Project Muse
- Digital E-Resources
- WEBOPAC
- New Arrival

ICHR PUBLICTION

- Indian Historical Review (Since 1974)
- ITIHAS (Shodh-Patrika)

SPECIAL PROJECTS

Indian Council of Historical Research (ICHR) promotes scientific research in History. Apart from regular granting of Research Projects, the Council undertakes Special Research Projects on various aspects of Indian History. The Special Projects aim to focus on a comprehensive approach to study the Historical aspects. The Council has made its contribution by undertaking Special Projects. These include:

Towards Freedom : Documents on the Movement for Independence in India.

Martyr's Project : Under this Project five volumes entitled: *Dictionary of Martyrs: India's Freedom Struggle (1857-1947)* covering various zones of Indian states have been compiled and edited. First three volumes have been published and remaining two volumes are under the process of publication.

1857 Project : In this Project, the ICHR made efforts to conduct various pictorial exhibitions and special seminars on the theme.

- Economic History of British Rule in India 1858-1947.
- Dictionary of Social, Economic and administrative Terms in India/South Asian Inscriptions

REFERENCES

- http://ichr.ac.in
- http://164.100.58.117/content/innerpage/history.php

9. LSE (LONDON SCHOOL OF ECONOMICS AND POLITICAL SCIENCE)

HISTORY

Supposedly the decision to found the school was made at a breakfast party on 4 August 1894. All believed in advancing socialist causes by reformist rather than revolutionary means, and the LSE was established to further the Fabian aim of bettering society, focusing on research on issues of poverty, inequality and related issues. This led the Fabians, and the LSE, to be one of the main influences on the UK Labour Party.

The School was founded by Fabian Society members Sidney and Beatrice Webb, Graham Wallas, and George Bernard Shaw, with funding provided by private philanthropy, including a bequest of £20,000 from Henry Hunt Hutchinson to the Fabian Society. In fact, Sidney and Beatrice Webb used the curriculum of the Institut d'Etudes Politiques de Paris (best known as "Sciences Po"), which covered the full range of the social sciences, as part of their inspiration for moulding the LSE's educational purpose. LSE was opened in October 1895 at number 9 John Street, Adelphi, originally as a night school to bring higher education to the working classes.

The School expanded rapidly and was moved along with its newly established library, the British Library of Political and Economic Science to number 10 Adelphi Terrace in September 1896. In 1902, The Coefficients dining club was regularly meeting in the Library, and they affected the development of LSE along with the Fabians and the Suffragettes movement (who also first met at LSE). In 1900, the School became officially recognized as a Faculty of Economics within the much larger University of London in Bloomsbury, and began enrolling students for bachelor's degrees and doctorates in the same year. At the same time, the LSE began expanding into other areas of social sciences, including, initially, geography (in 1902) and philosophy (in 1903), pioneering the study of international relations, as well as teaching history, law, psychology and sociology.

By 1902, it was apparent the School had and would continue to outgrow its Adelphi Terrace location, and moved to its present campus in Clare Market off the Aldwych and aside Kingsway-not far from Whitehall, in 1902. The Old Building, which remains a significant office and classroom building, was opened on Houghton Street in 1922.

In 1939, with the outbreak of the Second World War, LSE's Houghton Street campus became home to the Ministry for Economic Warfare, whilst following discussions between schools Director, Carr-Saunders and Winston Churchill, it was agreed to temporarily relocate the school to Cambridge, where it took over Peter house. Initially for a period of a year, the beginning of the Blitz led to LSE's post at Cambridge to be lengthened, returning to London in 1945.

At the other extreme, during these years Harold Joseph Laski, a professor of political science at the LSE was influential in British politics as an advocate of far left policies. Many renowned world leaders including John F. Kennedy (and his brother Robert F. Kennedy) studied under his guidance at the LSE.

LSE GOALS

LSE is one of the world's leading social science

universities. We have committed to a strategy that will build on our strengths, address challenges and maintain our worldwide reputation for excellence.

We have already achieved many of the goals set out in our 2014 review, including:

- Strengthening our faculty, this has resulted in remarkable success in the Research Excellence Framework and major improvements in most research-based and reputational rankings.
- Investing in our LSE Careers service for LSE alumni.
- Opening a new PhD Academy to nurture the next generation of leaders.
- Launching four new institutes, including The Marshall Institute for Philanthropy and Social Entrepreneurship and The International Inequalities Institute.
- Starting a major redevelopment of our campus, featuring a state-of-the-art 13 storey building overlooking a new public square.
- We have not been standing still. But rapid changes are taking place in higher education, and we need to change accordingly.

PRIORITIES FOR THE FUTURE

The LSE's future depends on enhancing our quality, our innovation, and our intellectual distinctiveness as a leading institution for social science. Our Strategy sets out a roadmap for how we intend to meet these challenges.

Our strategic priorities are to:

Education : We will lead in the provision of excellent disciplinary and interdisciplinary education. See our Education Strategy for details.

Strengthening and supporting faculty and staff : We will continually improve faculty quality, research performance and intellectual innovation and enhance the quality of our professional service staff.

Equity, diversity and inclusion : We will strengthen our commitment to equity, diversity and inclusion and take relevant action throughout the institution.

Leading globally in social science : We will lead and continue to be recognized as leaders in innovative, international, interdisciplinary and issue-oriented social science.

Diversifying our revenue streams : We will be enhance and diversify our revenue streams.

Developing our campus : We will secure an estate & other facilities commensurate with our standing and aspirations.

VISION

In considering the vision and direction of travel needed to remain a world-leading centre of excellence from now until 2030, the LSE communities were asked questions spanning six strategic themes:

- LSE's Founding Purpose
- LSE Education
- LSE Research
- Global Engagement and Impact
- Alumni Engagement
- Staff Engagement

SUBJECT DISCIPLINE

- Accounting and Finance
- Anthropology
- Economic History
- Economics
- European Institute

- Gender
- Geography and Environment
- Government
- Health Policy
- International Development
- International History
- International Relations
- Language Centre
- Law
- Management
- Mathematics
- Media and Communications
- Methodology
- Philosophy
- Psychological and Behavioural Science
- Social Policy
- Sociology
- Statistics

ORIGINS OF THE LIBRARY

The British Library of Political and Economic Science were founded in 1896, a year after the London School of Economics and Political Science. Arriving at a time when the social, legal and economic environment was becoming increasingly significant; providing materials from all over the world; the Library would enable such research and the 'laboratory' of the social sciences was born.

Sidney and Beatrice Webb led early fundraising efforts, capitalizing on their links to the Fabian Society and the London County Council. They were also motivated by the difficulties they had experienced during their own Academic research. The Library was initially housed in Adelphi Terrace, with the support of Miss Payne -Townsend, member of the Fabian Society and future wife of George Bernard Shaw, who sub-let the upper two floors of the building. The availability of larger accommodation in Clare Market led to further fundraising, culminating in the 1902 formal opening as pass more Edwards Hall, named after one of the Library's philanthropist supporters. In 1910 the first full-time Librarian took over from Sidney Webb. As the School itself grew the Library's acquisitions expanded; reinforced by major deposited collections, work began on a subject catalogue. The onset of World War II temporarily halted Library developments, with the collections moving to storage outside of London to avoid bomb damage. In 1945 the Library returned to activity, with many significant private collections and papers donated in the subsequent decades, and collections built to support LSE research and teaching.

LIBRARY SERVICES

Photocopying Services : Take your own photographs of items. Flash photography and scanners are not permitted.

Interlending Services : LSE staff and students can use the Interlending service if the material needed for your research is not held by the Library.

Data Protection guidance Services : Under the EU General Data Protection Regulation (GDPR 2018) researchers are responsible for the personal data they obtain and the subsequent use they make of it.

Self-service machines : Books should be borrowed and returned at the self-service machines. Follow the on-screen instructions or ask a member staff if you would like assistance.

Requesting material from store and archive collections : Complete a form in the 4th floor reading room or email us your requirements. Email requests take 2 working days for us to process.

Women's Library Reading Room : On the 4th floor of the Library, The Women's Library Reading Room is the space for using LSE and The Women's Library archives and special collections. Read about access to archives and special collections

Enquiries Desk : Enquiries staff is your first stop for help with the Library and its services. You can also contact the team by email or on Twitter

Exhibition Gallery : Visit our exhibition space by the entrance to LSE Library. Exhibitions change termly and are an opportunity to explore themes within our unique and distinctive collections. View information about our exhibitions.

Dissertation binding : Print & Copy Helpdesk staff can bind your work for you while you wait - it normally only takes a few minutes for this to be done. This service is offered throughout the year and is often used by students wanting to have their dissertation bound. We offer 'plastic comb binding' only so check your department requirements to ensure this meet expectations. A single set of plastic comb binding normally costs £2.50.

Lockers for LSE students : Library lockers can be hired for the academic year for a fee of £5. Due to the limited number of lockers available in the Library, lockers are allocated via a lottery system.

Support for people with disabilities : We are committed to providing full access to the range of services and facilities that we offer.

Physical access to the building : Access to the Library building is via a set of automatic doors, activated by the press of a button. Automated glass gates provide access through the entrances to the Main Library, LIFE area and the Course Collection area on the 1st floor.

Borrow, renew and request books : Visit this desk to get general help with borrowing, requesting material and any other issues to do with your Library account.

LSE Digital Library : Search LSE Digital Library for digitized material from the Library's collections and also born-digital material that has been collected and preserved in digital formats.

Data and statistics : There are 3 broad types of data services provide at LSE Library:

- Printed statistical data
- Online data
- Offline data
  - Microfilm or digital copies Services
  - New Arrivals Services
  - Thesis & Dissertation Services

RERERENCES

- http://www.lse.ac.uk/
- http://www.lse.ac.uk/library/about

10. SSRC (SOCIAL SCIENCE RESEARCH COUNCIL)

HISTORY

The SSRC was founded in 1923 by visionaries in the fledgling fields of anthropology, economics, history, political science, psychology, sociology, and statistics. The organization was shaped by the need to cross the boundaries that separated these disciplines from each other, university scholarship from public affairs, and the social sciences from the humanities and the natural sciences. It fosters innovative research, nurtures new generations of social scientists, deepens how inquiry is practiced within and across disciplines, and mobilizes necessary knowledge on important public issues.

The SSRC is guided by the belief that justice, prosperity, and democracy all require better understanding of complex social, cultural, economic, and political processes. We work with practitioners, policymakers, and academic researchers in the social sciences, related professions, and the humanities and natural sciences. We build interdisciplinary and international networks, working with partners around the world to link research to practice and policy, strengthen individual and institutional capacities for learning, and enhance public access to information.

The SSRC is an international, interdisciplinary network of networks dedicated to galvanizing knowledge and mobilizing it for the public good. For more than ninety years, the SSRC has navigated these borders, emerging as both a pivotal force in the academy and a respected contributor to the public good. Today, our work remains focused on enhancing the capacity of scholars and institutions and on building research networks that cross regions and disciplines to produce and communicate new knowledge.

SSRC BASIC COMMITMENTS

The SSRC approaches its work guided by five basic commitments:

1. Fostering innovation : We work on problems that need new approaches; we act as a catalyst for new thinking. We seek to mobilize the most creative and knowledgeable researchers and to help research institutions be more dynamic. Renewing existing expertise, putting knowledge to work on new problems, and generating novel data and theories are all crucial to advancing social science for the public good.

2. Investing in the future : We ensure the future of knowledge production through nurturing new generations of researchers, enabling practitioners to act on scientific knowledge, enhancing cross-fertilization among intellectual fields, developing capacity where it is most lacking, and facilitating the internationalization of social science.

3. Working internationally and democratically : Better understanding of basic social processes is a resource for improving the lives of all. It should be available to all. Participation in the production of scientific knowledge should also be as broad as possible. We support the internationalization of social science and opportunities for under-represented groups both as matters of equity and as requirements for ensuring that the production of knowledge is informed by different contexts and perspectives.

4. Combining urgency and patience : We bring researchers, practitioners, policymakers, and broader publics together to focus on topics of pressing public importance from health to human rights. But since even the most urgent problems are seldom solved overnight, we must learn even as we act, and we must continually renew existing knowledge.

5. Keeping standards high : Practical action, policy, and debate on major public issues all need to be informed by the best possible knowledge. This is produced by emphasizing scientific quality, engaging important public questions, and ensuring openness to critical analysis. Theory and research can then command the attention of those who approach practical issues with different values or agendas.

PURPOSE

The SSRC's organizational capacities focus on four intersecting purposes:

1. Supporting Innovation in Social Science Scholarship : By connecting disciplines and methods, the SSRC advances fresh ways to inquire, expand, and integrate the craft of social science.

2. Building Interdisciplinary and International Networks to Address Public Issues : The Council's experience and standing allow it to convene leading researchers and practitioners—from policymakers and UN leaders, to architects and artists, to journalists and activists—to generate new knowledge and explore solutions to pressing public matters.

3. Nurturing Scholars and Strengthening Institutions : Through fellowships, workshops, and mentorship, the SSRC identifies and supports the most promising young professionals across the social sciences. While supporting individual scholars, the SSRC is also deeply committed to improving worldwide conditions for knowledge production at an institutional level through capacity building, resource sharing, and networking.

4. Communicating and Explaining Social Knowledge : Relying upon diverse forms ranging from books and digital forums to conferences and public events, the Council seeks to deepen the comprehension of social science by journalists, policymakers, practitioners, and citizens. Through strengthening institutions and exploring digital frontiers, we also work to expand scholarly access to knowledge, particularly in areas where access has traditionally been limited.

TOOLS

- Graduate and postgraduate fellowships
- Convening policymakers and scholars
- Cross-disciplinary engagement and innovation
- Conferences and workshops
- Mentorship for young scholars
- Books and other publications
- Digital forums and resources
- Lectures and public events

PROGRAMS, FELLOWSHIPS & PRIZES

- AAS-SSRC Dissertation Workshop Series
- Abe Fellowship apply
- Abe Fellowship for Journalists apply
- African Peace building Network Book Manuscript Completion Grant
- African Peace building Network Collaborative Working Group Research Grants
- African Peace building Network Individual Research Grants
- China-Africa Peace Fellowship
- Conflict Research Fellowship
- Digital Literacy Initiative Travel Bursary
- DPD University Initiative
- Drugs, Security and Democracy Fellowship
- Global Scholars Initiative Writing Workshops apply
- International Dissertation Research Fellowship
- Japan Society for the Promotion of Science (JSPS) Fellowship
- Korean Studies Dissertation Workshop
- Korean Studies Workshop for Junior Faculty
- Mellon Mays Predoctoral Research Grants
- Negotiating Agreement in Congress Research Grants
- Next Generation Social Sciences in Africa: Doctoral Dissertation Completion Fellowship Apply
- Next Generation Social Sciences in Africa: Doctoral Dissertation Proposal Fellowship Apply
- Next Generation Social Sciences in Africa: Doctoral Dissertation Research Fellowship Apply
- Rachel Tanur Memorial Prize for Visual Sociology
- Sloan Scholars Mentoring Network Grants

- Social Media and Democracy Research Grants Apply
- The Albert O. Hirschman Prize
- Transregional Research Junior Scholar Fellowship: Inter Asian

LIBRARY SERVICES

- New arrivals services
- Thesis & dissertation services
- Inter library loan services
- Digital resources services
- Borrow, renew and request books services
- Data and statistics services
- Enquiries Desk services
- Photocopying Services
- Reservation Policy
- Online Payments
- Book Alert
- Web OPAC
- Audio/Video collection:
- Reports, Working Papers Services
- Library orientation
- Internet services
- Literature search services
- Digital projects services
    - CAKP Resource Hub
    - The Cities Papers
    - The Democracy Papers
    - The Immanent Frame
    - Items
    - Kujenga Amani

— Learning in Higher Ed
— Next Generation Social Sciences
— Parameters
— Research Matters
— Reverberations
— Sloan Scholars Mentoring Network
— DPDF Workspace
— Transregional Virtual Research Institute

REFERENCES

- https://www.ssrc.org
- https://www.ssrc.org/about/mission

Unit-IV

PLANNING OF SOCIAL SCIENCE RESEARCH LIBRARY

23

Planning of Library

INTRODUCTION

Planning is the deliberate, preferred manner of preparing for library service in the future. It is the responsible means of fulfilling future community library needs. A long-range plan, based on knowledge of the community, community expectations, resources of the community, and realistic projections of the future needs of the community will enable the library trustees and administration to perform their responsibilities better by providing efficient and progressive library service.

Every library shall develop, prepare and be guided by a long-range plan. (Planning for Library Excellence Revised).

What Is A Plan?

- A summary of the current status of the social science research library. Look critically at what the library does now. A plan is reality pushed into the future. By assessing the current situation, obvious needs and directions can be identified. Don't be afraid to brag about a good library.
- An assessment of community needs. A library's first responsibility is to address the needs of its community. It is basic planning to know what the community needs

are. The American Library Association has developed a number of tools that can help identify useful statistics and statistical sources for understanding a library's community.

- A statement of the library's mission, goals, and objectives. Once the library's overall role and mission are defined, specific goals with measurable objectives can be set. All decisions should be made in view of the plan.
- An ongoing process. Planning is an ongoing process. No plan is perfect. Unexpected events necessitate changes in any plan, and changing times present new problems and suggest new approaches to meeting library goals. Unless some crisis requires immediate updating of the plan, the plan should be updated on an annual basis.

TOOLS & TECHNIQUES OF SOCIAL SCIENCE RESEARCH LIBRARY PLANNING

How Is A Plan Developed?

There is no one best way to plan. Planning requires commitment, time, and organization.

1. Preparation for planning requires
   - Clarifying planning purposes and methods.
   - Defining responsibilities.
   - Allocating resources to planning.
   - Establishing a planning schedule.
2. Gathering the information for planning requires
   - Reviewing community needs for library services including cultural, educational, and informational resources of the community.
   - Looking at the demographic and economic data of the community.

- Identifying factors in the library's environment that may affect the provision of services.

3. Analyzing the information allows
   - Understanding of the community needs for library service.
   - Realizing objectively what the community has and what the community lacks. Defining the library's role in the community.
4. Development of a library's mission, goals, and objectives allows
   - Responsiveness to the community's needs, interests, and priorities.
   - Prioritizing programs and directing efforts toward tasks leading to the attainment of the stated objectives.
   - Evaluation of where your library is in relation to the total plan.

BENEFITS OF A PLAN

- Allows rational justification of your budget with governing authorities.
- Helps you prioritize programs and direct efforts to attaining objectives.
- Motivates the staff and board.
- Encourages coordination and accountability.
- Gives a clear measure for success.
- Assures enough lead time to undertake projects effectively.
- Leads to steady growth by encouraging yearly evaluation.

RECIPE FOR A PLAN

A plan is a flexible document seasoned by specific local needs. Most plans include the following:

- Description of the library's service area and communities
- Summary of data supporting library's needs
- Statement of general goals and specific objectives
- Details of services, programs, personnel, collection, and facilities desired
- Identification of priorities
- Timetable for achieving goals and objectives, both short- and long-range
- Cost projections for implementing the Plan
- Projections of resources
- Assignments and responsibilities for implementing the Plan
- Publicity campaign to accompany changes
- Provision for evaluation and reassessment at specific intervals

PHASES OF A PROPOSED SOCIAL SCIENCE RESEARCH LIBRARY BUILDING

1. Formation of library building committee : It is desirable to form a small building committee to handle the full process of library building. This committee may consist of representative from all concerned groups as well as the architect and the librarian. A building committee should be appointed to assist in the preparation of a concept programme evaluation of building plans. The building committee should consist of the following:

- The architect.
- The librarian.
- The library consultant.
- Interior designer.
- Head of the institution.
- Others.

Responsibility of Library Building committee : The responsibilities of library building committee are:

- The building committee should be charged with the responsibility for ascertaining the library's needs and for accumulating necessary data.
- The committee should consult as widely as necessary to determine the needs of the library.
- The committee should acquaint itself with the experience of other libraries with respect to new buildings.
- It should visit, if possible, some newer libraries and examine library building plans.
- With the assistance of the librarian and library consultant, the committee should make detailed estimates of the requirements of the different library units.

2. Arranging the library building programme : After building committee has completed it's planning it set down in writing, for the guidance of architect, a detailed, explicit statement of the requirements of the library. This statement may be prepared by the librarian by the library consultant, or by the architect in consultation with librarian or by the building committee itself. Space requirements should be given in detail. These requirements may be stated under such headings as: Space for books, space of readers (Seating), space for staff, and space required for other purposes.

3. Space estimates : In early stages of planning it is helpful to make some rough estimates of space requirements in terms of floor area. These estimates can be used in calculating probable cost of construction and they can be kept in mind when building sites are being considered. There is no standard measure that can be followed everywhere. A probable estimate for public and for university library are given below:

In Public Library

- For Magazine and periodical reader: 12 foot of superficial space each.
- Borrower estimated to be present one time: 20 square foot
- Normal Books: 10 volumes per square foot. But in reference section 7-8 volumes per square foot.

In University Library

- For library materials: 1 square foot per 15 volumes.
- Undergraduate students: 25 square foot per student.
- Graduate students: 35 square foot per student.
- Faculty Member: 75 square foot per member.
- Staff, counting and anticipated size: 100 square foot per person there are space requirements for stairways, corridors, ventilating of air conditioning and other accommodations.

4. The preliminary plans : The preliminary plan represents the most important phase of the whole planning process. The architect may produce a rough drawing of the main floor. The librarian has an important role in this preliminary plan. He should examine critically the architect's first drawing to determine whether adequate provision is being made for each library functions and whether the building as a whole will be sufficiently flexible and expandable for future use. After establishing the arrangement between the architect and librarian, the architect may draw the detail plan. If the cost estimates are satisfactory and no important problems remain, the preliminary plan will be approved and the architect will be authorized to prepare large plan and specifications.

5. Final plans and specifications : Final plans will consist of floor plans, elevations and sections and details of the structure. These will provide graphic illustrations of the building from several physical view points. The general constructions plans will be supplemented by separate set of drawings illustrating the design of the heating, ventilating and air-conditioning systems. There will be additional drawings illustrating the detailed design and location of many general and special features of the building such as stacks furniture etc. This plan will be supported written specifications describing the type and quality of materials to be used and any other information necessary for the builder. Then it can be placed for final approval of the committee.

6. Selecting the site : Where to locate the new buildings is an important question.

According to K. Metcalf, five major factors should be considered in selecting a sit.

Those are:

- Is its size adequate?
- What is its relation to neighboring buildings and to the whole population and traffic flow of the institution?
- What orientation is possible for a library building erected on it?
- Are there advantages or disadvantages in the slope of the land?
- What complications will arise from the nature of the ground beneath the buildings?

Simply, the site should be large enough to accommodate the present building and pursuit future expansion. The site should have an excellent surroundings and quiet environment. The library buildings should be situated centrally with pleasant surroundings and convenient accessibility where no contamination of air, sound etc. will occur.

PLANNING RESPONSIBILITIES FOR SOCIAL SCIENCE RESEARCH LIBRARY

Planning for Library Excellence, Revised (Draft) should be consulted for building-related state standards and guidelines. Trustees, staff members, consultants, architects, interior designers, city councils, county boards, jurisdictional staffs, regional planning departments, and community members all fit into the picture.

Trustees

- Determine that a new building is needed.
- Provide leadership in the campaign to inform the community and secure necessary support for the project.
- Appoint a building committee and assign tasks.
- Select and hire library building consultant.
- Select and hire an architect.
- Obtain financing for the project.
- Select and purchase the site.
- Approve the written building program.
- Approve preliminary and final architectural plans
- Solicit and approve bid documents
- Approve all contracts and any change orders to the contract

Library Staff

The library director and staff actively participate in planning for construction projects by compiling information, surveys, and statistics; by helping to prepare a written building program; by preparing building applications and reports; and by maintaining project records. The library director must be a member of the building team for accomplishment of a functional plan to support the library program.

Library Building Consultant

The consultant is usually an experienced librarian who has participated in several building projects. The cost of a building consultant can usually be saved many times over in reductions in construction and operating costs. Working with board and staff the building consultant can provide any or all of the following services:

- Survey the library's space needs
- Write the library building program
- Project a preliminary project budget
- Provide site analysis and recommendations
- Provide advice on funding options
- Provide assistance in selection of the architect
- Review all plans prepared by the architect and provide a written evaluation
- Review needs, specifications, and layout for shelving, furniture, and equipment
- Provide a final inspection of the facility

The Library Building Consultant of the Library Development and Networking Division of the Library of Virginia can provide building consultation advice and guidance.

We're set to go. What's next?

The board, with its planning completed, money in hand, and architecture in the final stages of plans, should follow this sequence:

- Review every nuance of the building plan. Decide what features can be optional (bid alternates) so that separate bids can be taken on these items.
- Review estimated costs so that the construction bids do not surprise.

- Follow all local ordinances and structures. Zoning and building codes should be checked as plans are made, but enlist the help of appropriate officials in the plan review and in recommending contractors to be asked to bid.
- Follow correct bidding procedures, legal and ethical. Allow time for bidders to estimate closely. Invite enough bidders so that there is a range.
- Analyze bids ruthlessly. Be sure you are getting what was specified with no unsuitable substitutes. Accept the bid that most closely meets specifications as well as offering good value.
- All bids too costly? You can call for new bids to an amended set of specifications. You can also rule out the optional features (bid alternatives) that did prove to be too much.
- Create a team of board, director, architect, and contractor to follow progress and to make regular reports.
- Expect some changes. Discoveries will be made about unexpected problems and opportunities. The contractor may suggest, for example, that a new tile may be less expensive and serve just as well as that specified. If so, that's a credit you can apply to something that will cost more (such as discovering poor soil on the site).
- Expect performance. This building is going to be a fixture in the community for a long time and should be properly and expertly built. Some boards find that the contractor has taken the job as a fill-in. doesn't accept excuses!
- Watch the expenditure of funds in a professional manager. Payments should be made upon proper evidence, but promptly. If you need financial advice,

seek it from a good mortgage banker or experienced purchaser of construction.

- Meet frequently during the building process. Meetings keep you in touch with progress, permit decisions on changes, and provide the material for ongoing public relations in the community.
- Plan for orderly occupation of the building, when it's ready, with festivities and community involvement. Allow plenty of time for moving in, completing the landscaping and other amenities, and then showing off the newest and best community asset.

OTHER ENVIRONMENTAL FACTORS

This plan was developed in a context of rapid, far-reaching technological and social change. For the most part, these changes are extensions of trends observed over the last few years; their continuance confirms strategic initiatives already in place and informs future development. These drivers include:

- Social networking, web services, Web 2.0 adoption, mobile devices, and the associated effects on user expectations;
- Further expansion of digital content, and a nascent shift from e-only access to e-only publishing;
- A move towards cloud computing, and the outsourcing of commodity IT services;
- Redefinition in the library automation market, with companies from different sectors offering convergent suites of services;
- A move towards more open systems and integration with open-source solutions;
- Still more complexity in intellectual property issues with emergent publishing forms and business models;

- Blending of roles for consumers and creators of content (user-contributed content);
- Increasing tendency for user communities to create their own tools for discovering, disseminating, and managing information

SOME CONCEPTUAL PRINCIPLES OF PLANNING WITH SOCIAL SCIENCE RESEARCH LIBRARIES

The traditional library doesn't meet the changing needs on information provision of today's information society. Library buildings, which are planned on old norms and standards, do not satisfy today's situation. Summarizing the results of above-mentioned research, we can formulate some principles of research library's activity and its architectural solutions.

1. Global and Special Collections : The Social Science Research Library to assumes the collection and preservation of print and other analog materials, as well as digital materials, together with a specialized staff of subject librarians, catalogers, and curators working with faculty and students to develop and interpret collections and services.

2. Digital Collections : As faculty and students work increasingly in virtual environments, deep and effective digital collections and services are essential. The Research Libraries will aggressively develop licensed, purchased, locally-created, and born-digital collections and related services to meet the re-search and teaching needs of the Social Sciences.

3. Effective Interfaces and Improved Access : This plan places a new emphasis on simplifying and improving access to digital and print resources and services. Research libraries will substantially improve search, discovery, and delivery, both in terms of improving local interfaces and by exposing social science resources to other search engines and discovery tools.

4. Planning of the building has to be flexible and simple : The planning of the building has to be flexible and simple in the general plan. There have to be possibilities of extension or transformation. That's why is advisable to use as much as possible movable columns, equally located ventilation, heating and aeration systems. The construction of light screens should also be easily movable from one to another to create a large space.

5. An internal garden in the middle of a building : It is advisable to design an internal garden in the middle of a building. This solution together with vertical and horizontal cabling allows an architect to create an optimal and aesthetic interior. Through the internal garden it is possible to achieve an architectural wholeness of the building and the interior.

6. Locate the storages on the underground floors : It is advisable to locate the storage-spaces on the underground floors and premises that need daylight on the over ground floors. The underground storage-spaces can be characterized by the following advantages: the possibility of rational usage of the collection, to locate it operatively, to organize more credible security of the collection, and make it much easier to maintain a proper temperature and humidity regime. The underground storage-spaces make it possible to design a compact building, and better its constructional, economic and exploitative indicators.

7. The Social Science Research Library has to exist in harmony with its natural and urban environment : The library has to become an organic part of the natural and urban environment.

8. The Social Science Research Library has to be comfortable : Comfortableness of service is one of the most important indicators of Social Science Research Library activity's value. This indicator includes: easy access to the library building, rational planning of the building and impressive architecture. There should be created a good working environment in the library: arranged individual carrels for intensive working and studying users, and well illuminated working places with dividing screens separating each place. Comfortableness also includes: providing the library with soft furnishing, plants, aquariums, soft carpet, large windows, balconies, premises for communication of people with different interests, and provisions with sound and video equipment. There is one more important demand for comfortableness. This is the accessibility of the collection. The collection has to be located according to library's collection profile, library's strategy and expectable users. The whole collection, arranged in subject groups, has to be located in different areas of open stacks.

9. A New Type of Social Science Research Library : Lastly, this plan expands the definition of a social science research library to include the work – focusing on the purposeful use of technology in learning and teaching, on partnering with researchers and scholars to share new knowledge, and on addressing the relationship between copyright law and the work of the University.

The social science research libraries participate in all of these initiatives, with a special focus on transformative change through strategic partnerships.

REFERENCES

• http://www.howard.edu/library/planning/Lib-Planning.pdf

24
Information Systems and Networks in Social Sciences at National Level

1. DELNET (DEVELOPING LIBRARY NETWORK)

INTRODUCTION

DELNET was started at the India International Centre Library in January 1988 and was registered as a society in 1992. It was initially supported by the National Information System for Science and Technology (NISSAT), Department of Scientific and Industrial Research, Government of India. It was subsequently supported by the National Informatics Centre, Department of Information Technology, Ministry of Communications and Information Technology, Government of India and the Ministry of Culture, Government of India.

DELNET has been established with the prime objective

of promoting resource sharing among the libraries through the development of a network of libraries. It aims to collect, store, and disseminate information besides offering computerised services to users, to coordinate efforts for suitable collection development and also to reduce unnecessary duplication wherever possible.

DELNET has been actively engaged with the compilation of various Union Catalogues of the resources available in member-libraries. It has already created the Union Catalogue of Books, Union List of Current Periodicals, Union Catalogue of Periodicals, CD-ROM Database, Database of Indian Specialists, Database of Periodical Articles, Union List of Video Recordings, Urdu Manuscripts' Database, Database of Theses and Dissertations, sample databases of language publications using GIST technology and several other databases. The data is being updated in these databases and is growing rapidly. All the DELNET databases have been resident on DELSIS, an in-house software developed on BASIS Plus, an RDBMS, the product of Information Dimensions Inc. of USA which has been provided to DELNET courtesy National Informatics Centre, New Delhi.

DELNET provides an array of facilities. DELNET'S relentless efforts in resource sharing have proved extremely effective. It has contributed a lot towards the modernization of libraries in India.

OBJECTIVES OF DELNET

The Main Objectives of DELNET are:

- To promote sharing of resources among the libraries by developing a network of libraries, by collecting, storing and disseminating information and by offering computerised services to the users.
- To undertake scientific research in the area of Information Science and Technology, create new systems in the field, apply the results of research and

publish them.

- To offer technical guidance to the member-libraries on collecting, storing, sharing and disseminating information.
- To coordinate efforts for suitable collection development and reduce unnecessary duplication wherever possible.
- To establish /facilitate the establishment of referral and / or research centres, and maintain a central online union catalogue of books, serials and non-book materials of all the participating libraries.
- To facilitate and promote delivery of documents manually or mechanically.
- To develop specialized bibliographic database of books, serials and non-book materials.
- To develop databases of projects, specialists and institutions.
- To possess and maintain electronic and mechanical equipment for speedy communication of information and delivery of electronic mail.
- To coordinate with other regional, national and international networks and libraries for exchange of information and documents.

DATABASE OF DELNET

Union Catalogue of Books : DELNET maintains an online union catalogue of books available in its member-libraries. This union catalogue is continuously updated and is growing in size. The information can be retrieved by author, title, subject, conference, series, etc. It has 2, 45, 45,450 bibliographic records. The request for inter-library loan can be placed through the online system.

Union List of Current Periodicals : DELNET has created union lists of current periodicals in science and technology, social sciences and humanities. This database is available online to DELNET users. It now lists 37,847 periodicals and is regularly updated and new titles are added annually. It is a major resource for Document Delivery Services.

Union Catalogue of Periodicals : DELNET maintains a union catalogue of periodicals, which contains full holdings data of the libraries. At present, the database contains 20,235 records.

Database of Periodical Articles : The database has details of articles which can be searched under the title, author, compiler, name of the periodical and subject. The database is being extensively utilized by the researchers and scholars. At present the database contains 9, 84, 809 records.

CD-ROM Database : A bibliographic database of CD-ROMs available with the member-libraries is being compiled. It has 58,831 records.

Union List of Video Recordings : This is a database of video cassettes available in DELNET member-libraries and has about **6,000** listings.

Union List of Sound Recordings : This union list consists of audio cassette records available in member-libraries. This database has **1,025** records.

Database of Theses and Dissertations : A database of Theses and Dissertations submitted to Indian Universities has been started, which covers various subjects. The database has **1, 02, 096** records.

Union List of Newspapers : The database has 70 records and contains information about the newspapers including title, name of the editor, published from, E-mail address and also the Web address of the INTERNET edition if available on the WWW.

Database of E-books : It has nearly 1613 records.

Profile of Member-Libraries : A directory of member-libraries is available and contains information about them.

DELNET also provides access to:

- Cambridge Dictionaries online.
- Networked Digital Library of Theses and Dissertations.
- ODLIS: Online Dictionary of Library & Information Science.
- GISTNIC Databases.
- MEDLINE & other databases of NLM.
- U.S. Patents: Full Text.
- Full Text Medical Journals.
- Open Access Journals.
- Engineering & Technology E-Journals: Table of Contents.
- Full-Text Medical Books.
- Full-Text Engineering & Technology E-journals.
- Learning Resources for LIS Professionals.
- Digital Libraries of the World.

SERVICES OF DELNET

Inter-Library Loan And Document Delivery Services: DELNET is offering inter-Library loan & Document Delivery Services to its member libraries. ILL requests can be registered online for books. For the resources not available in the union catalogues and journal articles, requests can be sent to DELNET through E-mail. DELNET has also prepared ILL Guidelines for use by the member-libraries. The services are quite popular among the member-libraries.

ILL Online (For members in Delhi)	Actual photocopying charges, if any, and courier/postal charges for books procured from outside Delhi will be extra.
ILL Online (for members outside Delhi)	Actual photocopying charges, and courier charges will be extra

Retro Conversion : DELNET offers retro conversion facilities to the libraries through specialized agencies and also facilitates the use of modern tools such as CO-ROM's and online facilities for retro-conversion.

Reference Services : DELNET maintains a referral centre which provides reference facilities to participating libraries. This centre also looks after the access to the central databases and provides prompt replies.

Professional Service/Training : DELNET arranges tutorials, workshops, lectures, and training programmes every year from time to time besides the National Convention on Knowledge, Library and Information Networking (NACLIN).

DELNET also offers : Announcements of the International Federation of Library Associations and Institutions (IFLA) and Library Science jobs globally. This information provides inputs to library and information professionals for improving their talent and professional expertise.

Technical Support : DELNET adopts the latest dependable technologies in information science. This helps libraries to get advice from DELNET to adopt technologies that emerge periodically. This also saves expenses and time of member-institutions. DELNET offers technical support to member institutions in the selection of:

- Hardware
- Software
- Communication Links
- Database creation
- Technical problems faced by member-libraries from time to time.

DELNET CONSORTIUM OF E-JOURNALS

- Gale Cengage Learning Packages

- **IESTC:** List of Engineering E-journals
- **IMC:** List of Management E-journals
- **IPC:** List of Pharmacy E-journals
- **IMedC:** List of Medical E-journals

- Pro-Quest Packages
  - List of Engineering/Technology E-journals
  - List of Management E-journals

MEMBERSHIP FEE

DELNET at present has 5985 libraries as its members, of which 270 libraries are in Delhi, 5690 outside Delhi in 33 States and Union Territories and 25 in overseas countries. Libraries interested in joining DELNET should apply on a prescribed form. The fees for membership are kept very low. At present the rates are as follows:

INDIA and Other SAARC Countries

Admission fee (one-time)	Rs.5,000/-
Institutional Membership Fee (Mandatory)	Rs.11,500/-per annum

Non-SAARC Countries

Admission fee (one-time)	U.S.$ 100/-
Institutional Membership Fee (Mandatory)	U.S.$ 500/-per annum

FUNCTIONS & ACTIVITIES OF DELNET

The main functions and activities of DELNET are:

Resource Sharing : DELNET saved foreign exchange worth Rs. 10 million by rationalizing subscriptions to foreign periodicals during 1991, 1992 and 1993 through resource sharing. This was mainly achieved in the fields of physical science, medical science and agricultural sciences.

Online Databases : DELNET has around twenty databases available online for their users which include Union Catalogue of Books (in member libraries), Union List of Current Periodicals, Union Catalogue of Periodicals, database of Indian Specialist (Who's who), multilingual Book Database, etc.

DDS : DELNET members can place their Inter-library loan requests through their ILL online facility, which is available on the union catalogue of books database. In 1991, a courier service was started on contract basis with a private agency for inter library lending among the participating libraries but it was not very effective. Later, DELNET introduced its own courier service with the financial help of NIC. The service is well used.

Development of Software : Earlier DELNET provided CDS/ISIS software for storage and retrieval purpose, developed by UNESCO through NISSAT, but presently it is distributing its own software DELSIS. It has also created software, viz. DELDOS and DEL-WINDOWS for creating MARC records.

Standardization : A standardization committee of DELNET has been meeting from time to time. DELNET uses CCF for interlibrary exchange of bibliographic data, accept AACR-II for cataloguing and LCSH is recommended for thesaurus.

Seminars, Conferences, Workshops and Training : DELNET also organizes national workshops, seminars and meets on library networking from time to time. DELNET has been organizing National Annual convention on Library and Information Networking (NACLIN) regularly. With the assistance of NISSAT and NIC it regularly conducts training programme on DELNET services, software, e-mail, subject heading of library of congress, AACR II, Internet, etc.

Publications : DELNET has been publishing a newsletter since January 1994 in order to spread the message and to increase awareness about library networking in India. It also publishes NACLIN Proceedings, Director's Report, etc. regularly.

Mailing Lists and Forum : DELNET has created a Listserv service called DEL-LISTSERV to provide the current awareness service to the users and allow the member libraries to receive the latest daily information from the internet automatically in the form of electronic mail. It also maintains other Listserv service such as Net-happenings, Med-clips, IFLA, LIBJOBS, etc.

Others : DELNET System for Information Services (DELSIS) is a powerful library networking software developed by DELNET. DELSEARCH is again, a database access mechanism developed by DELNET. DELNET is the first network which provides Email service in this country that was started in 1991. It provides this service through National Information Centre (NIC). The future of DELNET is very promising. Its membership with India and outside India is going to take a quantum jump. The DELNET databases are growing in number and size and as a variety of information on South Asia these are becoming available through DELNET. It is expected that all institutions outside India specializing in South Asian studies will take DELNET membership.

AREAS OF RESEARCH

DELNET has been conducting research in the following areas from its inception:

Use of International Standards : DELNET was the first institution in India to introduce MARC 21 standards among the libraries. Special training programmes are also organized from time to time in the use of MARC 21 Standard.

Open Source Software : DELNET is giving training in the use of KOHA - an Open Source Integrated Library System and DSPACE for building Digital Libraries. DELNET is glad to provide consultancy to the libraries on implementing these Open Source Software.

National Bibliographic Database : DELNET undertook the compilation of the National Bibliographic Database with the support of the Department of Culture, Government of India in 1998 as a Pilot Project. Fifty thousand records of books: 20,000 in English, 15,000 in Tamil and 15,000 in Punjabi were created at the Punjabi University, Patiala and International Institute of Tamil Studies, Chennai. At Andhra University Library, Visakhapatnam, 15,000 records in English and 10,000 records in Telugu were also created. Similarly 25,000 records each were created at the Asiatic Society, Mumbai and the Asiatic Society, Kolkata.

Creation of Union Catalogues and Union Lists : DELNET has been creating research tools for scholars and users in the form of union catalogues and union lists and these are widely used. The details are given in the section on Services.

REFERENCES

- http://www.delnet.nic.in/

2. INFLIBNET (INFORMATION LIBRARY NETWORK)

INTRODUCTION

The Information and Library Network (INFLIBNET) Centre was established as a project of IUCAA in 1991 and was recognized and as an independent, autonomous Inter-University Centre (IUC) of the University Grants Commission (UGC) in May 1996. Major activities and services of the Centre include automation of academic libraries and information centres, creation of union databases of resources (IndCat) available in academic libraries, promote resource sharing among academic libraries, promote information access and transfer, support scholarship, learning and academic pursuits. The Centre acts as a nodal agency for networking of libraries and information centres in universities, institutions of higher learning and R & D institutions in India with an aim to promote scholarly communication.

The technology being a driving force in the contemporary education system, the UGC has taken-up a major initiative for the benefit of academic community in universities under it s purview. The initiative called "UGC-INFONET Digital Library Consortium" provides access to selected scholarly electronic journals and databases in different disciplines. The Centre is responsible for execution and monitoring of this initiative. The Centre also extends access to e-resources to all Govt. / Govt.-aided colleges under a project entitled "National Library and Information Infrastructure for Scholarly Content (N-LIST)" funded by the MHRD under its National Mission on Education through ICT.

The Centre, on behalf of the UGC, has taken-up a number of new initiatives for the benefit of the academic community. These initiatives include:

Shodhganga : A reservoir of Indian Theses and Dissertations.

Shodhgangotri : A repository of synopsis submitted to the universities for registration under Ph.D. programme.

OJAS@INFLIBNET : An open access journal publishing platform.

Shibboleth : based access management system

Open source software R & D.

InfoPortal : A comprehensive gateway to all Indian electronic scholarly content.

E-PG Pathshala : E-Content for PG Courses.

Measuring Research Output of Indian Universities.

MISSION AND VISION

- Leveraging on the latest technology, create a virtual network of people and resources in academic institutions with an aim to provide effective and efficient access to knowledge through perseverance, innovation and collaboration.

- Provide seamless, reliable and ubiquitous access to scholarly, peer-reviewed electronic resources to the academic community in all educational institutions with a focus on services and tools, processes and practices that support its effective use and increase value of this information.
- Build and strengthen ICT infrastructure in educational institutions with value-added services.
- Develop tools, techniques and procedures for secure and convenient access management enabling users to access information in electronic format from anywhere, anytime.
- Develop resource selection guides and online tutorials for effective delivery and usage of e-resources.
- Facilitate creation of open access digital repositories in every educational institution for hosting educational and research content created by these institutions.

AIMS AND OBJECTIVES

The objectives of the Centre, as per the Memorandum of Association (MOA), are as follows:

- To promote and establish communication facilities to improve capability in information transfer and access that provide support to scholarship, learning, research and academic pursuits through cooperation and involvement of concerned agencies.
- To establish information and library network-a computer communication network for linking libraries and information centres in universities, deemed to be universities, colleges, UGC information centres, institutions of national importance and R & D

institutions, etc. avoiding duplication of efforts.

- To facilitate academic communication amongst scientists, engineers, social scientists, academicians, faculty, researchers and students through electronic mail, file transfer, computer/audio/video conferencing, etc.
- To undertake system design and studies in the field of communications, computer networking, information handling and data management.
- To establish appropriate control and monitoring system for the communication network and organize maintenance.
- To collaborate with institutions, libraries, information centres and other organizations in India and abroad in the field relevant to the objectives of the Centre.
- To promote R&D and develop necessary facilities to create technical positions for realizing the objectives of the Centre.
- To generate revenue by providing consultancies and information services.
- To do all other such things as may be necessary, incidental or conducive to the attainment of all or any of the above mentioned objectives.

PHYSICAL INFRASTRUCTURE

The INFLIBNET Centre has moved in January 2013 from its premises in Gujarat University Campus to its new Institute Building constructed at Infocity, Gandhinagar on the land measuring 10,000 Sq. Mtrs. allotted to the Centre by the Government of Gujarat, free-of-cost. The new building is located in the Infocity, Gandhinagar amidst reputed institutions such as NID, DAIICT and NIFT. The building of the Centre is designed by internationally acclaimed architect and renowned academician Dr Balkrishna V Doshi of Vastu-

Shilpa in consultation with other experts in the field of sustainable, eco-friendly and energy efficient building. Services of M/s. Katira Construction and M/s Malani Contractors, civil contractors, were hired for constructing the Administrative & Academic Blocks and Residential Blocks of the Building respectively and M/s. Ananjiwala Consultants, Project Management Consultants for quality control and for supervising the construction activity. The work for air-conditioning of the building is done by M/s Voltas and M/s. Siemens is system integrator for IT and low voltage infrastructure.

The construction of the Institutional building was started soon after the Bhoomi Pooja on 27th October 2009. The Foundation Stone for the Building was laid by the then Hone'ble Chairman, UGC and President, INFLIBNET Council Prof. Sukhadeo Thorat on 27th January, 2010. In the first phase, total built-up area of 1, 20, 000 sq. ft. has been completed that include Academic and Research Blocks, Administration, Library, Auditorium and Lecture Halls. In the second phase, 65,000 sq. ft. built-up area was completed including Hostels, Guest House, Staff Quarters, Director's residence, etc.

SERVICES AND TECHNICAL ACTIVITIES

The Centre undertakes a number of scientific and technical activities based on its functional requirements. Major R & D and human resource development activities are undertaken according to the requirements of the library and academic community including student, faculty and research scholars. Major services and technical activities undertaken by the Centre are given below:

1. Automation of University Libraries

The University Grants Commission, on recommendation of the INFLIBNET Centre, had supported

142 universities during IX Plan period and 24 universities during XI/XII Plan periods for automation of their libraries with software and training support from the INFLIBNET Centre. The total funds being allocated to 24 universities for automation of their libraries during XI/XII Plan Period is Rs. 195.60 lakhs including Rs. 6.50 lakhs for purchase of equipment (PCs, Servers, Accessories, Scanner, etc.) and Rs 1.65 lakhs recurring grant for five years. The Centre proactively helped universities that were funded for library automation during IX Plan Period to automate their libraries. Specialized training programmes were organized on topics related to library automation, standard bibliographic formats, tools and techniques and retro-conversion. An induction training programme on library automation was organized 24 university libraries that were given funds for library automation during XI/XII Plan Period.

2. IndCat: Union Catalogues of Indian Universities

The development of union databases of various library resources i.e. books, journals and theses has been one of the most important activities of the Centre since its inception. The union database named "IndCat: Online Union Catalogue of Indian Universities" created by the Centre is an outcome of the financial and logistic support offered to 166 universities by the UGC under its library automation scheme mentioned above. The number of records available in the IndCat database is as follows:

Books : 128+Lakhs bibliographic records from 157 university libraries with around 73.76 lakhs unique records.

Thesis : 2.5+Lakhs doctoral thesis submitted by 287 Indian universities/institutions.

Current Serials : 33,184 journal titles currently subscribed by 213 participating university libraries including journals from the UGC INFONET Digital Library Consortium.

Holding : 50,164 holding information of the serials from the 89 participating university libraries.

CEC's Video Database : 14,909 bibliographical records of educational video programmes produced by the CEC and its 17 EMMRCs.

The graphical user interfaces for IndCat was developed in-house by the Database R&D Group. These interfaces facilitate users to browse bibliographic information stored in union databases by subject category or by name of the university or chronologically by years and explore it by keywords, word in title, name of author or editor, etc. The interface also allows users to conduct search for a document in a single university, or universities in a geographical region or state. As such, in addition to being a Union Catalogue of resources available in university libraries, IndCat serves as a virtual catalogue for each participating university libraries. Most search interfaces for the union database support searching with varying degree of capabilities ranging from "simple search" to "advanced search" with Boolean operators. The Union database of books provides for downloading of selected bibliographic records in MARC21 format and porting them to MARC21-compliant integrated library software. It also facilitates the download features for CCF and ISO format.

All the union databases mentioned above are developed in an offline, i.e. universities send their bibliographic data to the Centre periodically in a batch mode. The Centre merges such records into its union catalogue after checking their correctness, their availability in other universities, etc. Efforts are being made to perform these activities in online mode. The Centre has already implemented the online mode for serial database.

The Centre has recently developed a new interface for Union Catalogue using open source enterprise search platform called 'Solr-based search interface'. The interface facilitates full-text search, hit highlighting, faceted search and dynamic clustering and database integration. It also facilitates users to conduct a single search across databases of books, theses and journals available in major university libraries in India. The beta version incorporates all the databases namely Books, Theses, Serials and CEC's Videos, hosted into IndCat server.

2.1. Subsets of Books Database

The union catalogue of books has two subsets namely GujCat and NERCat that are separately designed on demand of the concerned regions:

GujCat : The GujCat, a subset of IndCat, is unified online library catalogue of books available in major college/institute/university libraries within Gujarat state. GujCat contains bibliographic description, location and holdings information of books available in 33 libraries in Gujarat. A separate dedicated web-based interface is designed to provide easy-access to the merged catalogues of libraries in Gujarat. GujCat is a major source of bibliographic information that can be used for inter-library loan, collection development as well as for copy cataloguing and retro-conversion of bibliographic records within Gujarat.

NERCat : The NERCat, an online catalogue of books of eight universities in North-Eastern Region, is another subset of IndCat. The interface restricts the search within bibliographical records of the libraries resources available in the universities of the north-eastern states. NERCat is useful for the inter-library loan in the region.

2.2. Online Copy Cataloguing (OCS)

OCS is a Window-based application, developed by the Centre that facilitates libraries to interact with the Union Catalogue of Books (IndCat) and catalogue their new acquisitions online with an aim to promote co-operative cataloguing and avoid duplication of efforts. The OCS, on one hand, facilitates libraries to search and browse bibliographic records of documents available in IndCat and download selected records directly into SOUL 2.0 or any MARC21-compliant software. The holding information for the bibliographic record being downloaded from the IndCat gets updated automatically in the process. On the other hand, the interface facilitates creation of a new record for a document that is not available in the IndCat. This new record gets saved into local integrated LMS as well as into the IndCat. Besides, online cataloguing and copy cataloguing, the interface also facilitates bulk uploading and downloading of bibliographic records of books from IndCat.

2.3. CEC's Video Database: An INFLIBNET-CEC Collaborative Endeavour

The INFLIBNET Centre and Consortium for Educational Communication (CEC), in its endeavor to reach out to the unreached, are collaborating for dissemination of textual and visual resources through use and application of ICT. The INFLIBNET Centre and CEC, two Inter-university Centre of the UGC, provide information support for education and research to colleges and universities through their services and facilities. The INFLIBNET specializes in textual-based information retrieval services through its union databases and by facilitating access to full-text and bibliographic e-resources through consortium arrangements. The CEC concentrates on creation and dissemination of multimedia-based learning e-resources. Both the organizations make intensive use of Internet, Web and other communication technology to develop and disseminate their services. While both the institutions work primarily for the same goal, albeit separately, two institutions, in their endeavor to cooperate, coordinate and collaborate in the process of creation, development and dissemination of their resources and services, has recently launched Web-based interface to the CEC's Video Database consisting of 14,909 bibliographical records of educational video programmes produced by the CEC and its 17 EMMRCs. The interface was formally launched by Prof. S.K. Thorat, the then Chairman, UGC on 4th Dec., 2010.

3. Software for University Libraries (SOUL) (http://www.inflibnet.ac.in/soul/)

The SOUL 2.0 (Software for University Libraries) is state-of-the-art integrated library management software designed and developed by the INFLIBNET Centre with experience gained by the Centre over the years based on requirements of colleges, universities and other academic libraries. While the first version of the SOUL Software was released in Chennai at the CALIBER 2000, the 2nd version of SOUL Software named "SOUL 2.0" was released by Prof. S. K. Thorat, the then Chairman, UGC in January 2009. SOUL 2.0 is user-friendly Window-based software developed to work under client-server environment. The software is suitable not only for the academic libraries but for all kinds of libraries. The Unicode-based and MARC21-compliant SOUL 2.0 has six integrated modules, i.e. Acquisition, Cataloguing, Circulation, Serials Control, OPAC and Administration. The software is compliant to international standards such as MARC 21 to facilitate data transfer and exchange; Unicode to facilitate handling of multilingual content, SIP and NCIP for RFID compliance, FRBR to support functional requirement for bibliographic records, etc. The new version was received well by the libraries in India. The software has more than 2700 installations across the country. The Centre has developed SOUL Query Management Software for effective and efficient handling of queries from its users.

3.1. SOUL Query Management System (SQMS)

SOUL Query Management System (SQMS) is designed to handle and manage user's query about SOUL Software. The system is used for extending online support to the users of SOUL software and for handling queries from SOUL users. SQMS consists of two modules i.e. System User and SOUL Users. System User Module is designed for use of administrator to monitor and manage the queries fed to SQMS. System User Module provides system user's list, queries received list, query details, query status, query track, etc. SOUL User Module is designed for use by the end users for registering their queries. All SOUL users are end user of this system. Users can perform operations like feed queries, check status of their queries, add contact person details from the institute including their institute details, etc.

3.2. SOUL Support Services

The Centre has appointed seven SOUL Coordinators in different geographical regions of the country. Besides, the INFLIBNET Centre coordinates activity of maintenance and promotion of SOUL Software in the state of Gujarat and Rajasthan. The Centre uses multiple methods to reach out to the SOUL users and resolve their query in real time including a dedicated helpline (079-2623-8300), Google-chat and Team Viewer for remote access to SOUL servers of users.

3.3. UGC-INFONET Internet Connectivity Programme

Connectivity is one of the crucial infrastructural requirements for providing access to e-resources to universities. The UGC-INFONET Internet Connectivity Programme was launched in 2002 for bringing qualitative changes in academic infrastructure of higher education. The programme was renamed as UGC INFONET 2.0 with switching over of ISP from ERNET India to BSNL i.e. 1st April 2010 with an aim to provide higher and scalable Internet bandwidth to universities. In the new scheme 10 Mbps Internet bandwidth was being given to more than 180 universities on fiber-optic leased line. The INFLIBNET played an important role of monitoring and liaisioning between the BSNL and the universities. Since UGC Infonet 2.0 was using Fiber backbone, it paved the way for successful establishing National Knowledge Network (NKN) infrastructure in these 180 universities that provides 1 GB connectivity to all universities. As on 31st March, 2012, all universities have migrated to NKN / NME-ICT and are availing 1 GB/120 MB Internet bandwidth. The UGC Infonet 2.0 stands subsumed into National Knowledge Network. A new format for UGC INFONET is proposed to the UGC for better utilization of NKN by beneficiary universities.

4. Consortia-based Subscription to E-resources

The INFLIBNET Centre has set-up two separate consortia, namely UGC-INFONET Digital Library Consortium and N-LIST to extend access to e-resources to universities and colleges respectively. Two separate consortia were established not only to cater to the diverse needs of two sets of institutions, namely universities and colleges, but also to satisfy the requirements of different funding sources and economic models. A brief description of the two consortia is given below:

4.1. UGC-Infonet Digital Library Consortium & its Associate Membership Programme

The UGC-Infonet Digital Library Consortium was launched by Dr. A.P. J. Abdul Kalam, the then President of India in December 2003. The Consortium provides current as well as archival access to more than 8,000 core and peer reviewed electronic journals and 11 bibliographic databases from 28 publishers including university presses, scholarly societies, commercial publishers and aggregators in different disciplines. The programme has been implemented in a phased manner. In the first phase that began in 2004, access to e-resources was provided to 50 universities who had Internet connectivity under the UGC Infonet Connectivity programme. In the second phase, 50 more universities were added to the programme in the year 2005 as additional universities got Internet connectivity through UGC-INFONET programme. So far 206 universities that come under the purview of UGC have been provided differential access to subscribed e-resources. These e-resources cover almost all subject disciplines including arts, humanities, social sciences, physical sciences, chemical sciences, life sciences, computer sciences, management, mathematics and statistics, etc. The Centre has also initiated Inter-Library Loan (ILL) through JCCC (Journal Custom Content for Consortium). The JCCC provides article-level access to all the articles published in journals subscribed by the UGC-Infonet Digital Library Consortium as well as in journals subscribed by 26 university libraries designated as ILL Centres of the INFLIBNET Centre. Two new resources, namely Elsevier's Science Direct and Wiley Inter Science journals were added based on the demand of user's community from 2011 onwards.

4.2. Associate Membership Programme of the UGC-INFONET Digital Library Consortium

Success of UGC-Infonet Digital Library Consortium in the universities led to the demand for extension of the Consortium resources to the universities that are not under the purview of UGC. The Centre has initiated its Associate Membership Programme in 2009 with an aim to extend access to e-resources subscribed by the Consortium to private universities and other research institutions. Under the scheme, private universities and other research institutions can enroll themselves as "Associate Member" of the Consortium and subscribe to resources of their choice available through the Consortium. The rates of subscription to e-resources are same as applicable to the Consortium for its core members. Associate members are charged a token amount as annual membership fee. More than 177 members have enrolled themselves as associate members of the UGC-INFONET Digital Library Consortium and are subscribing to various resources of their choice through the Consortium.

4.3. Access to E-Resources for Walk-in Users

The Centre has more than 20 Internet enabled PCs dedicated for the walk-in users including students and researchers for accessing electronic resources subscribed under the UGC-Infonet Digital Library Consortium. The license agreements signed with the publishers of e-resources provides access to e-resources for "walk-in" users. The INFLIBNET Centre, as the coordinating agency for the consortium, gets complementary access to all e-resources subscribed under the Consortium. Students from Gujarat University and Central University of Gujarat and its affiliated colleges and students from the nearby universities and colleges are welcome to access e-resources subscribed under the Consortium. Around 1000 users per annum visit the Centre for accessing e-resources.

4.4. RSS Feeds Aggregation Services

The Centre has developed and installed RSS Feed Aggregation Service on its website. The service is targeted to users of the UGC-Infonet Digital Library Consortium. The RSS Aggregation Service facilitates RSS links to open on the website of the Centre for all electronic journals that are covered in the Consortium and have option for RSS feeds. Resultantly, the users, instead of copying RSS feeds into their RSS Feed Readers, can visit the INFLIBNET website and read the current contents of all the journals subscribed under the UGC-Infonet Digital Library Consortium. These

RSS Feeds are arranged according to subject categories as well as alphabetically. Moreover, journals covered under the RSS Feed Aggregation Services can also be searched according to the subject category and by words in journal titles. The RSS Feed Aggregation Service at the Centre offers the following options:

- INFLIBNET's News RSS
- Search for RSS Feeds
- Subject-wise/Publisher-wise RSS Feeds
- My RSS: Select your own set of journals and get their RSS feeds
- My Feed Reader

4.5. N-LIST (National Library and Information Services Infrastructure for Scholarly Content)

The Project entitled "National Library and Information Services Infrastructure for Scholarly Content (N-LIST)", being jointly executed by the UGC-INFONET Digital Library Consortium, INFLIBNET Centre and the INDESTAICTE Consortium, IIT Delhi, provides for access to scholarly content to colleges, universities as well as centrally funded technical institutions through its four distinct components i.e.

- UGC-INFONET e-resources to technical institutions (IITs, IISc, IISERs, NITs, etc.).
- INDEST e-resources to universities.
- E-resources to Govt./Govt.-aided as well as non-aided colleges.
- National Monitoring Agency at the INFLIBNET Centre to manage access, monitor, promote and impart training to promote optimal usage of e-resources and for monitoring all activities involved in the process of providing effective and efficient access to e-resources to colleges.

5. Open Access Initiatives

Open access initiatives taken-up by the Centre includes OJAS, a platform offered to faculty and researchers in universities to host their open-access journals, and three institutional repositories, namely ShodhGanga, Shodh Gangotri and IR@INFLIBNET. These initiatives are described below:

5.1. Shodhganga: A Reservoir of Indian Theses

Shodhganga is a digital repository set-up for submission of electronic version of theses and dissertations by research scholars in universities in India and make them available in open access to the world-wide academic community in response to the UGC Notification (Minimum Standards & Procedure for Award of M.Phil./Ph.D Degree, Regulation, 2009) where-in the responsibility of maintaining the digital repository of Electronic Theses and Dissertations (ETDs) is assigned to the INFLIBNET Centre. ShodhGanga is set-up using DSPACE that uses internationally recognized protocols and interoperability standards. The repository provides a platform to research students in universities to deposit, reuse and share their theses and dissertations. Organization of ShodhGanga reflects academic structure of participating universities to facilitate submission of theses in the respective Department/ Centre of a university. Ingestion interface of DSPACE has been customized to meet the specific requirements and make the process of submission easy and simple. The customized ingestion interface is simple to use and involves lesser number of steps in comparison to default submission interface of DSPACE. The interface facilitates submission of theses either by university administrators, university representatives or researchers themselves once they get themselves registered.

The interface also facilitates self-registration of scholars wherein user gets e-mail alerts and notifications at different stages of workflow. The ShodhGanga Website provides all information relevant to the students, research supervisors and university authorities with regard to ETDs including their responsibilities, access policies, submission process, metadata structure, etc. Considering the fact that process of adaptation of the UGC Notification, 2009 may take time for universities, research students are encouraged to submit electronic version of their Ph.D theses into the ShodhGanga on voluntary basis. Once the submission of theses is mandated by a university, process of submission of theses can be monitored by respective universities so as to ensure that correct and final version of all the theses from a given university are submitted into the Repository.

As on 1st June, 2013, researchers from 133 universities have started submitted their theses into the repository and 118 universities have signed MOU with the INFLIBNET Centre on Shodhganga and total number of theses submitted into the repository has grown to 7,606.

5.2. ShodhGangotri

A Repository of Synopsis submitted to Indian Universities for Registration in Ph.D Programme "ShodhGangotri" is a new initiative that compliments "ShodhGanga". While ShodhGanga is a repository of full text thesis submitted to universities in India, "ShodhGangotri" hosts approved synopsis of research topic submitted to the universities in India by research scholars for registering themselves under the Ph.D programme. Under the new initiative called "ShodhGangotri", research scholars / research supervisors in universities are requested to deposit electronic version of approved synopsis submitted by research scholars to the universities for registering themselves under the Ph.D programme. The repository, on one hand, would reveal the trends and directions of research being conducted in Indian universities; on the other hand, it would avoid duplication of research. Synopsis in "ShodhGangotri" would later be mapped to full-text theses in "ShodhGanga". As such, once the full-text thesis is submitted for a synopsis, a link to the full-text theses would be provided from ShodhGangotri to Shodhganga.

5.3. *IR@INFLIBNET*

The Centre has established an institutional repository called IR@INFLBNET using DSPACE, open source software accessible at http://ir.inflibnet.ac.in/. The papers published in the proceedings of the CALIBER and PLANNER, are uploaded in to the repository in PDF format. The Repository also includes course materials, newspaper clippings, etc. The repository has 1,274 full-text articles.

5.4. *Open Journal Access System*

The Open Journal Access System (OJAS) at INFLIBNET Centre uses Open Journal System (OJS), an open source solution developed by the Public Knowledge Project through its federally funded efforts to expand and improve access to research. The OJS is designed for managing and publishing scholarly journals online. It is a highly flexible editor-operated journal management and publishing system that has been designed to reduce the time and energy devoted to the clerical and managerial tasks associated with editing a journal, while improving the record-keeping and efficiency of editorial processes. OJS also supports content in multiple formats including text (structured and unstructured), audio, video, graphics and animation, etc. and reading tools for content. It seeks to improve the scholarly and public quality of journal publishing through a number of innovations, from making journal policies more transparent to improved indexing. OJS is compliant to Open Archives Initiative Protocol for Metadata Harvesting (OAI-PMH).

The INFLIBNET Centre has installed and configured

Open Journal System on servers at INFLIBNET to facilitate hosting of electronic versions of journals into open access mode with all processes of submission, peer-reviewing, editing, layout designing and publishing built into it. The initiative encourages universities and institutions that are publishing journals in print format to use OJAS @INFLIBNET for hosting electronic version of their journals free of cost on servers at the INFLIBNET Centre. The initiative also encourages faculty in universities to start their own open access journals using the platform offered by the INFLIBNET Centre. Journals hosted on OJAS @INFLIBNET are accessible to all users world-wide without any restrictions. Currently, Open Journal Access System @INFLIBNET hosts fourteen journals from different universities and other institutions.

6. Shibboleth-based Access Management System

The INFLIBNET Centre, as one of its core mandate, provides access to scholarly e-resources to universities and colleges in India under the UGC–INFONET Digital Library Consortium and N-LIST Programme. At present, access to e-resources in universities is IP-authenticated and, as such, access is restricted within the confine of a given university campus due to lack of proper authentication mechanism. The Centre is working towards deploying appropriate access management tools, enabling users to access e-resources from his/her campus, home or even while travelling. The Shibboleth is standard-based open source middleware software that provides Web-based single sign-on (SSO) access across all subscribed e-resources or within organizational boundaries so as to enable users to access e-resources from anywhere irrespective of his / her physical location. It allows web sites to make informed authorization decisions for individual access to protected online resources in a privacy preserving manner. Implementation of such a solution requires setting-up of proper user authentication and access control mechanism ensuring trust relationship between publisher, identity providing agency and the user institution.

The Shibboleth working architecture requires each participating institution to set-up their identity provider services (IDP). Looking at the present scenario, universities and colleges do not have requisite technical knowhow and ICT infrastructure, as such; the INFLIBNET Centre took-up the task of acting as an IDP for all its core and associate members, including universities and colleges under its umbrella. The implementation of Shibboleth technology at INFLIBNET Centre would function in the following manner:

- The service providers (publisher) will recognize INFLIBNET Centre as a trusted organization for authenticating the user and give an option on their Web sites to select INFLIBNET as an IDP.
- When a user chooses INFLIBNET as its IDP, he / she would be re-directed to IDP link at INFLIBNET Server.
- After verifying user's credentials, IDP at INFLIBNET will pass "user attributes" to the publisher which would include user's institute, department and role as faculty / student / researcher.
- Once authenticated, user gets access to his / her authorized e-resources. Unauthenticated users are denied access.

Shibboleth implementation at the INFLIBNET Centre was tested with Shibboleth test site and IDP service was tested with three publishers, namely Royal Society of Chemistry, Cambridge University Press and Institute of Physics. Proposal for setting up INFLIBNET Access Management Federation (INFED) was approved by the Governing Board of the INFLIBNET Centre. INFED and its website (parichay.inflibnet.ac.in) has been set-up with all requisite documentation.

7. Open Source Software R & D

Open source software is computer programs where source code is made available to the general public for use and / or modification from its original design free-of-charge. Open source programs are typically created as a collaborative effort in which programmers improve upon the code and share the changes within the community. There are a number of open source software in the field of library and information science that are available free of cost. The Centre has created R & D facilities and working groups to study and contribute actively to the open source movement. Moreover, the Centre has taken a cautious decision to move all its crucial operations to open source software. To begin with, Open Office was implemented in place of MS Office in the Centre. Open Source Laboratory was set-up at the Centre with PCs loaded with different versions of LINUX operating systems including Redhat, Fedora, Ubuntu etc. and Library Management Software like NewGenLib and Koha were installed on these machines. DSPACE, E-Print Archives and Greenstone Digital Library Software are also installed for testing and developing digital library for various applications in the Centre. All the union databases of the INFLIBNET Centre that were earlier hosted on MS-SQL have been moved to MYSQL, open source relational database management software. All the websites of the INFLIBNET Centre including UGC-INFONET Digital Library Consortium, SOUL, IndCat, N-LIST, OJAS, etc. are designed using open source software such as Apache, MYSQL, Tomcat, PHP, Java Script, PERL, etc. The ingestion interface for "ShodhGanga", setup using DSPACE, was custom-developed using open source tools to facilitate online submission of electronic theses into the repository. The Centre's Website offers RSS Feed Aggregation services implemented using PHP and MYSQL. Various open source Web 2.0 tools have also been implemented such as INFLIBNET Blog using Word Press, INFLIBNET Wiki using

Media Wiki, INFLIBNET Chat using PHPChat etc. to facilitate better interaction and collaboration between users and staff of the INFLIBNET Centre. Open source PHPBB is setup for INFLIBNET Bulletin Board. Apart from implementing various open source software, the Centre has also contributed following utilities to the open source community.

7.1. Conversin Utilities: CCF to MARC21 and Excel to MARCXML

CCF to MARC21 and Excel to MARCXML conversion utilities were developed and contributed as open source software for the benefit of libraries having MARC 21 compliant Library Management Software. Using CCF to MARC21 conversion, libraries can migrates CCF based records into MARC21 format which can be transported to any MARC21 compliant Library Management Software. Excel to MARCXML can be used to convert bibliographic records into MARCXML. Once the data is converted in MARCXML, the bibliographic records can be easily imported into SOUL2.0 or any other MARC21-compliant LMS without any data loss.

8. VIDWAN: Subject Expert Database

VIDWAN is a premier database of profiles of scientists / researchers and other faculty members working at leading academic institutions and other R & D organisations involved in teaching and research in India. It provides information about expert's background, contact address, skills and accomplishments. The University Expert Database was launched in the year 1999 that contained profiles of the subject expert serving in the universities and other academic institutions in India. In the year 2001, the Centre developed another database called Expert Database in Science and Technology with financial support from the National Information System for Science and Technology (NISSAT),

DSIR that contained profiles of experts working in the R & D organizations, particularly in science and technology areas.

These two databases were merged in the year 2012 and rechristened as VIDWAN: Expert Database. The database contains around 9,000+ profiles of the subject experts from various domains from 650 institutions.

9. Info-Port: A Subject Gateway to Indian Scholarly Internet Resources

Info-Portal : A Subject Gateway to Indian Electronic Resources is designed and developed by the INFLIBNET Centre to serve as a comprehensive gateway to all Indian scholarly content. The gateway open-up the Indian scholarly content scattered over the Internet through an integrated interface that support search, browse and multiple listing of more than 1,700 e-resources. The Info-Portal uses "Subject Gateway Management System (SGMS)" as hosting platform. The SGMS, designed and developed at the INFLIBNET Centre, facilitates entry of Internet resources and extending its access to users. SGMS supports browsing of Internet resources by Dewey Decimal Classification (DDC) Scheme. The main functional components of SGMS are:

Dewey decimal classification (DDC) Search : Internet resources fed into SGMS are organized accordingly to DDC classification (from 000 to 900). On clicking at main classes, sub-classes are displayed as per the DDC classification scheme. Users can see the list of electronic resources available under the sub-classes with brief description of each resource.

Search Cloud : Keywords that appear in DDC are shown as link in search cloud. Most frequently used keywords appear on homepage of SGMS with number of hits for that keyword. Users can access resources by clicking on the keyword that appears on the search cloud. Keywords that are searched more frequently are displayed in larger and bolder size as compared to other keywords.

Free-Text Search : Searches can be performed on words that appear in title of resources, keywords that are assigned to Internet resources and words that appear in the description of e-resources, etc.

Alphabetical Listing : Users can browse list of subjects arranged alphabetically.

Resource Type Search : User can also browse Internet resources by type i.e. corporate website, e-book, e-journals, personal websites, portals, etc.© INF

10. Bibliometric and Scientometric Studies

The Bibliometric Group was set up to study the impact of access to e-resources on research productivity in universities in India. Research profiles are being developed for every member university. These profiles include research output of a university including annual and cumulative growth of research publications over a period of four decades, impact of research in terms of citations received, H Index, focused areas of research of a university including its strength and weaknesses, international and national collaborations in different disciplines, correlation between number of articles downloaded from e-resources and number of research articles produced by researchers in a given university. Web of Science is being used for source as well as for citation data. Research profiles for 50 universities have already been completed.

11. E-PG Pathshala: A Gateway to All Post Graduate Courses

The INFLIBNET Centre has been assigned the task of coordinating all activities involved in production of e-contents at postgraduate level in 77 subject areas under the initiative called e-PG Pathshala funded by the MHRD under its National Mission on Education through ICT. The Centre is responsible for the technical as well as administrative coordination of this project. An open source Learning Management System called "A Tutor" has been configured to host e-contents created in this project and developed e-Pathshala Management System to manage the administrative workflow as well as a platform that facilitate interaction among the team members of each subject and track the progress made by contributors, i.e. paper coordinators, content writers and reviewers. Development of e-contents in 35 subjects has already been started. Moreover, the Centre has taken the responsibility for content creation for two subjects i.e. Library Science and Information Technology (in coordination with Gujarat University). The guidelines for execution of projects under e-PG Pathshala and as well as guidelines for content writers along with templates for content creation was developed and approved by the UGC. A national workshop involving subject coordinators, content writers and members of the standing committee was organized. Besides, seventeen subject-based workshops were organized for subject coordinators, paper coordinators and content writers. As on 1st June, 2013, twelve e-modules have been developed and are hosted on the LMS.

12. Human Resource Development and Consultancy

Imparting training to manpower working in the university and college libraries in the use of IT is an important objective of the Centre and has been given due priority. 535 training programmes, workshops and seminars focusing on the library automation and networking have so far been conducted till 1st June, 2013 benefitting 42,942 participants. INFLIBNET Regional Training Programme for Library Automation (IRTPLA) and User Awareness Training Programmes on e-resources subscribed under the UGC-INFONET and NLIST project were conducted across the country in collaboration with the universities. National and international conventions called PLANNER in North-eastern regions and CALIBER in various states in India are being organized biannually as part of the human resource development activities. The Centre has also conducted 105 Training Programmes on SOUL Installation and Operations for Libraries.

REFERENCES

- http://www.inflibnet.ac.in
- http://indcat.inflibnet.ac.in
- http://www.inflibnet.ac.in/soul
- http://www.inflibnet.ac.in/feed
- http://nlist.inflibnet.ac.in
- http://shodhganga.inflibnet.ac.in
- http://shodhgangotri.inflibnet.ac.in
- http://ir.inflibnet.ac.in
- http://www.inflibnet.ac.in/ojs
- http://parichay.inflibnet.ac.in
- http://vidwan.inflibnet.ac.in
- http://infoport.inflibnet.ac.in
- http://epgp.inflibnet.ac.in

3. NASSDOC (NATIONAL SOCIAL SCIENCE DOCUMENTATION CENTRE)

INTRODUCTION

National Social Science Documentation Centre (NASSDOC), was established in 1969 as a Division of the ICSSR with the objective to provide library and information support services to researchers in social sciences; those working in academic institutions, autonomous research organizations, policy making, planning and research units of government departments, business and industry etc. NASSDOC also provides guidance to libraries of ICSSR Regional Centres and ICSSR supported Research Institutes.

FACILITIES AVALIBLE AT NASSDOC

- Documentation Library and Reference Service.
- Collection of unpublished doctoral dissertations, research project reports, current and old volumes of social science journals of Indian and foreign origin.
- Literature Search Service from printed and digital databases, i.e. CD-ROMS, floppies, online database etc.
- Study grant to doctoral students for collection of research material from various libraries located in different parts of India.
- Compilation of short bibliographies on request.
- Financial assistance is provided for taking up bibliographical and documentation projects.
- Document Delivery Service is provided by procuring books and journals on Inter-library loan or by photocopying the documents.
- Short-term training courses are organized for the research scholars, social scientists, librarians and IT professionals to acquaint them with the latest information and communication technology.
- Cyber Cafe, to facilitate access to internet resources on social sciences

NASSDOC SERVICES

Library and Reference Service : The ICSSR-NASSDOC library has a collection of reference sources viz. bibliographies, encyclopedias, doctoral theses, research project reports, books on social science research methodology, computer and information technology and research surveys and on all social science disciplines. The collection is augmented by bound volumes of periodicals, Indian/foreign periodicals including ICSSR publications and other abstracting and indexing journals in social sciences, newsletters and annual reports of organizations. Government reports/serials and institutional publications are also acquired.

Bibliography on demand : Bibliography On Demand is a support service provided by NASSDOC to the social science research community. Normally, the requests for this paid service are received from scholars living in cities and small towns where library and documentation services are severely limited. Bibliography is a list of published books, periodical articles, etc. as well as unpublished PhD theses and reports. There are charges for use of the service.

Literature search service from electronic resources: NASSDOC has a collection of CD-ROM/on-line-based information sources. These are used for searching literature/ references. Some of the most used CD-ROM/ On-line databases in NASSDOC are:

- Dissertation abstracts on disc (Humanities and Social Sciences)
- EconLit
- International Political Science Abstracts
- POPLINE
- PsycLit
- Sociological Abstracts
- PsycINFO
- ISID CD-ROM database

Online Databases : NASSDOC subscribes to the following online databases:

- EconLit
- ERIC
- International Political Science Abstracts
- LISA

- Sociological Abstracts
- Social Services Abstracts
- PsycINFO

Acquisition of Ph.d theses : NASSDOC acquires unpublished Ph.D. theses in social sciences accepted by Indian universities. Since 2003 NASSDOC has revised its thesis acquisition policy when it was decided to pay a scholar for a copy of their Ph.D. thesis.

Document Delivery/Inter-Library Loan Service : A document delivery service is provided through an interlibrary loan or by photocopying papers published in periodicals. NASSDOC borrows books, periodicals, reports etc. from other libraries to meet the demands of the research scholars. NASSDOC as a member of DELNET (Developing Library Network) can access databases hosted by the DELNET on its website. NASSDOC can get documents on inter library loan through DELNET from the member libraries.

Reprography service : Photocopies are provided from the NASSDOC collection and also from its own network, if the document is not available within the premises.

CAS : NASSDOC provides a current awareness service by bringing out publications. Photocopies of references included in the CAS publications are provided. Following are the serial publications of NASSDOC available at the sales counter of the ICSSR:

- New Arrivals
- Bibliographic Reprints
- Conference Alert
- Doctoral Dissertation Abstracts

Study grant scheme : Under this scheme, Ph.D. research scholars get financial assistance from ICSSR to consult libraries and archives that are located in other cities. Traveling allowances and a daily allowance are paid to the scholars for this purpose.

Grants-in-aid to bibliographical and documentation projects : Under this scheme NASSDOC provides financial assistance to conduct research in the field of Library and Information Science and compilation of research/reference tools for social scientists. Project proposals fall under one of the following categories:

- Research in fields like bibliometric analysis, information seeking behavior, and library users' study.
- Compilation of user guides, directory, annotated bibliography or union catalogue.

Continuing Education Programme : In order to familiarize librarians, information experts and social scientists, with the techniques of information technology, NASSDOC organizes training workshops, seminars and lectures under its Continuing Education Programme in different parts of the country.

Preservation of documents/microfilming : NASSDOC has started microfilming of its Ph.D. thesis collection. NASSDOC has a collection of microfilms/ microfiches of Ph.D. thesis, some of the Indian and foreign journals, Economic Working Papers, Union Catalogues, Government Publications and rare publications are available for consultation in the Microfilm Section in the Reading Room at ground floor.

Retro Conversion of Catalogue Records : The catalogue database of the library has been converted into machine readable or electronic form with the help of an agency. In total 6000, catalogue records have converted using UNIMARC so that this data can be exchanged with other libraries. RFID Technology. Radio Frequency Identification (RFID) technology has been introduced for inventory management of books and members. The technology obviates the need for human intervention in issuance of books/

journals to the members in the library. The components used in RFID are electronic chips, which are pasted on books; membership cards (i.e. smart ID cards); two mid-range readers and pad antenna.

UNIMARC : For making the software compatible for exchange of catalogue records UNIMARC utility was purchased. To make the catalogue available online on the web, purchase of the WEBOPAC add-on facility is under process. This facility has been implemented within NASSDOC building but not on Internet scale, due to lack of infrastructure.

Internet : Internet connectivity has been provided to officials and scholars in the library. Internet is used for electronic communication, accessing and retrieving information from the subscribed online databases and from other Internet resources.

Indian Social Science Literature in Electronic Form : Under the project, started in 2003-2004, digitization of Indian Social Science Periodical Literature was undertaken. The purpose was to digitize Indian Social Science Literature published in 119 periodicals since their inception to 1970. It has 97492 references. Two disciplines i.e. Economics and Political Science have been taken for this project. The product has been completed and the database has been released in CD-ROM (INSPEL). The references in CD-ROM can be searched by name of the author, title of the article, subject of the article, name of the journal in which article has been published. Free search (i.e. the term may exist in any field) can also be conducted. The search results can be printed, saved, or exported to MS word. INSPEL has been developed in Visual Basic as front end for circulation on CDs.

Cyber Cafe : To facilitate access to internet resources on social sciences.

LIBRARY MEMBERSHIP

Institutional Membership : This is open to autonomous organizations, corporate houses, and research wings of public/private bodies with the annual fee of 4000/-. An institutional member can borrow five books at a time for a period of one month.

Consulting Members : Consultation facility is available for academicians, research scholars, students and members of general public that may include retired persons and other categories of readers. Consultation membership fee is Rs. 200 per annum (minimum Rs. 50 for one month).

Borrowing Members : Borrowing facility can obtain by paying Rs. 1000/- against security deposit fee along with annual member ship fee of Rs. 200/-. Two books are issued to individual members at a time for a period of one month.

NASSDOC DATABASES/PUBLICATION

NASSDOC is engaged in creation of databases and information locating tools. Some of these tools are available for sale.

- Library databases
- Directories
- Indian social science periodicals literature
- Union catalogues
- Bibliographies
- Current awareness service periodicals

PROGRAMMES

Study Grant Scheme : Financial assistance to PhD Scholars for consulting libraries and archives anywhere in India.

Grants-in-Aid to Bibliographical and Documentation Projects : Financial assistance for research in Library and

Information Science and compilation of research/reference tools for social scientists.

Continuing Education Programme : Short-term training workshops / seminars / interactive sessions / lectures for the social science community & Library and Information Science Professionals to upgrade their knowledge. Provides also grant to organize workshops/ seminars/lectures etc.

Apprenticeship and Internship : Practical training for library and information Science students.

REFERENCES

- https://www.icssr.org/nassdoc

4. SENDOC (SMALL ENTERPRISES NATIONAL DOCUMENTATION CENTRE)

INTRODUCTION

The Small Enterprises National Documentation Centre (SENDOC) was set up in 1970 when NI-MSME, was SIET, to energies MSMEs in India and the developing countries around the world with information and knowledge. Since then, it has been functioning as a clearing house of information both for entrepreneurs and extension agents. The Centre has emerged as a one - stop global and IT powered information centre for a wide spectrum of MSMEs, academia, students, research institutions, industry associations and entrepreneurs.

OBJECTIVES

The objectives of the Centre are to collect, store and disseminate techno-managerial information pertaining to MSMEs and to conduct need and demand based training programmes.

STRENGTHS

The library of the SENDOC possesses 70,000 books, 18,000 back volumes of journals, 30,000 reports, 65,000 journal abstracts, 7,500 product profiles, and subscribes to 140 national and international periodicals. It has also a collection that provides information on statistics, economics, production, finance, marketing, technology, machinery and equipment, raw materials, consultants, Government policies and programmes, exports and imports, investment, trade and area literature, licensing, etc. Experts working in the Centre scan and arrange information systematically for quick retrieval using LIMS (Library Information Management System) package. The information is accessible through our website www.nimsme.org.

SERVICES

Some of the important services provided by the Centre are:

- Inter-library lending of documents
- Lending of books
- Reference Services (Preparation of bibliographies)
- literature search
- Newspaper clippings (on select items)
- Technical enquiry
- Reprographic Services
- Consultancy service,
- Product profiles
- Organizes training programmes for clientele on cost

PUBLICATIONS

SENDOC plays a crucial role in the publication of the primary research journal SEDME (Since 1974) which is dedicated to small entrepreneurs and academia who wish to express and exchange their thoughts on any facet of MSMEs.

LIBRARY MEMBERSHIP

The membership to SENDOC library is open to students pursuing post graduation studies and researchers.

Sr. No	*Category of Members*	*Library Membership Fee*
01	Individual	Rs.500/- for one month
02	Researchers	Rs. 2,500/-

REFERENCES

- http://www.nimsme.org/page.php

25

Information Systems and Networks in Social Sciences at International Level

1. DEVINSA (DEVELOPMENT INFORMATION NETWORK FOR SOUTH ASIA)

INTRODUCTION

DEVINSA is a regional network for resource sharing on socio-economic information among the participating members of the South Asian countries as Bangladesh, India, Maldives, Nepal, Pakistan and Sri Lanka. The Marga Institute in Sri Lanka acted as the coordinating centre. DEVINSA was launched by the Committee on Studies for Cooperation in Development in South Asia (CSCD) in 1986 to develop an information base for their research needs. The six South Asian countries participate in DEVINSA through the Information Centres of the member institutes of CSCD. The International Development Research Centre (IDRC) of

Canada provides financial support. DEVINSA is a multidisciplinary, computerized database of bibliographic information on socioeconomic development in South Asia.

In the first phase of its programme during 1986-88, it created computerized bibliographic database of selected published and unpublished socio-economic literature on South Asia produced within and outside South Asia, to improve bibliographical control, document delivery and dissemination.

In the second phase of its programme during 1989-92, it introduced microcomputer processing techniques in all the focal points, upgraded the skills of personnel manning the systems. In the third phase of the programme after 1992, it promoted marketing of DEVINSA services with monthly bibliographies and cumulative index to make DEVINSA a self-sustaining proposition. However, when IDRC withdrew its support and the Marga Institute could not sustain the programme and the publications and DEVINSA suffered.

OBJECTIVES

- To bring under bibliographic control all information on socioeconomic development in the region.
- To apply the concepts of international cooperative information systems at the regional level
- To provide a range of products and services to users of current socioeconomic information

PRODUCTS & SERVICES

DEVINSA Development Abstracts : A monthly abstracting journal based on national inputs received from DEVINSA focal points, and includes a selection of over 200 abstracts and reviews of interest to social science institutions, researchers and analysts. It is available in print as well as on floppy.

International Document Delivery Service : Most of the documents included in the DEVINSA Development Abstracts are available at the Coordinating Centre and the other focal points.

Database Searches and Downloading Services : Requests for database searches should specify coverage by geographical area, year of publication and subject categories.

2. DEVSIS (DEVELOPMENT SCIENCE INFORMATION SYSTEM)

INTRODUCTION

DEVSIS is the first and foremost organization which has a philosophy of universal development and understanding. The purpose was to develop the global information system for socio-economic development. The development of science information system is needed not only for dissemination of information but also for the universal development. There is a growing need to creat the systems, institutions and the instruments which would help the movement towards this new economic and social order.

DEVSIS is a cooperative venture where all the nations of the world work together. Each country collects and processes development information available within their territory. It is a global information system. The system is decentralized to some extent. DEVSIS is the mission-oriented system.

DEVSIS is one of the projects that have been designed to advance towards the goal of pooling knowledge and experience acquired in the process of development, and making them available to those who need them. Before the development information system, there were some reports which stressed the need for global, inter-sectoral, interdisciplinary development information systems and programmes.

The preliminary design of the DEVSIS system has been prepared by a steering committee appointed by six co-sponsoring organizations: The International Development Research Centre (IDRC), the International Labor Office (ILO), the Organization for Economic Cooperation and Development (OECD), the United Nations Department of Economic and Social Affair (UN/ESA), the United Nations Educational, Scientific and Cultural Organization (UNESCO). Each country participating in DEVSIS has the responsibility to contribute standardized records of relevant document generated within its territory. The DEVSIS central unit will convert these records to machine readable form, merge them with the contribution to other national units, and produce a monthly index publication called DEVINDEX. In addition, the central unit will make the same collection of data available on magnetic table in a form that can be searched in a computer.

OBJECTIVES OF DEVSIS

The main objectives of DEVSIS are to:

1. Improve access to economic and social development information to individual and institutions, especially in developing countries of the world.
2. Achieve coordination between the existing information facilities including libraries.
3. Provide information services to users working in the development field at national, international, government and non-government level.
4. Be responsive to the expressed needs of its users and following reviews and evaluation to adjust effective needs.
5. Encourage all the nations of the world to give consideration to development information as an integral component of the national information policies.

6. Foster building and utilization of national and international resources needed to meet the goal.

PRODUCTS AND SERVICES

The principal outputs are expected to be available on magnetic tape as well as in printed form DEVINDEX, the main bibliography of current development literature, with indexes; and the file on magnetic tape. It is recognized that users in developing countries often face difficulties in having access to documents. The central unit will therefore, maintain a microfiche back-up file for all documents and reports not restricted by copyright law, and copies of documents can be obtained from this file. Participating centres can use DEVSIS output (On magnetic tape, printed form, and on microfiche) to produce specialized products and services for their own users communities i.e. bibliographies on specific subjects, selective dissemination of information (SDI) and recurring bibliographies.

FUNCTIONS OF DEVSIS

DEVSIS is a global, decentralized, and mission-oriented system. It concentrates on the information that has been caused to be generated by the development community itself with some additions of information from other related sectors, especially in which the information related to various activities connected to economic planning, education etc. and other activities of the government agencies and NGOS in a particular country.

From this magnetic tape base, a number of information services are possible. Among these is retrospective search, selective dissemination of information (SDI) and recurring bibliographies.

COVERAGE OF DEVSIS

The coverage is divided into two main categories.

1. So far, maximum utility DEVSIS is hospitable to information in different languages. DEVSIS mainly deals with social sciences. Terminology is not exact in social sciences as in the case of sciences. There is also less university in the significance of information in social sciences.
2. There are five categories of information DEVSIS covers:
   (a) **Basis economic and social information and data :** This group of information includes the statistical and other factual information.
   (b) **Theories, models and methodology :** This group of information includes models, methodologies, tools, techniques of study.
   (c) **Development, policy, plans and strategies :** This group of information consists of documents issued by various organizations, official plans, reviews and evaluation of development programmes.
   (d) **Studies on and for development tactics :** This group of information consists of pre-investment studies, development resources and operational experiences.
   (e) **Studies of consequences of development efforts and activities :** This group of information comprises economic impact, social impact and evolutionary reports on social development strategies.

REFERENCES

• http://www.devsis.org/page.php

3. APINESS (ASIA-PACIFIC INFORMATION NETWORK IN SOCIAL SCIENCES)

INTRODUCTION

The marvelous development in the field of communication and technology during the past two decades has greatly facilitated the people living in distant parts of the country, region or world to come closer to each other, think together and work together to achieve premeditated goals. And now an effort has been made in the Asia-Pacific region to set up a cooperative mechanism aiming at conservation of knowledge and its dissemination in the field of social sciences. The organization has been named as Asia-Pacific Information Network in Social Sciences. The present write up briefly enumerates the history of the network, its programmes and activities and what it aims to achieve.

AIMS

- Assist development of infrastructure at national level.
- Promote an inter-institutional arrangement rather than acting as a supra-national centre (the National Contact Point of each participating country should have its own circle of interactions guided by common interests and patterns of priorities).
- Promote a system of national, regional and international links.
- Decide priorities for development of information infrastructure.
- Promote a system of financial resources raised from member countries and from national, regional, international agencies and organizations interested in networking programmes.

EVOLUTION

UNESCO has helped many Asian Countries to acquire the institutions and structures indispensable to modern economic and social development, one of the principal methods used to achieve this is the convening of meetings, bringing together governments and individuals beset by similar problems to exchange experiences and attempt common solutions.

The history of APINESS may be traced to may 1973, when UNESCO organized the first Asian conference on teaching and research in social science. That conference mooted the idea of Association of Asian Social Science Research Councils (AASSREC) and also recommended action for promotion of exchange of information between the countries. Subsequently a number of UNESCO sponsored meetings held at New Delhi 1976, and manila 1977-78 stressed need for developing regional centres for Social Science Research and documentation. After a series of discussions and consultations on the feasibility of implementation of the proposal, it was concluded that it would be more appropriate to develop an inter-institutional programme rather than create a new regional centre. However the follow up efforts made at the New Zealand regional conference and UNESCO general at Belgrade in 1980, coupled with the undertaking given by six countries of the region to support cooperative programmes in social sciences, did not bear any fruit.

At the second conference of ministers responsible for the application of science and technology to development and those responsible for economic planning in Asia and the Pacific (CASTASIA II), held in manila in March 1982, recommendation was made for the "Creation of scientific and technological network for Asia and the Pacific for the exchange of information and experience". The network was to facilitate access to and use of information by scientists, engineers and other involved in developmental activities. The proposed network thus intended to include institutions of social science disciplines engaged in developmental activities.

In 1993, an Asian Regional Seminar on Information Science was organized by UNESCO in collaboration with the institute of library science of the University of the Philippines, which made 19 recommendations, one of which, among others, invited UNESCO regional unit for social and human sciences in Asia and the Pacific (RUSHAP) to "Extend its activities to include promotion of regional documentations and information services and assist national centres in strengthening and consolidating their activities". Consequent to this recommendation UNESCO commissioned a feasibility study for setting up the regional network. This study was carried out by Ursula G. Picache, of the institute of library science (Philippines). Her study was circulated among national commissions in the region and the member councils of AASSREC. This study was discussed at the 6th general conference of AASSREC in 1985 in Bali, Indonesia, and again at the executive council APINESS emerged and it was decided to collaborate with UNESCO in establishing the network. A regional meeting of experts, representing social science research councils, national libraries and documentation centres from 17 countries, was held at Bangkok 1986, under the sponsorship of RUSHAP and AASSREC which finally launched the network.

THE FRAMEWORK

The APINESS infrastructure would be broadly based on the ASTINFO model because of their identical objectives and programmes within their distinctive specialized fields.

MAIN CONSTITUENTS

The constituents of this system would be:

1. National Contact Point (NCP) : Each member state

will establish or designate an existing centre to act as a national contact point within the APINESS frame work. NCP would provide secretariat assistance for undertaking networking activities. About 14 countries have so far designated NCPs.

2. National Advisory Group of NCP (NAG) : NCP will set up a national advisory group to assist and advise it on networking programmes. NAG will provide representation to government departments, academic bodies, professional organizations and organizations having liaison with various organizations of U.N., like UNESCO, WHO, UNIDO, FAO, UNISIST etc. The exact composition of NAG is, however, to be decided by each country. NAG will review activities undertaken and submit proposals to UNESCO for assistance.

Functions and activities of NCP:

- To keep liaison with other national and international bodies/networks in pursuance of APINESS programmes.
- To coordinate, stimulate and monitor the progress of networking activities.
- To collaborated with UNESCO in all matters relating to the APINESS project.
- To facilitate assist consultant/expert missions in the country, organized under APINESS project.
- To identify national/regional/international institutions /systems and services located in the country, which could become participating centres of APINESS.

3. Regional Advisory Group (RAG) : APPINESS is thus conceived as an inter-institutional arrangement with emphasis on decentralization. It does not envisage creation of a centre of centres, but will encourage each network participate to act as a centre with its own counterpart centres to develop a system of interactions. APINESS will attempt to strengthen national infrastructures through regional cooperation. The secretariat of APINESS is presently based at UNESCO's regional unit for social and human sciences in Asia and the pacific, Bangkok.

ACTIVITIES

To promote networking spirit NASSDOC, as one of the NCPs established exchange programme with the institutions in member countries. It also brings out APINESS newsletter three times a year to disseminate information about the network's activities.

A number of projects listed below have also been taken up under APINESS programme.

- Working groups on: documentation and information services.
- Annotated bibliography on India 2000 A.D.
- State of art report on social science research in India.
- Information analysis centres.
- Data banks.
- Data archives.

ACHIEMENTS AT NATIONAL LEVEL IN INDIA

Indian national commission for cooperation with UNESCO has designated National Social Science Documentation Centre (NASSDOC) as the National Contact Point (NCP) for APINESS activities in India. To advise NCP in planning APPINESS programmes the National Advisory Group consisting of eminent persons has been set up.

NASSDOC as per approved APPINESS action programme has take up the following activities:

- Compilation, publication and distribution of APPINESS newsletter.
- Compilation of India 2000: An annotated bibliography. The document has been published by UNESCO

regional office, Bangkok.

- Collection of data for two UNESCO world directories. These are "Directory of Social Science Research Institutions" and "Selective Inventory of Information Service".
- Compilation of the state of art report on Social Science trends in India involving analysis of Social Science bibliographies published in India since 1970.
- Extension of support for setting up women information network by centre for women's development studies, New Delhi.

SERVICES

- SDI
- Preparation of state of art reports and processing.
- Repackaging of Social Science Information
- Documentation and information services.
- Data archives.

CONCLUSION

APINESS has been set up with laudable objective. Achievement of these objectives will obviously depend upon active cooperation and commitment of the participating national centres who will be the real custodian of the network. The task is no doubt formidable taking into consideration financial constraints and resultant long neglect of Social Science Research and its dissemination in the region, but it is surmountable. With the expected active cooperation of international organizations, like UNESCO, WHO, ESCAP, UNDP, IDRC etc., APINESS is expected to bring countries of the region closer to each other through better exchange and dissemination of information and thereby promote mutual understanding and respect, universal solidarity, justice and progress.

REFERENCES

- https://uia.org/s/or/en/1100029586